CULLOTTA

The Life of a
Chicago Criminal,
Las Vegas Mobster,
and Government Witness

CULLOTTA

The Life of a Chicago Criminal, Las Vegas Mobster, and Government Witness

Dennis N. Griffin
and
Frank Cullotta

With contributions from
Dennis Arnoldy

Huntington Press • Las Vegas, NV

**Cullotta: The Life of a Chicago Criminal,
Las Vegas Mobster, and Government Witness**

Published by
   Huntington Press
   3665 S. Procyon Ave.
   Las Vegas, NV 89103
   Phone (702) 252-0655
   e-mail: books@huntingtonpress.com

10-Digit ISBN: 0-929712-45-5
13-Digit ISBN: 978-0-929712-45-1

Design & Production: Laurie Shaw

Photo Credits: Frank Cullotta, Dennis Arnoldy, Kent Clifford, Dennis N. Griffin, Gene Smith, Illinois Department of Corrections, *Las Vegas Review-Journal*, Las Vegas Metropolitan Police Department

Dedication

To the memory of my mother Josephine, who passed away in 1990. And to Ashley, my granddaughter, who left us in 2005. She was the light of my life.

Frank Cullotta

Acknowledgments

The information contained in this book was derived from many sources, primarily from Frank Cullotta himself and retired FBI agent Dennis Arnoldy. But there were many others who contributed to this project and I want to mention and thank them here. They include, but are not limited to, former Clark County Sheriff John McCarthy, Commander Kent Clifford, Detective David Groover and Lt. Gene Smith, former Strike Force Special Attorney Stanley Hunterton, and former FBI agents Joe Yablonsky, Charlie Parsons, Emmett Michaels, Donn Sickles, Lynn Ferrin, and Gary Magnesen.

The newspaper archives of the Las Vegas-Clark County Library District held stories from the *Las Vegas Sun, The Valley Times,* and *Las Vegas Review-Journal* that provided key information regarding events and incidents of the Tony Spilotro era in Las Vegas. A series of 1983 articles by Michael Goodman of the *Los Angeles Times* further illuminated those times. My special thanks go out to Las Vegas TV station KVBC for allowing the use of their investigative report of Tony Spilotro's trial for the killings of Billy McCarthy and

Jimmy Miraglia (the M&M Murders).

The Illinois Police and Sheriff's News Web site www.ipsn.org provided a wealth of information relating to organized-crime history in both Chicago and Las Vegas. The well-researched book *Of Rats and Men* (John L. Smith) was an invaluable resource. The movie *Casino*—in which actors Joe Pesci and Robert De Niro portray characters based on Tony Spilotro and Frank "Lefty" Rosenthal— proved to be extremely informative.

Others deserve mention, but for various reasons they desire to stay in the background. Respecting their wishes, they will remain nameless, but not unappreciated.

Denny Griffin

Contents

Part Three—Witness Protection and Beyond

Dennis Griffin and Frank Cullotta

Foreword

Frank Cullotta is the real thing.

I found that out when I was working on *Casino*, a book about the skim at the Stardust Hotel in Las Vegas. The story was about Anthony Spilotro, the mob boss of Las Vegas, and his relationship with Frank Rosenthal, the man who ran the mob's casinos. Cullotta was an invaluable source for me, because by the time I started writing the book, Spilotro had been murdered and Rosenthal, who'd miraculously survived getting blown up in his car, was reluctant to give interviews.

But Frank Cullotta was alive and he'd not only known all of the major characters central to the book, he'd been one of them. He and Spilotro had been boyhood pals back in Chicago and it was Spilotro who convinced Cullotta to migrate west to a felony paradise. Cullotta had run the robbery, extortion, and murder departments for Spilotro's Vegas mob.

Spilotro and Cullotta extorted cash from every illegal bookmaker, drug dealer, and burglar operating in Las Vegas. Those who refused wound up buried in the desert. Soon, no one refused and

Spilotro became the indisputable boss of Las Vegas.

The police called Cullotta's high-tech burglary crew "The Hole in the Wall Gang," due to their penchant for breaking into buildings by blasting through walls.

The gang operated with very little trouble for years. Ultimately, however, one of the crew turned police informant to stay out of jail. He blew the whistle and Cullotta and his Hole in the Wall Gang were arrested in the middle of burglarizing Bertha's, a large Las Vegas jewelry store.

The size and sophistication of the Cullotta crew surprised many in Las Vegas, especially when it was revealed that Cullotta had access to all the local police and FBI radio frequencies, not to mention a former Las Vegas police sergeant stationed outside Bertha's as a lookout. While sitting in jail, Cullotta concluded that he'd been set up by Spilotro to take a hard fall. After much agonizing, he decided to roll and testify against his former partners and friends.

By the time I contacted the Justice Department, Cullotta had already testified and served his time. He was now a free man. The only way for me to personally contact him was through Dennis Arnoldy, the FBI agent who had debriefed Cullotta in safe houses and federal prisons.

Arnoldy said he couldn't guarantee anything. Cullotta was in the Federal Witness Program living "somewhere in America." But Arnoldy did say he'd somehow get Cullotta my number.

When Cullotta called the next day, I was surprised to find that he wasn't hiding somewhere in America. In fact, he was in Las Vegas, the city where some of the most dangerous men in the state had already tried to kill him. He suggested that we meet in the morning in the parking lot of a Las Vegas shopping mall not far from the Strip.

The next morning I was there. No Cullotta. I checked my watch. He was five minutes late. Then, suddenly, Cullotta appeared. He just popped up. I was startled. I didn't see him coming until he was right on top of me. He stood close. He was solidly built and wore a small narrow-brimmed canvas rain hat. I was even more surprised when I realized he was alone. No federal marshals or FBI agents were watching his back. He leaned against a car fender and listened to my pitch about the book. He agreed to meet again, but mostly he said he wanted to make sure I got it right, especially the part about why he decided to testify against his former pals.

Cullotta turned out to be an invaluable resource. His memory was phenomenal. He's the kind of person who remembers his license-plate numbers from decades ago, and this is a man who usually owned three or four cars at once. Equally important to me, Cullotta had been either a participant in or an observer of most of the book's important events. He either set up or committed robberies and murders. He was often the third person in the room during domestic disputes between Spilotro, Rosenthal, and Rosenthal's wife, with whom Spilotro was having an affair. In fact, Spilotro's fear that Cullotta would report back to the bosses in Chicago, who'd forbidden the affair, caused Spilotro to try and kill Cullotta. The failed murder attempt turned Cullotta into a government witness.

One of a non-fiction writer's major concerns is knowing if the people you're interviewing are telling the truth. That problem becomes even more acute when dealing with cops, lawyers, and crooks, to whom lying is not unknown.

In Cullotta's case, however, he'd already been debriefed by the FBI and testified under oath in court about everything we were discussing, which could all be checked in the public record or in the volumes of FBI summaries. I felt confident that Cullotta was telling the truth, because his extraordinary immunity deal depended upon it. Cullotta's freedom would end the minute he was caught in a lie and he'd immediately be sent to prison, where he was bound to get killed. Therefore, I was in the unique position of interviewing someone whose life literally depended upon his telling the truth.

Martin Scorsese, the director with whom I wrote the script for *Casino*, realized Cullotta's value immediately and hired him as a technical advisor during the production of the film, which was shot on location in Las Vegas.

Before he could start working on the film, however, Universal Pictures insisted that Cullotta hire a bodyguard. They would pay for the extra protection, but they insisted he have security around the clock.

Cullotta hired an attractive young security guard he knew who had a serious crush on him. He also got her to carry two guns. As a convicted felon, he couldn't legally carry a gun. There was no law, however, that said someone couldn't carry a gun for him.

Cullotta had either been involved in most of the mayhem depicted in the film—his character as Joe Pesci's right-hand man was played by Frank Vincent—or knew the participants well enough to help the actors and director with the kinds of details necessary to capture the characters and mood.

During the film, the Joe Pesci character decides to kill one of the gang's associates who had become an informant. Pesci sends a hit man to do the job, but chaos erupts and the hit man winds up chasing the informant all around his Las Vegas house, in and out of rooms, until he finally kills him near the swimming pool and dumps the body into the water.

Dennis Griffin and Frank Cullotta

Before shooting the scene, Scorsese asked Cullotta how such a bizarre murder might have happened. Cullotta explained that Jerry Lisner, the victim, had failed to go down after he'd been shot because, "I didn't have a silencer at the time and I had to use 'half-loads,' bullets where you take out some of the powder to lessen the noise.

"Lisner and I are coming out of the den and I pull the stick out and pop him two times in the back of the head. He turns around and looks at me. 'What are you doing?' he asks me. He takes off through the kitchen toward the garage. I actually look at the gun, like, 'What the fuck have I got? Blanks in there?' So I run after him and I empty the rest in his head. It's like an explosion going off every time.

"But he doesn't go down. The fuck starts running. It's like a comedy of errors. I'm chasing him around the house and I've emptied the thing in his head. I'm thinking, what am I gonna do with this guy? I grab an electric cord from the water cooler and wrap it around his neck. It breaks.

"Finally I catch him in the garage and he hits the garage door button, but I hit him before it goes down and it's like he just deflates.

"There was blood all over the place. My worry was that I'd leave a print in blood somewhere on his body or clothes. I hadn't worn any gloves, because Lisner wasn't dumb. He wouldn't have let me in the door if he saw me wearing gloves. Because of the danger of my prints being on his body or clothes, I dragged him to the pool and slid him, legs first, into the water. He went in straight, like a board. It was like he was swimming."

Scorsese dismissed the actors. He had Cullotta recreate the Lisner murder scene on film. The man you see in the film, chasing the victim around the house, emptying bullets into his head, and finally tossing him in the pool, is the real Frank Cullotta, the same man who did the actual murder for which he was given immunity. I cannot think of another film in which the killing being depicted on screen is reenacted by the man who committed the original murder.

It was much later, after the movie was done, that most of the people working on the film realized what had happened that day. But by then Cullotta was writing his own book and living somewhere in America.

Nicholas Pileggi

Introduction

During the 1970s and into the mid-1980s, the dominant organized-crime family operating in Las Vegas hailed from Chicago. Known as the Outfit, they removed large amounts of money from the Sin City casinos they controlled before it was ever recorded as revenue. This particular form of theft was referred to as the "skim." They also received income from street crime rackets such as burglary, robbery, and arson. This era was dramatized in the 1995 movie *Casino*.

Las Vegas law enforcement was aware of the mob's presence and the need to rid the streets and casinos of its influence and corruption. But the two agencies with the primary responsibility of battling the criminals—the FBI and the Las Vegas Metropolitan Police Department—were experiencing their own difficulties. The feds had image problems due to agents accepting comped meals and shows from the casinos they were supposed to be monitoring. The Las Vegas Metropolitan Police Department was sent into chaos in 1978 when FBI wiretaps recorded two of its detectives providing information to the mobsters. But changes were on the way.

The FBI began importing fresh troops from other offices to replace agents who were either reassigned or took early retirement as a result of the fallout from the comp scandal. And in November 1978, the voters of Clark County elected a new sheriff, a reformer who vowed to clean up Metro's Intelligence Bureau and declared war on organized crime. It wasn't long after the new sheriff took office in 1979 that the two agencies began to cooperate and launched a full-court press against their organized-crime foes.

Also in 1979, there was a personnel change on the criminal side. A career thief, arsonist, and killer from Chicago arrived in Vegas to take charge of the mob's street crimes. That man was Frank Cullotta.

Cullotta had been invited to Sin City by the Outfit's man on the scene, Tony "the Ant" Spilotro. Cullotta's friendship with Spilotro dated back to their days as young toughs and thieves on the mean streets of the Windy City. His duties included assembling and overseeing a gang of burglars, robbers, arsonists, and killers. The crew Cullotta put together became known as the Hole in the Wall Gang, because of their method of breaking into buildings by making holes in the walls or roofs. In addition to stealing, the gang provided muscle in enforcement matters and otherwise did Spilotro's bidding. For the next three years, Tony, Frank, and their crew ruled the Las Vegas underworld.

During that time the battle between law enforcement and the mobsters ebbed and flowed, with victories and setbacks for both sides and no apparent winner. But in 1982, a 1979 murder and a failed 1981 burglary contributed to a major turning point in the war: Frank Cullotta, Spilotro's lifelong friend and trusted lieutenant, switched sides and became a government witness. Suddenly,

Dennis Griffin and Frank Cullotta

the law had a source who not only knew the workings of the gang from the inside, but was willing to talk about it.

Having a cooperating witness with Cullotta's knowledge could provide the government with the breakthrough it needed to bust the mob's back, but only if his information was credible. It was a sure thing that any criminal defense attorney would challenge Cullotta's veracity. It would certainly be brought out during any court proceedings that the government's chief witness was a career criminal and an admitted killer, a man who had made a deal with prosecutors in order to obtain a lighter sentence. Under those circumstances, how much value would Cullotta actually be?

To address those issues, government lawyers decided not to use any information Cullotta imparted to them or their investigators as the basis for charges or in court, unless it was double- or triple-checked for accuracy. The man assigned the task of determining Cullotta's truthfulness was Dennis Arnoldy, the FBI's Las Vegas case agent for the Spilotro investigations.

For the next five years, Arnoldy debriefed the erstwhile gangster, obtaining the intimate details of life inside Spilotro's crime ring, and transported him to appearances before various grand juries, courts, and commissions. During that time a personal relationship developed between the two men that continues today.

In my book *The Battle for Las Vegas—The Law vs. the Mob*, I told the story of Spilotro's Las Vegas years primarily from the law-enforcement perspective. That book contained many insights that were disclosed to the general public for the first time. While researching *Battle*, I had the opportunity to talk with Frank Cullotta and became convinced that his life story would be a fascinating read and provide the other side of the Las Vegas mob story. It turned out that Frank had already been having the same thoughts.

Now, he has taken this opportunity to tell the tale. Some people, including his own brother and sister, might not be pleased to see it in print. But Frank believes that this is the only venue available to him to get his account on the record. In these pages, he discloses criminal activities for which he has either received immunity or the statute of limitations has long since expired. The story takes the reader beyond *Battle* and into the often dangerous, sometimes humorous, but always exciting real-life world of cops and robbers.

This book is by no means an attempt to make excuses for Frank's conduct. He did what he did, he is what he is. It's highly unlikely that this straight-from-the-shoulder account of his career as a criminal will make him a candidate for sainthood.

The story begins with Frank's early years growing up in Chicago, where he embarked on his decades-long career as a criminal. As Frank advanced from juvenile crimes into burglary and armed robbery, he met and became friends with other hooligans, one of whom was Tony Spilotro. The two men again joined forces in Las Vegas, where Frank was Tony's main man.

Although Spilotro got most of the notoriety, it will become clear here that Frank was an accomplished criminal in his own right. He planned and carried out the most daring robberies and burglaries committed by the Hole in the Wall Gang. In addition to thieving, Frank and his crew served as Tony's enforcers, shaking down bookies and drug dealers and plotting or committing murders.

To get a feel for the two men and their relationship, Frank relates some of their individual and joint escapades in Chicago, including the true circumstances behind the so-called M&M murders. The movie *Casino* contains a scene based on those killings, in which actor Joe Pesci's character places a man's head in a vise and squeezes until the victim's eye pops out.

Next Frank takes us to Las Vegas and tells the real story of life inside Spilotro's Sin City gang, their battles with the law, and why he switched sides. Dennis Arnoldy adds insights from the law's perspective, providing the reader with the unique opportunity of examining specific events from opposing viewpoints.

If you're a true-crime or organized-crime enthusiast, a *Casino* fan, or simply interested in Las Vegas history, I don't think you'll come away disappointed from reading *Cullotta*.

Denny Griffin
Las Vegas, March 2007

Part One

From the Windy City to Sin City

1

Murder in Las Vegas

At approximately 4:30 a.m. on October 11, 1979, a dead man was found floating face down in the swimming pool of his residence at 2303 Rawhide Avenue in Las Vegas. He'd been shot in the head several times by a small-caliber handgun. The corpse was that of 46-year-old Sherwin "Jerry" Lisner. His wife Jeannie, a cocktail waitress at the Aladdin, found the body. She'd left work early, after becoming concerned when her husband failed to answer her telephone calls, and made the grisly discovery.

According to investigating police officers, Lisner had put up quite a fight. Bullet holes were discovered throughout the dwelling and blood was found on the walls and floor leading from the garage, through the residence, and out to the pool. Although the house had been ransacked, the cops didn't believe robbery or burglary was the motive. They declined to speculate on the reason Lisner was killed, but they did have a theory on how the murder went down. The killer knocked on the garage door, surprising Lisner. When he answered the knock, the shooting started. Although wounded, the victim attempted to escape his assailant, running through his home with the would-be killer in close pursuit and bullets flying. After a valiant effort to survive, Lisner's luck ran out when he reached the pool. No murder weapon was found and no suspect named.

But the police had their suspicions on the why and who of it. They knew that the dead man had mob connections and was in legal trouble. He'd been arrested by the FBI on July 11 and charged with interstate transportation of stolen property, aiding and abetting, grand larceny, and conspiracy. Free on $75,000 bail, Lisner was scheduled to go on trial October 29 in U.S. District Court in Washington, D.C.

Lisner was also believed to have been acquainted with Chicago Outfit enforcer and Las Vegas organized-crime kingpin Tony Spilotro. And it was rumored that the deceased had been negotiating with the FBI to work out a deal in the federal cases pending against him in Washington. Could those negotiations have included providing incriminating information against Spilotro, one of the FBI's prime targets?

Metro investigators knew all this and suspected that Spilotro might well be behind the killing. However, they couldn't immediately prove their suspicions and kept their thoughts to themselves.

As it turned out, the cops were pretty close to the truth in their idea of what occurred at Lisner's house that night. But they were wrong about Lisner being surprised by the arrival of his killer; he'd expected him. And the victim had drawn his last breath in his living room, not outside by the pool.

There was no error, however, in law-enforcement's belief that

Tony Spilotro was behind the murder. When the soon-to-be dead man answered his door that evening, he invited his murderer inside. In a matter of moments the visitor began to fire a total of ten bullets aimed at his host's head, with several finding their mark. The assassin wasn't Tony Spilotro himself, but he was there at Tony's behest. The man was Spilotro's trusted associate who ran a crew of burglars and robbers known as the Hole in the Wall Gang. His name? Frank Cullotta.

The Early Years

Frank Cullotta was born in Chicago on December 14, 1938, the son of Joseph and Josephine Cullotta. He had two siblings: older sister Jean and a younger brother Joseph. The family lived in a working-class and mostly Italian neighborhood called the Patch. His father had a unique job. He drove the work car—getaway car— for his crew of burglars and robbers. Joe Cullotta exhibited a cold businesslike demeanor to all, including his family. He also had a violent temper. Any love and warmth the children experienced in the Cullotta household came from Josephine.

Joe Cullotta, age 38, was killed when the car he was driving crashed during a high-speed police chase when Frank was about nine years old. In addition to his own memories, as Frank grew up relatives and associates of his father told him story after story of Joe's exploits and expertise as a criminal. The elder Cullotta was considered by friend and foe to have been the best wheel man in Chicago. He was also highly dangerous, capable of mayhem and murder.

Josephine Cullotta herself never discussed her husband's criminal activities with her children, either before or after his death. She limited her comments about him to simply saying that he was a good man. But Frank witnessed his father slap his mother around on more than one occasion. And Joe's violence toward his family wasn't limited to his wife; the children were also victims of his anger.

One of the things that set Joe off was when one of the kids got a bad report card. Josephine made an effort to keep that kind of news from her husband, but if he did find out, there was hell to pay. On one occasion when Frank brought home a derogatory report, Joe got wind of it and went into a rage. Josephine tried to calm her husband, to no avail. Frank dove under his bed as his father headed toward him.

At that point his sister intervened. "I'm not going to let you hurt him, Dad," she said, stepping in front of her father to block his path.

Joe Cullotta glared at his daughter in disbelief. "Oh yeah? Here," he snarled, as he kicked her and sent her sprawling down the stairs. Although she suffered the consequences, Jean's heroic action saved Frank from a beating.

Joe Cullotta's ferocity wasn't limited to his family. Young Frank personally witnessed his father in action in a situation that today would be called road rage. He was with his father driving on North Avenue when a couple of guys in another car got under Joe's skin. One of them spit out their window and some of it got on the Cullotta vehicle. Joe flew into a maniacal rage. He chased the other car down the street and ran it up on the curb. He then dragged the two occupants out and beat them senseless.

Dennis Griffin and Frank Cullotta

In spite of Joe's lack of affection and propensity for violence, he was a good provider for his family. He made sure they never wanted for anything. The Cullottas had new furniture every year and the kids had the best toys. Frank didn't learn until later that virtually everything his father provided was stolen.

The law was often on Joe Cullotta's tail. When the family was living on the east side near Grand and Ogden, a few doors from future Outfit boss Tony Accardo, Frank came home from school one day and found a police detective sitting in his house. His mother neither acknowledged the stranger nor provided an explanation as to why he was there. That cop stayed for several hours, then left when another one replaced him. This routine continued for several days. To add to the mystery, Joe Cullotta had apparently gone missing. If his wife knew where he was, she wasn't saying.

After about a week, the cops stopped coming and Joe Cullotta made his appearance. It turned out that Frank's father was a suspect in the robbery of the *Chicago Tribune*. He and his crew got away before the police arrived, but a witness had identified them. Joe was eventually captured and charged in that robbery, but he beat the case in court.

In spite of Joe Cullotta's sometimes abusive behavior toward his wife and children, Frank came to idolize his father and admire his success as a criminal. That adoration contributed to Frank's decision to follow in his footsteps. And once he started down that path, there was no turning back.

• • •

Frank's disdain for authority, for rules and regulations, became apparent early on. Going to school was problematic for him. He hated it. He considered the teachers to be a bunch of mean old biddies. There was another problem, too. Frank wore glasses. In those days kids who wore eyeglasses were looked on as freaks by some of their classmates. When nasty comments or dirty looks were directed at Frank because of his eyesight, he responded with his fists.

Ongoing difficulties regarding Frank's conduct resulted in his mother enrolling him in a Catholic school. The nuns were tough on him and routinely slapped his hands or knuckles with a ruler. On one such occasion Frank fought back; he took the ruler away from the nun and broke it over his knee. That incident resulted in expulsion and a return to the public school system.

The change of scenery didn't improve Frank's attitude toward school. When he acted up, the teachers made him sit behind the piano or put him in the closet. This made him even more hateful and defiant. He started coming to school late or not showing up at all.

When Frank's mother received calls or letters from the school about his behavior, she did what most parents would do: She punished him. He had to come straight home in the afternoon and be in the house by a certain time at night. Then she took away his allowance. To compensate, while walking to school he started stealing the money out of the bags customers left out to pay for their newspapers. Eventually, the paperboy got tired of finding the bags empty and began to keep an eye out for the thief. One day he spotted Frank in the act and the chase was on. Frank got away and started taking a different route to school.

Stealing the paper money accustomed Frank to having some cash in his pocket. He liked the feeling and knew he needed to find

Dennis Griffin and Frank Cullotta

another source of income. Like many other kids in his neighborhood, he decided to try his hand at shining shoes.

. . .

Frank started shining shoes up and down Grand Avenue. One day he noticed a kid about his age, though much shorter, shining shoes on the opposite side of the street. The competitors glared at each other for several seconds.

The stranger hollered, "What the fuck are you lookin' at?"

Frank replied, "I'm looking at you. What about it?"

Like a pair of Wild West gunfighters ready to do battle, the boys walked toward each other. Stopping a few feet apart in the middle of the street, they put down their shoeboxes.

The stranger said, "This is my fuckin' territory and I don't want you on this street. Understand?"

"I don't see your name on any street signs and I'm not leaving."

The challenge had been made and answered. Some pushing, shoving, and name-calling followed. As the confrontation ended, the other boy said to Frank, "I'm coming back here tomorrow and if I see you, we'll have to fight."

Not backing down, Frank said, "Then that's what we'll have to do."

Frank returned to the same spot the next day as promised, but the other kid wasn't there. In fact, the two didn't meet again until about a week later. Frank didn't think he'd intimidated his competitor. He figured the boy was around and they were simply missing each other.

The next time the two met, the stranger approached Frank, but he wanted to talk, not fight. "I've been asking around about you. What's your last name?"

"Cullotta."

"Was your father Joe Cullotta?"

"Yeah. So what?"

"Your father and my father were friends. Your old man helped my old man out of a bad spot one time."

As the boys talked, the stranger explained that his father ran a well-known Italian restaurant on the east side called Patsy's. Joe Cullotta frequented the restaurant and liked Patsy Spilotro. Joe had come to Patsy's rescue when he was being harassed by a gang of criminals known as the Black Hand. Frank's adversary-turned-friend was Patsy Spilotro's son Tony.

After listening to Tony's story, Frank remembered hearing about the incident at Patsy's restaurant. The Black Hand consisted of Sicilian and Italian gangsters who extorted money from their own kind and Frank's father hated them with a passion. Their method was to shake down business owners by demanding money in return for letting the business stay open. They were making Patsy pay dues every week. When Joe Cullotta heard about it, he and his crew hid in the back room of the restaurant until the Black Handers came in for the payoff. Then they burst out and killed them. After that Patsy wasn't bothered anymore.

Patsy's wasn't the only time Joe Cullotta had trouble with the Black Hand. In another incident, a member put a threatening note on Cullotta's door. When Joe saw that note, he went crazy. He found the guy who was responsible for the threat in a barbershop getting a shave. He walked up to the chair and blew him away, right in front of the barber. The Black Hand became aware that it was Joe Cullotta who killed their man, but they didn't retaliate. They may have come to the conclusion that he was a man better left alone.

Finally, the man in charge of the Black Hand was murdered while he was asleep in a hotel room. His wife, in the bed right next to him, wasn't killed. Frank heard that his father was in on the murder, but he never found out for sure. In any case, that killing marked the end of the Black Hand in the Cullotta neighborhood.

Frank and Tony Spilotro had some things in common other than their fathers having been friends. They were nearly the same age—Tony was seven months older—and neither liked school or had much respect for authority. Their main difference was the makeup of their families. Tony had five brothers and there's no evidence that Patsy Spilotro engaged in criminal activity.

. . .

In Tony Spilotro, Frank had made a friend who would play a major role in his future. At the same time, he was learning a lot about getting by on the streets. And his formal education continued to go poorly. He was sent to a vocational school where he tried to turn over a new leaf by staying out of trouble. That effort didn't last long, though. In fact, his behavior turned violent.

The new place was a trade school for boys who couldn't handle a normal academic environment. Frank liked working with his hands and was actually doing well in shop. But the principal, Mr. Jones, was a real tough guy. He was always on the kids about haircuts and wearing their pants too low. He regularly badgered Frank.

One day Mr. Jones stopped Frank in the hall and asked him to step into the bathroom with him to talk. Frank thought it was a little weird, but went along. Once inside, Jones said, "I've told you and told you about wearing your pants like that. Now get them up where I want them."

Frank stared back defiantly. "They're staying where they are."

Jones flew into a rage. "We'll see about that!" he yelled, pushing Frank and slapping him.

Frank kneed Jones in the groin. When the man doubled over, he kneed him in the head. Frank left Jones on the floor of the bathroom and walked out. No action was taken against him, possibly because Mr. Jones felt he was in the wrong for slapping Frank around and decided to let the matter drop. That wasn't the end of it for Jones, though. A couple of other kids were having similar problems with him and Frank's anger hadn't been completely sated. The trio decided to give the principal another lesson.

As Mr. Jones walked down a hallway during recess one day, the three boys threw a blanket over his head and pushed him into an empty classroom. He tried to resist, but he couldn't fight off three tough and angry kids. They tied him up and hung him out a window, dangling by his ankles. The police were called and someone identified Frank as being involved. He was expelled from the trade school and sent to a place that he found to be a hell of a lot worse.

• • •

Montefiore School was a reformatory for troublemaking kids who couldn't get along anywhere else. Two young men who fit that definition and found themselves in Montefiore were Frank Cullotta

Dennis Griffin and Frank Cullotta

and Tony Spilotro. Frank was the first to arrive, followed by Tony a week later.

The student body of Montefiore was primarily black. Tony and Frank were two of the half-dozen or so white kids in the place. They had a bad time of it and were regularly involved in physical confrontations with their black classmates. In addition to the fights, the two boys had to rely on public transportation to get to and from Montefiore. Using a bit of ingenuity, they solved that problem in short order: They began stealing cars.

Frank had already figured out how to hotwire his mother's car. He showed Tony how simple it was and Spilotro was impressed. The pair stole any car they wanted, drove to school, and parked a couple of blocks away. Most of the time they drove the same car back to their neighborhood.

Having their choice of vehicles was convenient, but it didn't resolve the problem of dealing with their fellow students. The combat continued.

One day as Frank came out of wood shop, he found Tony surrounded by four or five blacks. One of them wanted to fight Tony alone. "Come on, white boy," he said. "Just you and me."

When Tony accepted the challenge, the black kid picked him up and flung him over his head to the floor. Tony got up and outboxed his opponent. Then one of the other blacks said, "Let's kill the motherfuckers," and the gang started to attack.

Frank grabbed one of the long poles with a hook on the end that was used to open and close the upper windows. He swung it at the blacks and caught a couple of them in the head, giving him and Tony time to run out of the building. Frank didn't go to school the next day, but Tony did; he took a knife with him and stabbed one of the black kids, resulting in expulsion.

But Tony wasn't through with Montefiore yet. He, his older brother Vic, and Frank stole a car and went back to the school. They wanted to get the leader of the blacks, a boy named Jackson, who they believed was the instigator of all the problems. They pulled up to the schoolyard in the hot car around lunchtime. Vic Spilotro was armed with a 45-caliber pistol.

The three entered the building and found Jackson in the cafeteria. They yanked him outside, beating him with the gun as he was dragged to the car. Jackson's friends seemed stunned and didn't immediately react. After a few seconds they came outside, but didn't interfere as their leader was placed in the stolen car and driven away. Jackson was pistol-whipped and beaten, then dumped off back at the school.

Frank, Tony, and Vic were subsequently charged with the kidnapping and assault. Tony disappeared for a while and nobody could find him. However, he did show up for court and was released to work at his father's restaurant. Frank was thrown out of Montefiore and placed in a reformatory setting, where the kids had to live in cottages right on campus. The time he spent there was difficult on his mother. But she remained loyal and visited him every day.

Frank was eventually released from reform school and placed back in the public system. As soon as he reached the age of 16, he dropped out of school for good.

• • •

Josephine Cullotta cashed in some savings bonds her husband had left in Frank's name and bought him a used car, an Oldsmobile

Dennis Griffin and Frank Cullotta

98. To Frank it was big and beautiful. He loved it and washed it all the time.

One day while he was giving the car a bath, an old neighborhood acquaintance stopped by. The man's name was Bob Sprodak; he was also known as "Crazy Bob." Sprodak was a year or two older than Frank and it was common knowledge on the street that he always carried a gun.

"Nice-lookin' car you got there," Crazy Bob said. "I've got a car parked down the street, but mine's hot. You workin' anywhere?"

"My uncle's getting me a job at a newspaper stand downtown. I'll be starting any day now."

Then Sprodak did something that would change Frank's life forever: He reached into his pocket and pulled out a big wad of money.

Frank was impressed and curious. "Where'd you get that?"

"Sticking up places; I do armed robberies. I hold up taverns, restaurants, and gas stations. There's a lot of money in it and it's real easy."

Frank had more questions. "Do you work by yourself?"

"Usually, but you're welcome to come with me sometime if you want. Sometimes it's better to have another guy along."

"I don't know. It sounds pretty dangerous," Frank said. "What do you do if somebody fights back?"

"Then you shoot him."

Frank wasn't completely sold on the idea. "Okay, I'll think about it."

The next day Frank's uncle took him to the newspaper stand to start work. It was then that he learned there was a little more to the job than selling newspapers. "This is very important," the uncle said, holding up a cigar box. "Guys are going to come by here and give you money and slips of paper. They'll be for their bets on horse races. You take the money and slip of paper and put it in this cigar box. Whatever you do, don't mix the bet money up with the newspaper money. Got it?"

"Yeah, sure. What do I do with the bets and money after I collect them?"

"Just put them in the box like I told you. Somebody will stop around every so often and pick them up."

Frank tried the job for a while. But the weather was turning cold and he had to sell papers and collect illegal bets while standing next to a 55-gallon drum with a fire in it in order to keep warm. From time to time a car pulled up and a guy got out to collect the contents of the cigar box.

As it got colder, Frank thought more and more about Crazy Bob and that big wad of cash. He started to ask himself what the hell he was doing out there freezing to death for a few quarters when there was an easier way to make a lot more money. He told his uncle he was quitting.

"Quitting? What the fuck do you mean you're quitting? You can't just quit!" the uncle stepped in close, threatening him.

Frank wasn't intimidated. "This is bullshit. I know of better ways to make money than standing out here freezing to death. I'm all done."

With that decision Frank's life turned another corner. The days of stealing newspaper money and fighting with teachers and other kids were behind him. From then on, the cars he stole would be work cars, used in burglaries and armed robberies. The next phase of his career was about to begin.

3

Bigger Things

Anticipating large amounts of cash in his pockets, 16-year-old Frank Cullotta was ready for his first foray into major crime: He was about to become an armed robber. However, along with the potential rewards, there were also great risks. In the Chicago of that day, it wasn't unusual to encounter a pedestrian, tavern patron, homeowner, or store cashier who was armed and wouldn't surrender his money without a fight. And if caught by the police, the criminal penalties for a robber were much more severe than pilfering from the paperboy's moneybag.

Those concerns didn't deter Frank, though. He contacted Crazy Bob Sprodak about a week after giving up his newspaper-stand job and told him he was ready for action. The two decided they would stick up a saloon that same night. But as the score went down, Frank was haunted by an old nemesis.

Sprodak assured Frank that all they needed for the job were gloves to avoid leaving any prints, a hot car, and guns. Getting the gloves and car were no problem and Bob said he'd supply the guns. Neither man had his picture on file anywhere. Bob was clean and Frank's priors were all juvenile, so they wouldn't cause him any grief. He was feeling pretty good about things until he thought about his glasses. His mother always told him that he should be a good boy, because wearing glasses made him stand out in a crowd and people would remember him if he acted up. With that warning in mind, when Frank went to rob the tavern that night, he didn't wear his specs. He never considered that the bar might not be adequately lit.

Frank and Crazy Bob charged into the tavern. Bob yelled, "Everybody put your hands up and behave!" For emphasis, he let loose with a blast from his sawed-off shotgun. The pellets shattered several of the whiskey bottles behind the bar, creating a shower of broken glass and booze. Having everyone's attention, Bob ordered them to the floor.

Frank was positioned by the door to prevent anyone from running out. He watched as the bartender and patrons obeyed Bob's instruction and went to the floor, but one obstinate man just stood there. Frank yelled for him to get down, but he didn't budge.

"What's the problem?" Bob wanted to know.

Frank started toward the stubborn patron as he answered. "This bastard won't do what he's told. But he's going down now, one way or another."

A few steps closer now, Frank realized the guy who wouldn't follow his orders wasn't a person at all; it was actually a coat rack. With hats and coats on it through his bad eyes, it had looked like a person. Embarrassed, he hit the coat rack and knocked it over. As the robbers ran out of the building with their loot, the sound of

Crazy Bob's laughter was ringing in Frank's ears.

Although Frank's first armed robbery had been successful, he was concerned that if word got out about the coat rack, he'd never live it down. "You've gotta promise you'll never tell anybody about that goddamn coat rack," Frank insisted, as they drove away from the scene of the crime. "Promise?"

Crazy Bob chuckled, then turned serious. "Sure, Frankie. Your secret's safe with me." Then he laughed again. "Just make sure that if you ever decide to do any shooting on one of these jobs, you know where in the hell I am before you pull the trigger."

Frank continued to shun wearing his glasses on scores. But from then on he didn't go inside on tavern robberies unless he was sure the place was well-lit.

Chicago had a lot of bars and the pair started robbing two or three joints a night. It was exciting and they were making money, but Frank knew it was a dangerous occupation. He was sure it was just a matter of time until they ran into an armed bartender or customer. On top of that, Bob was getting more trigger happy, shooting up the places. He figured he'd better get away from Crazy Bob before something really bad happened.

After Frank quit doing armed robberies with Sprodak, he started pulling tavern jobs with another friend. It wasn't long before he'd put together a four-man crew. Following in his father's footsteps, Frank became the wheel man on these robberies. He did all the driving, while the rest of his gang ran into the saloons hollering like a bunch of cowboys. Even so, they were becoming more professional about it, wearing gloves and masks to protect their identities.

Frank's concern about armed patrons turned out to be well-founded during a tavern robbery in Cicero. This was one of several

Chicago suburbs that were heavily mob connected. Independent thieves had to be careful pulling jobs in such areas, because Outfit guys might be running or hanging out in the targeted establishment. Robbing connected businesses or individuals could be dangerous on the spot or have repercussions later on. Or both.

On that night Frank manned the work car while his crew entered the tavern to pull the job. They were only inside a few seconds when the sound of gunfire shattered the night. The door to the bar flew open and the robbers came running out to the getaway car. Two men from the bar were chasing them; both had guns and were shooting. As Frank pulled away from the curb, the windows in the car were shattered by the gunfire.

"Jesus Christ!" one of the crew hollered as a bullet creased his hair, then went right out the windshield. "Let's get the hell out of here!" another shouted, returning fire.

"We're not out of the woods yet!" Frank yelled, as the car gained speed. "We've still got to get out of Cicero and make it home. Keep an eye out for the cops and other cars," he added, calming down.

"It's going to be a long half-hour ride back to the neighborhood," someone else said.

"I think we're in the clear." Frank breathed a sigh of relief, after putting the tavern some distance behind. "I'm going to pull over and switch plates. Keep your guns drawn."

Things went smooth until they got near their area; then an unmarked police car pulled behind them and turned on the lights and siren. Frank pushed the accelerator to the floor and the pursuit was on. He turned a corner and found a car stopped in the middle of the street. It happened that Tony Spilotro and a couple of other guys were in the car that was blocking Frank's route. He yelled at them and Tony got the car out of the way, but the cops were gaining. Frank told his men to back them off. For the second time that night bullets whistled through the air. After a few shots the police car went out of control and hit a utility pole; the officers were uninjured, but stopped. Completing their escape, the thieves dumped the hot car and went home.

As for the robber whose hair had been creased by a bullet, it had been too close a call for him. That was his last robbery.

In spite of all the excitement, the take from the robbery wasn't that great, only about $500. The newspaper reports of the incident said that a couple of armed patrons had driven the robbers off. Frank never found out if the shooters were connected to the Outfit.

• • •

The next day, Frank and his boys were in their hangout, an Italian restaurant called the Pizza Palace, when Tony came in. They talked about what happened the previous night, the police chase and the cop car being wrecked.

"I think you fuckin' guys are crazy, but you've got balls," Tony said. "How'd you like to come in on a deal I've got working?"

At that time Tony was working his way up the Outfit ladder, pursuing his goal of becoming a main man. He was then part of a crew run by Outfit guy James "Turk" Torello. Unlike his buddy, however, Frank preferred to stay independent and call his own shots. In that respect he was a renegade. But even though he was leery of getting involved with Tony because it might mean hooking up with and being controlled by the mobsters, he was intrigued and wanted to hear more. "What kind of deal are you talking about?"

"Turk's got a thing going that's safer and pays better than the robberies you're doing. We call it the bank route."

"You mean sticking up banks?"

"No. All we do is lay on [watch] the banks, looking for messengers coming in to get money for businesses. These guys follow a routine. If you get behind them in line at the bank, you can tell how much cash they'll be carrying by the color of the bands holding the stacks of money they take out. Once you identify a messenger and know how big a score to expect, you can rob him a week or two later after he leaves the bank."

Frank liked what he was hearing, but was concerned about getting involved with Torello. "You're already with a crew. How do we fit in?"

Tony smiled. "I can work with Turk and you guys, too. There are a lot of banks around and I'm an ambitious guy."

Frank knew that if they threw in with him, Tony would make sure some of the money from their scores was kicked back to the Outfit. They wouldn't allow him to moonlight otherwise. Frank wasn't thrilled about having to pay the mob a tribute. In fact, the idea galled him. Still, it sounded like easy work with good earning potential. He glanced at his crew and got their nods of approval. "Okay, we're in," he said.

A few days later, Tony, Frank, and one of his crew drove to Kenosha, Wisconsin, where they did their first bank-messenger robbery. It was a $20,000 score. The only drawback was the travel; the distance back to Chicago increased their chances of getting caught. They decided to do future jobs closer to home.

For nearly a year Frank's gang, along with Tony, pulled a number of successful bank-messenger robberies in and around Chicago.

Dennis Griffin and Frank Cullotta

As it turned out, though, an unplanned caper led to the end of the bank-route heists.

One of Frank's crew was having a problem tailing a messenger and asked Frank for help. "I've been watching a guy at a bank in Oak Park. Every time he leaves the bank he walks through a tunnel and then I lose him. How about coming with me and help me follow him?"

"Sure. We'll use that big Lincoln of yours to scout it out. We'll figure out his route and take him later."

After parking the car in an alley nearby, they watched the tunnel at the time the messenger always made his run. True to form, he came along right on schedule. The appearance of the two thieves must have scared the messenger, though. As soon as he spotted them, he screamed, "Don't hurt me! Here! Take it!" Then he threw the moneybag at Frank. As the messenger disappeared back into the tunnel, the two thieves looked at each other in disbelief and broke into laughter. Then they grabbed the money and took off.

As they started to drive away, Frank noticed some guys in a car stopped at the end of the alley. Not sure who they were, the thieves decided to get out of the area quick. The Lincoln went by the other car fast, but not fast enough.

What had been one of the easiest scores of Frank's early career turned out to be costly in the end. One of the occupants of the other car noted the Lincoln's plate number.

•   •   •

At the time of the Oak Park incident, the Chicago Police Department's robbery detail was under the command of Frank Pape.

This legendary cop is credited with killing nine alleged criminals in the line of duty and was responsible for sending 300 more to prison. He survived a 39-year law-enforcement career and passed away in March 2000 at the age of 91.

One of Pape's detectives was Tom Durso, who was also an extremely tough guy. Durso and an associate, a reputed Outfit enforcer named Mike Gargano, used to shake down the thieves, demanding a cut of their scores. The word on the street was that if you failed to pay, you could end up dead. If you were a crook, these were good men to stay away from—for more than one reason.

As a result of the Oak Park bank-messenger job, Frank Cullotta had the misfortune of having encounters with all three of them. It was his first adult interrogation by the Chicago cops, one of the worst of many to come.

Things began to unravel for Frank when witnesses passed the license-plate number of his friend's Lincoln to the police. The cops traced the registration to Frank's partner, who was known to them. Durso and Gargano went on the prowl and picked up Frank and his buddy on the street. First they handcuffed and beat Frank's pal. He denied being involved in the Oak Park situation and stuck to his story. Eventually, he was released.

Next it was Frank's turn. Durso and Gargano put him in their car, then Durso stuck a gun in his face. "Where's the fuckin' money?"

Frank acted confused. "What money?"

"Cut the shit. You know goddamn well what I'm talking about. Where is it?"

"I don't know nothin' about any money. You must have me mixed up with somebody else."

"Listen, you prick, we could whack you right now and dump you out on the street. Nobody'd know any better and they wouldn't miss you, because you're just a scumbag crook."

Frank hung tough. "I tell you I don't know what the fuck you're talkin' about."

Frank's denials enraged Durso and Gargano, who worked him over pretty good. Further demands that he admit to the robbery and divulge the location of the messenger's money were unsuccessful. Frank was then transported to the station and up to the detective's office on the eleventh floor, where he was handcuffed to the back of a chair. A few minutes later, Frank Pape walked in. He said, "How ya doin?"

Assuming the question had been directed at him, Frank answered. "I'm doin' pretty good."

Pape had apparently been talking to Durso. He grabbed a phone book from a desk and hit Frank in the head with it. "Who's talkin' to you, you no-good cocksucker? When I tell you to talk, you talk. Otherwise, shut the fuck up. Understand?"

This time, Frank's *failure* to answer resulted in another crack in the head with the phone book. That was followed by a punch in the chest, knocking both him and the chair over backwards. Looking up at Pape, Frank said, "I haven't done anything wrong and don't even know why I'm here."

Pape said to Durso, "Get the cattle prods in here. I'm going to make this son of a bitch talk."

A few minutes later, the cattle prods were applied near Frank's testicles. The same questions were asked over and over: Tell us about the robbery. Who was with you? Where's the money?

Each time, the prisoner answered that he didn't know what his interrogators were talking about. Every denial was followed by a zap with the cattle prods. Screaming in agony, Frank told the cops what he thought of them, generating additional pain. But through it all he didn't talk. He didn't admit to anything.

After a while, Pape left the room. On his way out he said to Durso, "Throw this bastard out the window. Say he tried to escape."

Hanging out the window by his ankles, Frank prayed he wouldn't be dropped. Durso fired more questions at him as he hung upside down, but Frank kept his mouth shut. Eventually, he was pulled back inside where Frank Pape was waiting. He said, "Was your father Joe Cullotta?"

"Yes."

"Are you trying to be the man he was? You aren't going to make it. You'll never be the man he was."

Finally, Frank was turned loose. He'd made it through the session, but had definitely taken the worst of it. He'd meet up with Durso and Gargano again, though under very different circumstances.

• • •

On his way home, Frank stopped to see Tony Spilotro, who was then a partner with one of the Outfit guys in a restaurant called King Burger. Noting Frank's black eye, Tony asked, "What the fuck happened to you?"

"The cops picked me up for that Oak Park thing. There was Frank Pape, Durso, and his buddy Gargano." He raised his shirt to display the bruises.

"What'd you tell them?"

Dennis Griffin and Frank Cullotta

"I didn't tell them shit. If I had, I wouldn't be here now. I'd be locked the fuck up."

Tony was impressed. "That's good, Frankie. Fuck those assholes."

"You wanna know the worst part? They used cattle prods on me."

Tony couldn't believe it. "*What?* Those cocksuckers used cattle prods? Rotten bastards."

"Yeah, and now anytime a messenger gets robbed, they'll be looking for me. I've gotta give up the bank route, Tony. I've gotta find something they won't connect me with."

It didn't take long for Frank to find what he was looking for: a market for automobile spark plugs. He located a warehouse full of them and a guy called an "out," who'd buy the hot merchandise. Frank and an associate broke into the warehouse, but were spotted while loading up their work car. The police arrived just as Frank was making his getaway. A chase ensued.

Reaching speeds of a hundred miles an hour, Frank lost the cops without incident. After ditching the car, he and his partner split up on foot. But a police patrol picked up the other guy and he gave up Frank.

During court proceedings, Frank's lawyer worked a deal with the prosecutor. The charges were reduced from felonies to misdemeanors in return for a guilty plea. In 1956, shortly before he turned 18, Frank began his first adult incarceration, a one-year sentence in the House of Corrections, a City of Chicago facility. His sister and mother were disappointed in him. But his mother remained supportive and came to see him regularly. She was his only visitor.

Being locked up wasn't that much of a hardship for Frank. He'd been conditioned for it by his encounters with the juvenile system. In fact, the guards at the adult facilities treated the inmates better than in the juvenile lockups. And he knew several of the other inmates from his reform-school days. Throughout Frank's criminal career, he never did time in a place where he didn't know some of his fellow convicts from the streets.

By the time he got out, Tony and the rest of Frank's gang were working with the Outfit in Cicero. Continuing his desire to remain independent of the mob, Frank quickly hooked up with a couple of other guys and started a new crew. He also hooked up with a new girlfriend, Ann.

Ann was underage, so when they decided on a whim to get married, they had to elope. A few months later, Ann announced she was pregnant. Their daughter Angela was born about six months after that. Frank and Ann were not only too young to get married. They were also way too wild to settle into family life. Soon thereafter, Ann filed for a divorce.

• • •

Frank managed to stay out of jail for the next few years, but in 1960 he got busted again in conjunction with the burglary of a large appliance store. It was plain bad luck. Frank and another burglar made entry through the front door, unaware that an off-duty rookie cop walking to a store to get milk for his baby was about to pass by. The cop noticed the burglary and dropped a dime on the thieves.

After entering the building, Frank looked out the front window and saw cops all around the place. "Find a place to hide," his accomplice said. "You've got a record and I don't. Let them arrest me."

Frank climbed into the drop ceiling and concealed himself while the cops were arresting his friend. More bad luck: The ceiling gave way and Frank came crashing down right in front of the officers. He looked up and saw a bunch of guns in his face.

While being held in the Cook County Jail on the burglary charge, Frank found himself housed on a tier with Sam Giancana, head of the Chicago mob from 1957 to 1966. One of the other inmates introduced Frank to the Boss. Giancana told Frank, "I've heard a lot about you, kid. You remind me of myself; I was a wild kid, too. But you've got to learn to control that temper of yours. Maybe when you get out, I'll be able to help you some time."

Frank had no desire to join the Outfit, but he was flattered by the offer from the top mobster. He was also impressed with Giancana's clout behind bars: He lived like a king. He had his own stove and refrigerator; people cooked for him and washed and ironed his clothes; guards brought him filet mignon. During the four days they spent together, Frank got to share those delicious meals.

Another inmate of some note who shared those meals was Richard Cain, a Giancana associate and former cop. In the 1992 book *Double Cross*, co-authored by Giancana's half-brother Chuck and nephew Sam, the authors allege that Giancana was part of a CIA conspiracy to assassinate John F. Kennedy. They assert that Giancana said it was Cain, not Lee Harvey Oswald, who fired the shots from the Texas School Book Depository building in Dallas that day. Cain was murdered more than a decade later, in a Chicago sandwich shop on December 20, 1973, in an apparent mob hit.

Frank was able to get the burglary charge for the appliance-store heist reduced to a misdemeanor, but he was sentenced to the

House of Corrections for another year. The rookie cop who saw the break-in and sounded the alarm was subsequently transferred, then promoted, and ended up as warden of the county jail.

• • •

Frank estimates that, including his confinement in the reform school, by the time he reached his 22nd birthday he'd been locked up a total of about three and a half years. In spite of all those days of lost freedom, when Frank got out of the slammer, he had no intention of giving up the criminal life. He was still in his early 20s and he enjoyed the excitement of it. He believed he was already a good thief and would only get better. Living on the right side of the law didn't appeal to him at all.

It didn't take Frank long to get back in harness. Shortly after he hit the streets, Tony Spilotro introduced him to a guy who provided tips on potential burglary or robbery victims. The tipster said he had inside information from an insurance company that the home of the heirs to Dad's Old Fashioned Root Beer contained a large amount of valuables.

Frank knew the robbery would require a home invasion. When he got information that the husband and wife were out of the house for the evening, the gang made its move. They hid in the shrubbery along the driveway, waiting for the couple to come home. When the husband got out of the car and opened the garage door, the robbers charged them, took their keys, and escorted them into the house. A live-in maid was in her quarters and the two kids were sleeping in their rooms. Everyone was tied up and the thieves spent about three hours going through the place.

This time the score was a bust. Instead of an anticipated take of about $100,000, the thieves ended up with around $600 each. In spite of the paltry sum, the newspapers played the robbery up big. A few months later Frank heard that a couple of guys had been charged with the heist. Although innocent, they were convicted and sentenced to 15 years in prison.

Even though this adventure turned out to be a disappointment, Frank and Tony never gave up on using tipsters. On the contrary, they were a major resource for the duo throughout the years, particularly during their time in Las Vegas.

• • •

Frank, Tony, and their crews always went on jobs anticipating worthwhile scores. They gathered intelligence on potential victims and developed detailed plans to minimize the chances of being caught. In order to keep tabs on the cops, for example, the thieves carried police radios in the work cars to monitor their calls. There were no portable radios in those days, so the radio had to be plugged into the car's cigarette lighter, using an adapter. The driver had the police radio and a walkie-talkie; the guys doing the burglary had walkie-talkies.

The plans included a pick-up spot in case something went wrong. If it did and there was time, the burglars brought the stolen property with them to that location. But if the situation demanded an immediate escape, the loot was left behind. When there were no problems, the work car backed up to the building and the booty was loaded right there.

The crooks were after cash mostly, but on a bad night they took anything they thought they might be able to sell. They knew a fence who'd buy most of the junk. He didn't pay much, but anything was better than nothing.

They tried to be as professional as possible, but they were all in the midst of a volatile time of life in a dangerous business. And on occasion, there were personal scores to settle. Frank's first armed-robbery partner Crazy Bob Sprodak, for one, always seemed to wind up in the middle of a beef.

Sprodak came to Frank and complained that members of a gang known as the K Knights had roughed him up. He said that these were some big goons and he needed help in getting his revenge.

Tony and Frank told Bob they'd help him. The trio put together some Molotov cocktails and a couple of rifles, then stole a car. With Tony driving they pulled up in front of the K Knights' hangout, got out of the car, fired a few shots through the window, and tossed in the Molotovs. As the cops closed in, the three got away. But one of the K Knights was able to identify Frank and he was arrested two days later. He was charged with arson and attempted murder. His lawyer was able to get the arson rap dropped completely and the attempted murder reduced to a misdemeanor. For the third straight time Frank had avoided a felony conviction. However, he drew another year of incarceration, this time in the custody of Cook County.

During Frank's second stint in the county jail, he had a little easier time of it. By then, the warden was none other than the rookie cop who'd seen Frank and his crew breaking into the appliance store. He felt that Frank was responsible for getting him the prestigious position and visited the inmate every day. Any reasonable request Frank made of the warden was granted. He served his year and returned to the streets.

Before Frank went away, though, he and Crazy Bob pulled another caper. They were taking a load of merchandise to Frank's fence when a police car pulled alongside and the cop motioned them to pull over. Frank pretended he was about to comply, then slammed into a U-turn. The cop turned on his siren and the pursuit began. Frank was running red lights and doing eighty.

"The fucking cops are shooting at us!" Crazy Bob yelled. Just then a bullet passed through the car and struck the windshield. "Let me out of this goddamn car!"

Frank made a few more turns and wound up on a street that the cops had sealed off a couple of blocks ahead. He drove up onto the sidewalk and pulled into an alley. He and Bob bailed out while the car was still rolling; it hit a lamppost and stopped. They split up and eluded capture.

The escapade made the newspapers. Another high-speed chase, shots fired, and the bad guys got away. But this marked the end of Frank's affiliation with Sprodak. Just being around Crazy Bob provided a little more excitement than he wanted and from then on, Frank kept his distance. It was a good thing he did. Several years later Bob and a guy called Sausage Fingers were doing burglaries when one night they hit the house of a close associate of Tony Accardo, the Outfit boss. The mobsters went nuts. They rounded up all the known thieves, including Frank and his crew, and wanted to know who'd done Accardo's friend's place. Frank told them he didn't know anything about it.

Someone must have talked, though. Sausage Fingers was killed in his car right in front of his house and Crazy Bob disappeared.

One day as Tony and Frank were riding down the Eisenhower

Expressway, Tony pointed at the pillars under an overpass. He said, "Did you know that Crazy Bob is the foundation for one of them?"

Frank didn't want to believe it. "You gotta be kidding."

Tony laughed. "No, I'm not. Crazy Bob is holding up the fucking overpass."

. . .

Frank had been earning his living on the wrong side of the law for nearly 10 years. His scores were growing and his methods becoming more sophisticated, but his targets were riskier. Frank wasn't shy about hitting a jewelry store now and then, but they weren't easy to burglarize and the jobs required special planning. Frank came up with two ideas and used them both.

For the first plan Frank had his partner, a guy named Duke, dress up in a painter's uniform, complete with splotches of color on it. He even used a van that looked like a painter's work vehicle. The scheme called for Duke to enter the store and ask to see a piece of jewelry, then to mace both clerks. At that point Frank would come in and they'd tie up the clerks, put a closed-for-remodeling sign in the window, grab the merchandise, and run.

On the day of the caper there were only a couple of minor snags. When Frank walked into the store, the mace was still in the air and he and Duke both got it in their faces. It was annoying, but not debilitating. And as Frank was locking the door, a guy wanted to come in to get a bracelet. Frank told him the store was closed and sent him on his way. He and Duke cleaned out the vault and got away with a pretty good haul.

The second plot required Frank to do something he never

Dennis Griffin and Frank Cullotta

thought he'd do: dress as a Chicago cop. He'd have the whole uniform on—belt, badge, gun, everything issued to real cops. Frank took two other men on the job with him. One of them would assist Frank inside the store after he gained control of the employees; the other would man the work car.

Frank entered the store and asked to see the manager. He told the manager his car was parked illegally and he had to move it right away or get a ticket. When the manager and the clerks came out from behind the counter to check the parking situation, Frank pulled his gun and ordered them to the floor. He told them that no one would get hurt if they stayed still. The manager realized that something was fishy and was slow to comply. He looked at Frank and said, "You've gotta be kidding. You're not a real police officer."

Frank snarled, "It doesn't make any difference who the fuck I am. You'd better get on the goddamn floor, stay quiet, and don't look up."

When all the employees were under control, Frank used a walkie-talkie to contact the work car. His assistant came in and they loaded a duffle bag. In jewelry-store robberies, the safe was always emptied first to assure making off with the most valuable stuff—the diamonds. Then, time permitting, lesser items were taken. Watches were a low priority, because they could be easily traced by their serial numbers.

After cleaning the place out, the crew took the employees into a back room and tied them up with duct tape. Then they pulled the phones out of the wall and left with a good score.

• • •

Frank knew that a criminal who committed the same type of crime in the same manner for too long was asking to get caught. He switched his modus operandi on similar jobs every so often and didn't stay with any one particular type of larceny for a prolonged period. He was always on the lookout for different targets and techniques. Eschewing jewelry stores for a while, he set his sights on public pay phones, which took in a lot of money. The trick was to come up with a tool to open the coin boxes quickly.

Frank contacted a man with locksmithing experience and told him what he had in mind. The guy said if Frank brought him a pay phone, he'd see what he could do. Frank went out, ripped a phone off a wall, and delivered it to his colleague.

It took about ten pay phones before the problem was solved. The easiest way to get the boxes open was by punching out the locks. Frank and the lock man made a tool to put up against the cylinder. Using a five-pound sledge, they were able to knock in the lock, which released the latch holding the coin box in place.

Then Frank specially modified a work car for looting the pay phones. He installed a false gas tank and cut a hole above it in the rear floorboard. This enabled him to dump the coins through the hole in the floorboard and into the fake gas tank. The hole was then covered with a metal plate and carpeting.

To keep the phone company from learning how the coin boxes were being ripped off, thereby prompting them to improve their security, the thieves disposed of the empty boxes where they wouldn't be recovered.

After a few months Frank's locksmith friend developed a pick that made getting into the coin boxes even easier. But the phone company got its hands on one of the picks and changed the mecha-

Dennis Griffin and Frank Cullotta

nism, so it was back to the drawing board for Frank and his crew.

By then, however, Frank decided it was time to move on to greener pastures.

●　●　●

From pay phones, Frank progressed to "boosting." This two-person operation involved theft by trickery rather than force. The first person walked into a jewelry or department store and distracted the salesperson. Meanwhile, the accomplice removed the real merchandise from the display case and replaced it with phony stuff. By not leaving the cases empty, the clerks never even realized they'd been had.

Frank boosted with a girl named Debbie, who he thought was probably the best in the world at her chosen trade. She wasn't only attractive, she was fast. They weren't romantically involved; their connection was all business. The pair boosted all over Chicago. Once, they even went to Florida, though it required bringing all the stolen goods back to Chicago to sell. But they had fun, and the jobs were safe, clean, and easy.

Debbie was also sharp when it came to making and managing money. She owned her own home, had a new car, and sold boosted merchandise right out of her house. She knew a lot of people and they couldn't wait for her to get back from her trips so they could buy stolen goods at wholesale prices. She didn't believe in giving the stuff to a fence when she could make a lot more money selling it herself.

Debbie was about eight years older than Frank and real particular about whom she worked with. He considered himself fortunate that she teamed with him. Although they were making money and the jobs weren't particularly risky, boosting didn't fit into Frank's long-term plans. His goal was to become a big-shot thief, doing daring robberies and burglaries that were recognized by his peers as the work of a consummate professional. So he split with Debbie and got back into committing more serious crimes.

. . .

Though Frank and Debbie never became a couple, by this time he'd turned into something of a "thief about town." He loved to drink and party with women, who considered him a sport in return. He also developed a fondness for nice automobiles. Of course, both required a lot of money.

Frank thought nothing of using his ill-gotten gains to support a lavish lifestyle. It seemed to him that was what life was all about. For example, he bought a new car two or three times a year; sometimes he had four. He can't explain his affinity for cars, but he learned that having nice wheels made the guys jealous and attracted the girls.

Frank also tended to be generous with his money. He took care of his family financially. His mother wouldn't take cash from him outright. She knew how Frank made his living and didn't want that kind of money. To get around her attitude, Frank invested for her. He had her house refurbished, making it into a beautiful home.

In addition, he felt that if somebody was down, he should help them get back up again. He discovered he had to be careful when offering money to a proud man who was down on his luck or it could cause resentment. He made an effort to make people comfortable when accepting money from him.

The ladies actually enjoyed his company; it wasn't just because he spent a lot of money that they wanted to be around him. They found him to be understanding, easy to talk to, and not just after what he could get from them.

He also had another motive for bumming around with women: Frank knew that hanging out with the guys usually meant getting in a fight in one of the saloons, having his face messed up and his clothes ruined.

Some Outfit guys resented his popularity with the ladies, though. One night he got into a fight with a guy named Joey over a girl. Her name was Judy and she later married future Outfit boss Joe Ferriola.

Joey and another guy owned a disco lounge in the suburbs. Frank pulled in there one night and drew a few funny looks from the bartender and regulars when he walked into the lounge. He was sitting at the bar when Joey asked him to step outside to talk. When they got outdoors, Joey wanted to know why Frank had said this, that, and the other thing about him to Judy. Frank didn't know what Joey was talking about. And then Joey threw a punch. Frank threw him to the ground, with Joey's head bouncing off a car bumper as he went down. Frank got on top of him, but two of Joey's Outfit pals grabbed Frank; the three of them worked him over pretty good. When they let Frank go, he went to his car and drove home, but he was so angry, he was homicidal.

After washing up, Frank took a gun and drove back to the lounge to kill Joey, but his target had already left. The matter was over for that night, but Frank was far from ready to forget about it. He talked to Judy and learned that it had actually been a friend of his who'd made the comments Joey found offensive, but Joey wrongfully assumed they'd come from Frank. That explanation did little to calm Frank's anger, though.

About three days later and still enraged, Frank was driving down the street when a car with Joe "Gags" Gagliano in it pulled him over. Gags was one of the Outfit bosses and had heard about what happened at the disco. Fearing there might be more trouble, he wanted to talk to Frank.

Gags said, "Frankie, Joey was way out of line the other night. He knows he was wrong, so why don't you just forget about it. Okay?"

"Fuck him! I want a piece of that bastard, just him and me. If his buddies want in, I'll take 'em all on one at a time."

"It's all straightened out. Joey will never talk to you again or even look at you. I don't want for there to be any more problems. Let it go," Gags said.

The next day Frank saw Tony. "You know, I'm thinking about whacking Joey, that cocksucker," Frank said.

"I wouldn't do that, Frankie," Tony said. "Shit like that can start a fuckin' war. Know what I mean?"

"Are you telling me I've gotta live with the idea that I took a beating from Joey and his guys and didn't do anything about it?"

"Look, Frankie, you were asked nice to leave this thing alone. You don't want to offend anybody by ignoring that and going after Joey anyway. That could be bad news. Things might change some-day, but for now I'd let it go if I was you."

"Okay," Frank said. "It's over."

Tony Spilotro had given his friend good advice. Those who violated mob protocols were often subject to sanctions, including death. This was a fact that would hit Frank very close to home in the not-too-distant future.

• • •

Frank saw his ex-wife Ann around town from time to time, but rarely spoke to her, not even to inquire about their daughter Angela. Frank wanted to see his daughter, but Ann wasn't interested.

That changed in 1965 when Ann came looking for Frank. She was having problems with her new husband and needed money. They met at the Colony House Restaurant on Grand and Harlem. Ann brought along Angela. Confronting a daughter who was now nearly eight years old, one he hadn't seen since in over seven years, made for an uncomfortable encounter for Frank. Before the meeting ended, he gave Ann $2,000, hoping she'd spend some of it on Angela.

After that get-together, Ann and Angela dropped out of sight and Frank didn't see them again until 1975. During the intervening nine years, Ann went through three husbands. She told Frank she thought it was time their daughter, now almost 17, got to know her real father. He spent one whole day with Angela. They went through a photo album she'd kept over the years, then he took her for a ride and bought her some clothes, spending about $1,600 on her. It was a fun day.

Angela told Frank she'd learned how to drive, but didn't have a car. A few days later he bought her a Volkswagen. When he went to look her up about a week later, she and Ann were gone.

The M&M Boys

While Frank made sure to stay independent of the Outfit, his pal Tony Spilotro was determined to become part of it. Spilotro not only worked as a thief for Outfit-connected crews, he also began to develop his reputation as an enforcer when he went to work for a loanshark and mob associate named "Mad Sam" DeStefano.

DeStefano was known to friend and foe as being completely insane. While dealing with his enemies, his depravity knew no bounds. Mad Sam preferred to use an ice pick on his victims, but wasn't above knifing, shooting, or incinerating them, depending on his mood. Although he was unstable, the bosses kept him around because he was a good earner. In addition to being an accomplished torturer and killer, Sam reputedly had another talent: He could spot young up-and-comers who shared his proclivity for brutality. DeStefano apparently liked what he saw in Tony Spilotro and recruited him to help collect money from delinquent borrowers and assist in other enforcement matters. In that capacity, Tony was allegedly involved in the 1961 murder of a man named William "Action" Jackson.

Jackson, part of Mad Sam's loansharking operation, apparently became greedy. Sam thought Jackson was skimming money and wanted to make an example of him. It's believed that Spilotro and tough guy Chuckie Grimaldi, who later turned government witness, were part of the team Sam assigned to the task. According to sources familiar with the case, Jackson was taken prisoner by DeStefano's men and tortured for two days.

Jackson, who weighed more than 300 pounds, was stripped naked and hung on a meat hook. He was beaten and stabbed with ice picks. Strips of his skin were peeled off with a razor. And a blowtorch was used on his genitals. The inquisition ended when Jackson's heart finally gave out. Presumably, the grisly discovery of his mutilated body sent a clear message to anyone else considering stealing from Mad Sam.

Frank Cullotta first met Sam DeStefano in the North Avenue Steak House. He and Tony Spilotro were sitting at the bar when Sam came over. He must have been drunk, because he was ranting and raving about future Outfit underboss Jackie Cerone—who was later convicted for skimming money from Las Vegas casinos—and picking on everyone in the place. Frank found Sam to be an obnoxious blowhard and told Tony they had to leave. He couldn't stand being around him.

In 1963, Mad Sam got into a dispute with Leo Foreman, a real-estate broker and one of his collectors. Not long after, Spilotro and Chuck Grimaldi reportedly lured Foreman to the home of Mario DeStefano, Sam's brother, in Cicero. The two beat Foreman, then dragged him into the cellar where Mad Sam was waiting. Skipping an exchange of pleasantries, Sam got right down to business. He took a hammer to Foreman's knees, head, groin, and ribs. Next came twenty ice-pick thrusts, followed by a bullet to the head. The realtor's battered body was later found in the trunk of an abandoned car.

So, by the early 1960s, Tony Spilotro—only in his mid-20s and recently married to Milwaukee-born Nancy Stuart—had risen from school bully to a made man in the powerful Chicago Outfit. His reputation as a ruthless enforcer was in place and some of his best years were still ahead.

• • •

Tony tried to convince Frank that he should go to work for the Outfit. He said he was making all kinds of money muscling Jews, loansharking, sports betting, and running book joints. In fact, to help convince him, Tony recruited Frank for a big jewelry score he was lining up.

A jeweler from New York was bringing a big load of diamonds to town and would be robbed when the diamonds were delivered to a shop in the Maller Building, a high-rise that housed wholesale jewelry stores.

"The place we're going to hit is in the Maller Building on Wabash," Tony told Frank. "There will be four guys on the job, two doing the robbery and two inside men. I won't be there, but I'll get an equal split of the take. It's going to be a big score."

"Who else have you got besides me?"

"The two Jew brothers that own the store are in on the deal with us; they're our inside guys. You and I will pick the fourth man."

"Let's do it," Frank said.

They selected the fourth crew member, cased the Maller Building, and made their plans. On the appointed day, Frank and his accomplice, each carrying a briefcase containing a .45 revolver, entered the building, took the stairs to the second floor, the elevator to the seventh, and the stairs to the eighth. When they got to the store, they were buzzed into a lobby area. Frank's partner flashed a private-investigator's business card that allowed them to enter an inner room. In the second room were the two store owners and the New York jeweler. Frank and his partner forced the three to the floor, tied them up, and closed all the blinds.

As planned, the safe was empty, but Frank went through the motions of searching it to make it look good to the New Yorker. Then he searched the man's attaché case. Inside were packages and packages of diamonds; the thieves had found what they'd come for. For appearances sake, the robbers continued to look around for another ten minutes, then left.

After getting back to their car, Frank drove downtown while his associate opened up some of the packages. Suddenly the other man said, "Motherfucker! I think there's more here than they told us."

"Let's see," Frank said, glancing at the opened packages.

"What are we going to do?"

Frank shrugged. "We can't do anything. We already made our deal."

When they arrived at the designated meeting place, they turned all the diamonds over to Tony and a guy named Mike, who'd set up the job. The value of the merchandise wasn't mentioned. The following day the newspaper reports stated that the stolen diamonds had a value of $500,000. The cut Frank and the other guy got was based on a take of a lot less than that. But Frank knew better than to mention it. He told his confederate, "I'm not going to start a war by accusing Tony of shorting us."

The brothers who owned the store claimed the loss on their insurance and collected big. In addition, they got their cut from the score itself. But the cops were suspicious of them and put on a lot of pressure. One of the brothers couldn't handle it and eventually committed suicide.

. . .

Frank did a slow burn over getting shorted by Tony and the mob, but he kept his feelings to himself. Still, it reinforced his inclination to remain independent when shortly after the diamond heist, Tony again pressured Frank to join up.

"Frankie, you've got all that money now and you should put it to work for you. The stuff I'm involved in is better than robbing places all the time. Let me show you how to do it."

"I don't know. I do all right on my own and I don't have to answer to anybody."

"Listen to me, Frankie. Let me set you up with a few accounts you can loan your money to. You'll get back ten percent a week in interest. Even after you give the Outfit their cut, you'll make out pretty good. Trust me, I wouldn't steer you wrong."

Reluctantly, Frank agreed. "Okay, I'll give it a try."

Tony set Frank up to put his money out on the street. But the fledgling loanshark wasn't impressed with the business. He constantly had to chase guys to collect what they owed him. After about a year of having to holler, threaten, and break some heads, Frank came to the conclusion that loansharking just wasn't his bag. Instead, he hooked up with a couple of guys, Billy McCarthy and Jimmy Miraglia, to do commercial burglaries.

• • •

The newly formed trio of Cullotta, McCarthy, and Miraglia went on a robbery binge, hitting department and jewelry stores. Their efforts were usually successful and they made some hefty scores. In addition to the actual thefts, Frank and his crew spent a lot of time keeping their equipment in good working order and improving their methods whenever possible.

The thieves drove fast cars that were licensed to fictitious addresses. They used a currency-exchange guy who could get the license plates. He was expensive, but he got the cars licensed and that was all that mattered. In addition, the work cars were modified to conceal a variety of weapons, including handguns and sawed-off shotguns. The hiding places were under the dash, inside the door panels, and in back of the driver's seat.

Knowing what the police were doing was vital to their success. Frank had a talent when it came to electronics and he put it to use.

The police were starting to be equipped with portable radios. Frank thought it would be a good idea for his crew to have them, too. But he had to figure out how to put together a portable police radio.

He contacted a guy with radio expertise named Ronnie. They got together and went over numerous radio books. "I want something that's small and easy to conceal," Frank said.

"How small?" Ronnie asked.

"I want the radios to fit inside a camera case."

Ronnie thought for a while, then he smiled. "We can do it. All we have to do is build circuit boards."

In those days police calls weren't scanned like they are today, so the radio needed only one crystal. But Frank and Ronnie put in three so they could switch channels. For power they used four square "C" batteries.

The addition of the portables let the guys doing the burglaries listen to the police calls directly. That meant the work-car driver didn't have to have a radio himself; he'd be told by walkie-talkie if something was coming down. And if the work car was stopped by the police, the driver wouldn't be charged with illegal possession of a police radio.

Frank was concerned that if the cops found out about the radios, they'd change their procedures. For that reason it was important that none of the radios fall into police hands. He decided that any extra radios they made would only be sold to the best thieves, those with the least chance of being caught.

The thieves regularly removed safes from burglarized businesses and transported them to one of their garages. If the safe's doors were square, they were peeled open with a power tool. If the safe had round doors, the crew filled it with water or sand, then cut open the doors with an acetylene torch. The purpose of the sand or water was to protect any paper money inside the safe from burning up. Once in a while a few dollars burned, but the most work came as a result of the money being wet. The damp cash was first dried in a regular clothes dryer, then every bill had to be ironed to remove the wrinkles.

Frank's gang didn't confine its efforts to Chicago; they roamed as far away as New Orleans. A tipster claimed a Big Easy Sears store regularly held around $90,000 in cash on the weekends. With that kind of incentive, the thieves headed to Louisiana.

The burglars cased the store and located all the security equipment. Only the doors and windows were alarmed. They decided to bypass the alarms by going in through the roof. But when they went back the next day, they immediately ran into trouble. The roof was concrete and they couldn't get through it. As an alternative, the burglars pried up an air-conditioning vent and started down. The first guy made it okay, but Frank got stuck part way. The guy below pulled him by the ankles and the one above put his feet on Frank's shoulders and pushed him through.

When they got to the vault, another surprise awaited them: It was encased in an ADT alarm box they couldn't penetrate. McCarthy asked, "What the fuck are we going to do now?"

"There's no sense in going away blank," Miraglia said. "Let's take all the goddamn furs."

Frank disagreed. "Furs are too risky, and the stuff they carry here isn't top of the line. It's not worth it. Let's chalk it up as a bad day and get out of here."

Frank refused to go back into the vent shaft, so he busted out a window and used it as an exit. The would-be thieves escaped with their equipment, but from Frank's perspective it was a very bad trip.

Frank and his crew needed a quick score. Frank knew a woman who worked for the rapid transit company and she told him about all the money the stations had in their booths. People paid for their monthly passes on certain days and the money stayed in the booth

Dennis Griffin and Frank Cullotta

until a Brinks truck came for it near the end of the month. Frank cased one of the booths and watched as the passengers made their payments. When the time was right, he and one accomplice did the robbery. The booth had two doors and two female clerks working. The robbers kicked in the doors, dumped the money into a bag, and left. It was an easy $15,000 score, which eased the pain of the New Orleans fiasco.

$$\bullet \quad \bullet \quad \bullet$$

Frank also started to commit some crimes on the federal level, burglarizing post offices. The goal wasn't cash, but stamps. These jobs were a piece of cake.

Post offices weren't alarmed then. Entry was easy and safes were big. The burglars peeled off the safe's door panels using a portable power tool. Then they spun the dial, lined up the bolts, and opened the door.

Postage stamps were five or six cents at the time. Tony set Frank up with a guy who paid a penny per stamp. That may not sound like much, but those safes contained sheet after sheet of stamps. Frank did only two post offices burglaries, though. He knew the feds would start setting traps and he didn't want any federal charges.

$$\bullet \quad \bullet \quad \bullet$$

Jimmy Miraglia, Frank's friend and co-thief, hung out with a guy named Mike Joyce. Though the three men went out on the saloon circuit once in a while, Frank considered Joyce a loose cannon, an Irishman who turned into a lunatic with a few drinks in him. When feeling his oats, Joyce didn't hesitate to pull a gun and let the rounds fly.

One night Frank, Jimmy, and Mike were in a place called Nicky's MGM Bar in Cicero. Mike didn't like a song on the jukebox and wanted it changed. The bartender refused. Mike whipped out his pistol and shot up the jukebox.

"Cool it, you idiot!" Frank told him. "This place is Outfit-connected."

"Fuck 'em," Mike said.

Joyce got away easy on that one. All he had to do was replace the jukebox, but he was warned not to do it again.

Another time the same threesome was in another Outfit-connected tavern in Elmwood Park. Two big guys at the bar turned out to be pro football players. The football players were drunk and obnoxious. Mike was small and thin and had the "little-man complex." He decided to tell the football players to shut up. They picked him up and threw him outside. Pretty soon Mike came back through the door, but this time he was carrying two pistols. The fight was on and the other patrons joined Frank, Jimmy, and Mike in whipping up on the football players.

Again, the Outfit wasn't happy about it. They didn't want people like Mike coming into their places, waving guns around, and making a mess. Mike got another warning, more stern than the first. But he was a slow learner. Eventually, the Outfit had enough of Mike. They shot him in the head, cut off his penis and stuffed it into his mouth, then torched him and his car. He was burned almost beyond recognition.

What happened to Mike Joyce for annoying the Outfit should

have been a lesson to others. But Billy McCarthy and Jimmy Miraglia also proved to be slow learners.

• • •

One night Billy McCarthy was out drinking by himself. He went into the Black Door, a saloon in Rosemont owned by Frank Pondeleo, an associate of Paul "the Waiter" Ricca, second in command of the Chicago Outfit. Two brothers, Ronnie and Phil Scalvo, managed it for Pondeleo. Their father was closely tied to Tony Accardo.

Billy got into an argument with Ronnie that turned into a fistfight. Ronnie and Phil beat up Billy and threw him out of the bar. Billy found Jimmy and Frank and told them what had happened. He wanted to go back to the bar and get revenge.

Frank said, "I know how you feel, Billy, but you've got to forget about it. That place is connected and you can't fuck around with those guys. If we start any more trouble, they'll whack us all."

But Billy didn't listen. A couple of nights later, he and Jimmy went back to the Black Door to get even with the Scalvos. Instead, they got another beating. Frank saw them the day after and they were still in a rage. They wanted to kill the Scalvos and asked Frank to come in on it with them. Knowing how well-connected the Scalvos were, that was the last thing he wanted to do. On the other hand, Jimmy and Billy were part of his crew and he felt he owed them some loyalty. Reluctantly, he agreed, but with the understanding that the killings couldn't take place on mob turf.

Jimmy had a fictitiously licensed work car with a hopped-up engine and hiding places inside to stash guns. For about a week they went back and forth to the lounge watching the brothers, hoping to catch them alone and follow them away from the bar to hit them. But every time the Scalvos left the tavern, a cocktail waitress left with them. The Outfit frowned on killing innocent bystanders, so Frank's crew continued to wait for the right opportunity.

One night Frank and a girl were bowling when Billy McCarthy came into the alley looking for him. "Jimmy and I are going to the Black Door tonight. Do you want to come with us?"

Frank nodded toward his girl. "I'm on a date. But I can send her home and go along with you if you want."

Billy thought it over for a few seconds. "Never mind. You stay with her."

"Here, you'd better take the key to my garage, in case you need any guns. You know where they are." Frank handed over the key.

After Billy left, Frank and his date bowled a couple more games, but he felt uneasy. He asked the girl to drive him over to the Black Door. They pulled in to get gas at a station near the bar. There, Frank saw Jimmy's work car come around the corner and drive away. Afterward, Frank and his girl went to a motel and spent the night. When they left the motel the next morning, Frank turned on the car radio and heard a news flash about a triple murder in Elmwood Park, a suburb about seven miles from Rosemont. Two men and a woman had been gunned down in their car on a side street. No identities were given, but he was pretty sure who the dead people were. It looked like Billy and Jimmy not only killed guys who were connected, they also hit the waitress. Worse yet, they did it in Elmwood Park, a heavily Outfit-connected area. Frank knew if the Outfit identified Billy and Jimmy as the shooters, they were goners. There would be no warnings or second chances.

Frank saw Billy at the bowling alley the following night. He thought Billy looked pale and acted antsy. "What did you do with the guns you took from my garage?" Frank asked.

"We had to dump them."

"Did you and Jimmy use them to whack the Scalvos and the broad?"

"We didn't do that, Frankie. I'm glad they're dead, but it wasn't us."

Frank didn't believe him, but he didn't question him further.

A couple of days later Tony was at Frank's door. Tony said they had to talk and he didn't pull any punches. "I know you hang out with Billy and Jimmy. They had a problem with the Scalvo brothers and now the Scalvos are dead, along with a waitress. They [the Outfit] think you, Billy, and Jimmy were the hit men."

"I had nothing to do with that, Tony, absolutely nothing," Frank said.

"Look, Frankie, I've been sticking up for you with these people. I personally guaranteed them you weren't there, that if you knew anything you'd tell me, huh? But here's the way it is. You've got to give up Billy and Jimmy. If you don't, I can't save you."

Frank was annoyed that Tony was trying to score points with the Outfit bosses. But he knew he had no choice in the matter. If he tried to cover for Billy and Jimmy, he'd be dead, too. Frank told Tony what happened the night of the murders, that Billy and Jimmy had done them using guns they'd taken from his garage.

Tony seemed satisfied. "You done the right thing, Frankie. Those guys fucked up bad and now they have to pay. But you've got no problem; you're going to be okay."

When Tony left, Frank knew Billy and Jimmy had no chance.

Two days later Tony asked Frank to meet him at the bowling alley. Both men were nervous. Frank figured he'd be asked to set up his friends and it was Tony's responsibility to convince the Outfit that Frank was innocent of the Scalvo killings.

Tony said, "They want to talk to Billy McCarthy and they need your help in making the arrangements."

Frank knew that if he didn't cooperate, he, too, would be a dead man. "What do you want me to do?"

"Call Billy and ask him to meet you at the North Avenue Chicken House at eight o'clock tonight."

Frank got Billy on the phone and scheduled the meet. Tony made a couple of calls on the pay phone and told Frank, "Meet me at the Howard Johnson's on North Avenue at seven forty-five. Make sure you bring your car."

Frank knew better than to ask questions.

That night he met Tony and an Outfit driver named Saint at Howard Johnson's. Tony took Frank's car and left him with Saint. Saint popped his front radio speaker and pulled out a .38. Frank turned toward him and his right hand went behind his back, where he had a gun in his waistband. Saint, knowing Frank was ready to protect himself, put his gun in a less threatening position between his legs. About forty minutes later, Tony returned. He said to Frank, "Here's your car. See you later." Frank heard him tell Saint there hadn't been any problems.

The following morning, Billy's wife called Frank. "Where's Billy?" she asked.

"I don't know. I haven't seen him."

"Something's wrong, I know it. He always calls me if he's going to be late or isn't coming home."

"I'll keep my ears open. I'll call you if I hear anything."

Frank didn't know for sure what had happened to Billy, but in his heart he figured his buddy was dead. He got part of the story talking with Tony about ten days later.

"Billy's wife called me a few days ago looking for him," Frank said.

"Frankie, Billy's gone. It's all over. Forget about it, it's done. I don't want you to say anything to Jimmy about it, though."

"Can you tell me what happened that night at the Chicken House?"

"I guess so. Billy was in the restaurant looking for you. I told him you were outside waiting for him. I said, 'Let's go see him.' When we got outside, Billy saw the Outfit guys and went for his gun. I grabbed him around the neck and shoved him in the Outfit car. Frank, Billy went rather easily."

Frank saw Jimmy Miraglia in a restaurant a few nights later. "Have you seen Billy around?" Frank asked.

"No, no I haven't. Why?"

"Don't you think that's kind of strange? Maybe you ought to make yourself scarce."

"I'm not worried. I haven't done anything wrong."

Frank learned later that the next night, Jimmy was in a lounge and some Outfit guys were outside in their work car, laying for him. Jimmy got lucky that night when the police spotted the car and searched it. They found a stash of guns and arrested everybody. That should have been another message for Jimmy, who should have run like hell right then, but he didn't. They got Jimmy the next day.

Tony told Frank all about it shortly afterward.

"Jimmy was in a lounge when we got him. We took him in the liquor storage room and beat him, but we didn't kill him. We left him locked in the room and while we were gone, Jimmy got into the booze. He was drunk when we came back for him. We took him out and put him in the trunk of his own car. Saint and I were in the follow car. While we were driving Jimmy apparently pulled out the wires for the brake lights. When we saw the brake lights in his car go, out we motioned for the driver to pull over so we could find out what the problem was. As soon as we opened the trunk Jimmy jumped out and made a run for it. We caught him, knocked him out, and took him to where we were keeping Billy's body.

"Jimmy knew he was going to be killed. He asked to be strangled so his wife could collect some insurance money. We did what he wanted and dumped him in the trunk of a car along with Billy. Then we drove the car to another neighborhood and ditched it. A couple of days later somebody noticed the stench and called the cops."

Tony was in a talkative mood that day and divulged the rest of the story about the night Billy McCarthy was killed. He said, "He was one tough fucking Irishman. We beat that motherfucker with everything, but he wouldn't tell us who did the Scalvos with him. We finally got so pissed off we put his head in a vise and turned it. The kid's eyeball popped right out of his fuckin' head. Billy begged me to kill him. He gave up Jimmy's name just before he died."

Even though Tony told Frank he was off the hook for the Scalvo killings, Cullotta was too close to what became known as the M&M Murders for comfort. He remained very cautious for the next six months. He installed security lights around his house and garage. Every time he opened the garage door, it lit up like the Loop. He even had a remote starter put on his car. They were fairly new on the market and it cost about $800, but as far as Frank was concerned, it was one of the best investments he ever made. Every day he used that remote before getting in the car. When there was no explosion, he knew he was home free. He didn't tell anybody about the starter. He considered it a life-insurance policy.

Not that Frank didn't feel bad about the deaths of Billy McCarthy and Jimmy Miraglia. Billy and Jimmy had been his friends and he set them up to be murdered. But he'd tried to talk them out of the course of action that seemed destined to destroy them. After they refused to heed his warnings, Frank did what he had to do in order to ensure his own survival.

Tony stayed in touch with Frank regularly during that period. "Relax, Frankie," he said. "You did the Outfit a great favor with Billy and Jimmy. They accept you and they know they can trust you."

"I'm clean with them, right?"

"Yeah, sure. You ought to take advantage of this opportunity to get more involved with them."

"I don't think so, Tony. Thanks, but no thanks."

Tony laughed. "Well, the door's open. You can come and join me anytime you want."

Frank knew then that he was finally connected to the Outfit. He had Tony and a few other guys on his side, so the relationship was solid. If he made a big score, he'd have to kick back some money to them. Other than that, he could do what he wanted and didn't have to answer to anybody. That was good enough for Frank.

Crime Wave

Frank Cullotta put the M&M Murders behind him and continued his life as a thief. It was, for better or worse, his chosen career. He was good at it. It afforded him a lavish lifestyle, with new cars, fancy girls, and respect on the street. And he couldn't have held a straight job, even if he wanted to, which he didn't.

Staying true to his habit of frequently changing his M.O., Frank started hijacking trucks. Color televisions were a hot item at the time—new on the market with high price tags. Frank told a friend who was a dispatcher at a truck terminal to keep his eyes open for loads of color TVs. The dispatcher started calling Frank about once a month to give him information on particular loads to hijack. Once he took the loaded truck, he sold it at the best price available. If the entire load was fenced at one time, the take was minimal. To earn more money, Frank gave a television set to ten legitimate people he knew, along with ten more sets on consignment to sell to their friends. After all the TVs were sold, Frank collected the money and split it with his crew. Everyone made out on the deal.

Another hijacking involved a load of Max Factor lipstick, with an estimated value of $350,000. Frank got involved when an acquaintance named Skeets contacted him. The hijacking went smoothly, but after three weeks, Frank's crew hadn't been paid off. Apparently, Skeets couldn't find anyone to buy a hot load of lipstick.

Meanwhile, Frank mentioned the hijacking to Tony. "I heard about that job, but I didn't know you were part of it," Tony said.

"Yeah, but this fuckin' Skeets says he hasn't sold the load yet and we haven't seen our money."

"That's true. He's got the stuff stored where it's safe. I'll keep an eye on it and make sure you get the right cut," Tony assured him.

A buyer finally came forward, but he turned out to be an undercover agent for the FBI. The feds busted Skeets and all that money went down the drain. Frank and his crew never got a dime out of it.

Frank took advantage of another situation where he had inside help to steal money from an armored truck. The father of one of his friends worked as a janitor in a garage that serviced Brinks vehicles. The father told his son how careless the Brinks drivers were with their keys, the way they left them laying around.

Frank suggested that his friend's father grab one of the keys that fit the back door of an armored truck. Frank would get the key duplicated and return it before anyone realized it was missing.

The father came through and for the next week, Frank followed the particular truck on its route, always using a different car. Finally, the truck stopped at a big shopping mall and both guards went inside. Frank rolled up in the work car, unlocked the back door, and grabbed four bags of money. Frank's friend and his father received 20% of the take.

The next day, the newspaper reported the missing money. The report said the driver of the truck was being investigated; the next story said it must have been an inside job. A later article said the moneybags had probably fallen out the back door of the truck.

Frank's first armored-truck score had been a larceny from an unattended truck. His next effort was an armed robbery and he believes it was the first of its kind in Chicago.

Another thief named Peanuts approached Frank about a Brinks money-truck heist Peanuts wanted him to come in on. Frank lived in Franklin Park, close to where the robbery was taking place. In exchange for using his house, Peanuts agreed to let Frank participate in the robbery.

Peanuts explained that the robbery would take place in Norridge, a suburb adjoining Franklin Park. "We're going to hit the truck when it stops at a church rectory to pick up the money taken in on the weekend collections. The church is located in a secluded area with very little traffic."

Peanuts also explained the financial arrangements. "Five of us will actually pull the robbery. Two other guys won't be involved directly, but will receive equal cuts. Because of the size of the score—a half-million dollars or more—we'll have to make a kickback to the Outfit."

On the day of the robbery, Frank and two others went to the rectory. When a priest answered the door, he was grabbed and tied up. He said, "Boys, please don't do this."

"We're here for the armored truck, Father. We don't mean you any harm," Frank assured him, then gagged him and put him in another room. The intruders found the closet containing robes and other priestly clothing. One of the crew donned that garb, while another put on a Brinks uniform that had been brought along for the job.

The truck showed up. When the guard knocked on the door, the guy dressed like a priest let him in. The robbers held their guns on him while he was tied and gagged. The fake Brinks guard went out to the truck carrying a bag stuffed with clothes to make it look like it held money. He knocked on the door window, following Brinks procedure. When the driver popped open the door, he was grabbed, taken into the rectory, then tied and gagged.

Frank kept an eye on the priest and guards while the other two drove the armored truck into an adjacent cemetery to unload the money into one of the work cars that was waiting there. When they were finished, the gang took off for Frank's place.

When they got there, the many moneybags were brought down to the basement. The task of separating the money into stacks of various denominations was an all-night job. As dawn broke, the money was put into thousand-dollar piles and secured with rubber bands. The whole room was covered with stacks of money and there was over $3,000 in loose change. The overall take was about $360,000. Frank's cut was $50,000.

Frank was contacted one more time about doing an armored-truck heist. He listened to the plan and found out it would require killing the guards. He never went on an armed robbery with the intent of shooting anyone, particularly an innocent person. He knew that if things went sour during a stickup, he might have to use his

Dennis Griffin and Frank Cullotta

gun, but he would kill his victim only as a last resort. Under the circumstances, he decided to pass on the offer. He never did another armored-truck job.

• • •

Though Frank never formally joined the mob, his orbit in Chicago crossed theirs on many occasions. The Outfit sometimes needed an outside guy to resolve a problem the bosses were dealing with. It often involved intimidating or roughing someone up. But Frank clearly remembers the first time a made guy came to him wanting a person killed.

The Outfit guy gave Frank, and his friend Mikey, also known as Bushelhead, a picture of the man he wanted hit, along with his name, address, and vehicle information. The target had something to do with the Barber's Union and was causing a lot of problems.

Frank and Mikey drove out to where the man lived and looked around. For the next week or two they observed him, learning his habits. They checked things out very carefully, because they didn't want to hurt any innocent bystanders, especially children.

The guy they were after left his house at the same time every morning, so they decided to use a car bomb. On the morning of the hit, they opened the victim's car and Mikey went to work with the canister and blasting cap, while Frank stood lookout. A little while later, the victim got in the car, turned the key in the ignition, and the bomb detonated. The roof lifted off the car and rolled down a hill. The two hit men cleared out of the area fast.

The next day Frank got a thank you and $10,000 from his client. It had been a good hit and the Outfit was satisfied. For Frank, his first contract murder was strictly a business deal. He hadn't known the victim and had no feelings about him one way or the other. And the successful conclusion of the assignment was bound to enhance his reputation.

Frank also crossed paths with mob guys hanging around with Tony Spilotro. One night Tony called Frank over to his place. When he got there, Tony was playing gin with a tall slender man. It turned out the guy was Frank Rosenthal, also known as Lefty. Rosenthal was a big-time oddsmaker from Chicago who was living in Florida and was back in town for a visit. When the game ended, Tony had him stuck for about $30,000. Lefty had to wire Tony the money when he got back to Florida. He didn't dare stiff Tony Spilotro.

• • •

The next time he changed M.O.s, Frank returned to doing residential burglaries.

Phil, one of Frank's associates, had a list of all the coin collectors throughout the city and the suburbs. He knew their addresses, phone numbers, and even the value of their collections. Phil and Frank lined up a buyer for the coins, then began to steal them.

There were always three men on these jobs. Unlike the usual burglaries and robberies, the work car was left parked on the street unmanned. All three burglars went into the house and the driver stayed by a front window and served as a lookout.

The burglary of one second-floor apartment was particularly difficult. It was necessary to be extra quiet, so as not to awaken the old couple who lived downstairs. Frank and his men got into the apartment and found the safe. The three of them picked it up, got it to a side window overlooking the lawn, and threw it out. It didn't make much noise when it landed, but it sank into the lawn about two feet. It took a Herculean effort to get it out of the ground and into the work car. It was well worth it, though. The safe was loaded with rare coins that fetched a fortune.

Another crew of thieves from the Grand and Ogden area knew about Phil's coin-collector list and wanted some of the action. They'd helped Phil once when he was down and out. He asked Frank what he thought he should do.

"If you feel obligated to those guys, you should take them on a score. It's your list and you've gotta do what you think is right," Frank said.

"Would you come along with us?"

Frank didn't like a couple of guys on the other crew and wasn't interested in working with them. "No. There's enough of you. If you decide to take them on a job, I'll sit that one out."

Phil elected to do a job with the other gang. They chose a place in Northbrook, an exclusive neighborhood. Phil told Frank he had bad vibes about that location, but went along with the plan anyway. They walked into a trap.

Frank heard later what went down. Phil was the first one in the door with another guy right behind him. The third one wasn't even inside yet when the cops started yelling. Phil turned around and ran and the cops opened fire. A shot hit Phil in the back, passed through his lung, and hit one of the other burglars in the forehead. Phil got outside the house and made it about fifty feet before he fell over dead.

Frank never found out who tipped the cops, but he believes

that if Phil had listened to his instincts, like Frank had listened to his, he might still be alive today.

. . .

Frank also got leads from people who sold jewelry insurance to homeowners, and his crew continued to tear up the suburbs. They knew what valuables would be in the house. And in the neighborhoods they were working in, they usually found a lot more than jewelry. People hid their valuables in strange places. Cash was secreted under clothes hampers and in clothing storage bags. Jewelry was often found stashed inside walls, in light switch boxes. Still, Frank and his boys always seemed to find the loot.

But in Chicago, burglarizing upper-class houses in the suburbs could have unintended consequences. One time they burglarized a house in Elmwood Park. They found jewelry and about $500 in cash taped to the bottoms of dresser drawers in the bedroom. Unbeknownst to them, however, it belonged to an Outfit-connected bookie.

The next day word was out on the street. Frank knew he'd not only better not fence the stuff, but he should probably give it back. He went to an Outfit guy he knew and explained the situation.

The mobster said, "Don't you know better than to do burglaries out here in Elmwood Park? A lot of our people live here."

"I wasn't aware of that or I wouldn't have done it."

"Okay, I'll take your word on that. I'm going to give you a pass this time, but consider yourself warned. Don't let it happen again."

Frank gave him all the bookie's property and cash back and

thought that was the end of it. But as Frank found out when the Outfit guy called him later, the burglary victim's hands weren't clean either.

"Where's that five grand?" the Outfit man asked.

Frank was confused. "What five grand?"

"Our guy said you got him for five grand in cash. You only gave back five hundred."

"That's all the cash we got," Frank insisted. "Why would I admit to the burglary, offer to give everything back, then hold out on you?"

Frank's argument made sense to the mob bigshot. It turned out that the bookie wasn't aware that the burglars had already admitted to the job when he made his claim to his superior. He figured the theft provided a good opportunity for him to keep some of the bet money and report it as a loss.

The bookmaker wasn't killed, but he had hell to pay for quite a while for lying to the Outfit.

Sears and Roebuck bore the brunt of Frank's decision to resume commercial thieving. Sears had a number of outlets in Chicago and its suburbs. One of the gang entered the target store near closing time and hid, usually under a bed, until all the employees had left. Having a man already inside the building made these relatively easy scores.

• • •

Frank was out, in a bar on Rush Street, when he ran into Barton, an accomplished burglar with a good reputation among other thieves. "I've got a pretty good racket going, doing high-rise apartments," he told Frank. "I usually work alone, but you're welcome if you want to come along."

"Where are you working at?"

"On Lake Shore Drive, mostly. I'm getting a lot of tips and making some good scores."

Lake Shore Drive was the "Gold Coast" of Chicago. Anyone with a condo on Lake Shore had to have megabucks. But Frank knew all about the drawbacks of attacking high-rises. The buildings had tight security, and if you were able to get up to the apartments without being spotted, you still had to get back out with the loot. There was only one way out, too—usually in an elevator. If the cops showed up while you were on an upper floor, you were trapped. In spite of the risks, Frank told Barton he'd go along.

Frank always figured that a man's home was his castle while he was in it, and he didn't particularly like to do home invasions or have to confront tenants. But at times, there was no alternative. On one occasion, the tenant came home while Frank and Barton were in his apartment. They heard him put the key in the lock and were waiting when he opened the door. Frank stuck a gun in the man's face, took him down to the floor, and tied him up. The burglars took what they wanted and left. Afterward, Frank went to a pay phone and called the cops. He told them that a man was tied up in his condo and gave them the address.

Frank and Barton made some nice paydays hitting the high-rises, but they knew it was only a matter of time before they got caught. Pretty soon the risks outweighed the rewards and they let it go.

• • •

Frank's favorite car salesman knew what Frank did for a living. As it turned out, he was interested in supplementing his commissions.

One day the salesman asked Frank, "If I provide you with information for a robbery, how much would it be worth to you?"

"I pay my tipsters ten percent of the take. What have you got in mind?"

"Most of the down-payment money we receive is cash, usually several thousand dollars for each car sold. Whatever we take in on Friday or Saturday stays in the safe until Monday, so Sunday would be a good day to do something. Are you interested?"

"I'm interested. But what if we pick a slow week and there's not much money? I don't want to do a job unless I'm sure it's worthwhile."

"How much money does it take to be worthwhile?"

"At least forty grand."

"Tell you what. I'll make sure there's at least forty thousand or more in the safe so you don't waste your time. But in return for that I'd like to get fifteen percent."

"You've got a deal. I'll have my crew ready to move on short notice. You call me when you're sure the money's right."

The salesman called one weekend when he knew there was about $45,000 in the safe. The gang made their move that Sunday.

The dealership didn't have any alarms, making it an easy target. Frank's crew pried open the overhead door in the service department with a tire jack, just enough to slide under it, then used winches from the service department to get the safe out of the office and into the dealership station wagon parked inside. After that, they raided the parts department and took all the spark plugs. They used the station wagon to transport the safe, then ditched it.

The salesman had been right about the amount of money in the safe and got his 15% of the cash. The spark plugs were separate and he wasn't involved in that, so he didn't get a cut of those profits.

Frank continued to buy two or three cars a year from that same dealership and salesman. For a while he felt like he was playing with house money.

• • •

Along with jewelry stores, post offices, coin collectors, and car dealerships, Frank saw an opportunity with large supermarkets, which take in a lot of cash. He decided to go after one of the local Jewel Supermarket outlets and see what kind of score could be made.

Frank found a store he liked and watched it for several days. He learned that the last stop of the week for the money truck was on Friday. That meant by Sunday night the store's safe would be pretty full. He cased the store and found out where the safe was located, then found an alarm box mounted on an outside wall.

The next question was whether the alarm was wired into the police station. To get the answer he pulled a night break-in, making sure the alarm went off. He took a couple of cartons of cigarettes to make it look like a kid's job. Then he watched the store and listened to the police radio. There were no police calls, and no cops came. Finally, a neighbor must have reported the alarm and a patrol car showed up to check things out. Knowing the alarm wasn't directly wired into the police station, Frank silenced the system by ripping the alarm bell off the outside wall.

Frank's gang removed the safe from the store using a truck with a winch. Then they took it to Frank's house where the doors were opened with a torch. The safe was bulging with money. It inspired the gang to hit almost every Jewel store in the city. Their take on those jobs was always between $30,000 and $80,000.

These were easy scores, with the exception of one night when the police stopped the thieves after the burglary. They pulled over the truck with the safe in it; Frank was behind driving the follow car. It happened he knew that one of the officers could be dealt with.

"I was just telling my partner that Cullotta would be coming around the corner any minute," the cop said.

"Look, let us get the safe to where we can open it and see what we've got. I'll give you guys ten percent of whatever's in there," Frank suggested.

The cops were agreeable. Two days later they received their cut.

It wasn't only the cops who could be bought. For the right price, the system could be corrupted from bottom to top.

A local thief asked Frank to help him out with a burglary in nearby Bensenville. They got into the place and cleaned it out, but when Frank went to get the work car to load up, the police rolled by. They spotted the break-in and quickly more cops, with dogs, showed up. Frank ran away, leaving the car behind, and made it safely back to his house. He figured Phil got busted and contacted a bondsman to get him out. The bondsman told him it was too soon and to wait until the next day.

Later that same night, Frank drove his legitimately licensed car to a friend's house in Elmwood Park, parking on the street out in front. The next thing he knew, the Elmwood Park police were there. They said they had a warrant for his arrest for the burglary. He told them they were nuts; it was all bullshit. But they showed him the warrant, arrested him, and took him to their station.

Eventually, the Bensenville police picked up Frank and transported him to their place. One of the cops tried to get a confession out of him. He said, "If you don't tell me what I want to know, I'm going to send the dog in here. We sent the dog in after your friend and look what happened. He gave you up. That's why you're here now."

"You can stick your dog up your ass. If you think you've got something on me, book me. If not, let me go."

They booked him. Frank and his pal were tried separately and both were found guilty. The other thief got three years. Frank's more extensive criminal record earned him eight years for the same crime. Frank's lawyer filed an appeal and he bonded out pending the results.

Frank fought that conviction for two years, going through a total of four lawyers. The first one, the trial lawyer who lost the case, wasn't real good on appeals, so he hired another one. When the court rejected the appeal, the second lawyer didn't even tell him; he heard about it from the bondsman. Next, he hired a pair of lawyers and they got a six-month stay of his sentence to file another appeal. They said he'd probably have to take the case all the way to the United States Supreme Court and try to get a reversal on a civil-rights violation. He had to come up with $1,600 to pay for transcripts and other things to get the process going.

Frank met with the lawyers again two days later. They said

things were looking good, but he'd have to pay $14,000 in "guaranteed" money over the next couple of months.

"What the hell is guaranteed money?" he asked.

"That means if we win the appeal, the money is ours. If we don't, you get the money back."

Frank thought it over. The arrangement seemed to give the lawyers an incentive for doing a good job. But if he got his money back, it meant the appeal was lost and he'd be going to prison. In reality, though, what choice did he have? "I'll get you the money. You get me a reversal," he said.

The case dragged on and on. A couple of years later, Frank was in a lounge when an acquaintance gave him some good news. "Congratulations, Frankie, I see you won your appeal."

"What are you talking about?"

"It's in today's paper. They threw out your conviction."

Frank called one of his lawyers. "What's this I hear about my case?"

"Yeah, we've been trying to get a hold of you," the lawyer said. "Your conviction has been reversed."

"You don't sound surprised."

"I'm not. We knew you were going to win the whole time. That's why we went for the guaranteed money. We're in business to make money, not give it back."

It was now obvious to Frank that there'd been more in play than the skill of his lawyers. But he didn't really care how they'd done it or who got paid off. By the time the decision was announced, he'd invested almost $40,000 in the case, about enough money to have bought every item in the place he had been convicted of burglarizing. But it was money well spent.

. . .

By the late-1960s, Frank was an accomplished thief. Many of his scores resulted in big money. Did he have a nice nest egg set up? According to him, he didn't. That wasn't the way things worked in his world.

Most people might think that a successful thief like Frank had to have tons of money. Not true. There are twenty-four hours in a day and regular people work eight of them. After that, they usually have dinner, watch a little TV, and go to bed. They don't spend a lot of money every day.

On the other hand, a thief has all 24 hours to play with. He may be on the streets 16 or 17 hours a day. Some scores take only a couple of hours and he's got his money. And then he has got the rest of the time to spend it, often foolishly. That money can go pretty quick.

And a thief like Frank had expenses that the average guy didn't. Unless he worked alone, the score had to be split with his crew. And if he made a lot of money, the Outfit had to be cut in. Tipsters had to be taken care of; cops had to be paid off on occasion; lawyers and bail bondsmen cost a lot of money; there were the expenses of getting fictitious registrations for the work cars, and so forth. To keep up appearances, a professional thief had to dress well, have nice legit cars, and hang out in the right places. Those costs were in addition to rent, food, and utilities. And in Frank's case, he was pretty free with his money, taking care of family and friends. Maybe he could or should have had a lot of money, but he didn't.

Frank spent plenty on his family. His sister had married a good provider and didn't need financial assistance, but he felt obligated

Dennis Griffin and Frank Cullotta

to look out for his mother and younger brother. He didn't want them to be financially strapped in any way. He didn't realize that his brother viewed him as a hero—kind of a Robin Hood figure—and wanted to be just like him.

Frank was driving down Grand Avenue one day when he heard a news flash that a 10-year-old boy had been shot during the robbery of a convenience store. The suspect had been arrested and identified as Joe Cullotta, Frank's brother.

Stunned, Frank pulled into a restaurant to use the pay phone to find out where they were holding Joey. He was only inside a couple of minutes when two Italian detectives he knew came in.

"Frankie, we need to talk to you," one of the cops said. "We arrested your brother for robbery and we're holding him at the station. He's really worried about how you're going to react, so we told him we'd try to find you before you got the news somewhere else."

"I appreciate that. I really do. But Joey's a straight kid. What the fuck happened?"

"Why don't you come to the station with us and we'll explain everything on the way."

After promising he'd keep his composure and not take his frustration out on Joey when he saw him, Frank and the detectives headed out for the station. On the way the officers told him what they knew.

"According to your brother and other witnesses, Joey and another guy, who we're still looking for, were holding up the store when this kid who knew your brother came in and started to say hello to him. Joey panicked, grabbed the kid, and ran out of the store. As they were running, Joey's gun went off and the bullet caught the kid in the leg. Then Joey got really scared. He tried to find you and took the kid into a bar where he thought you might be, but you weren't there. The kid was bleeding and one of the Outfit guys in the place told Joey he had two choices: Take the kid to the hospital or kill him. He brought the boy to the hospital. We arrested him there and he and the kid gave us the whole story."

"How about the kid? How bad is he hurt?"

"He's going to be okay; it was just a minor wound."

Frank thanked the detectives for coming to get him. Although they had an adversarial relationship, these particular cops were human beings and understood what Frank was going through. He tried to give them money to show his gratitude, but they wouldn't take it.

When Frank got to see his brother, Joey started to cry. He gave Frank a lame excuse for why he'd pulled the robbery. Frank knew the story was bullshit, but Joey was still his brother. He arranged for his bail and hired a lawyer.

Frank had all he could do to keep from laughing during the initial meeting he and Joey had with the attorney. The lawyer didn't mince his words when he addressed the younger Cullotta. "Don't try to put yourself in the same category as your brother. He's been stealing since the day you were born. Here you are, a Johnny-come-lately, trying to be a crook, a tough guy. Well, you're not. You're just a dumb son-of-a-bitch."

Afterward they discussed Joey's case. The lawyer said that even though there'd been a shooting, it was an accident and the boy hadn't been seriously hurt. He thought he might be able to get Joey off with probation as a first-time offender. As the attorney predicted, Joey was sentenced to five years probation.

Frank wanted Joey to get into something legit, where he could make an honest living. Joey enrolled in school to become a barber. But instead of being satisfied to cut hair in a shop with a couple of chairs, he went on to become a successful hair stylist and made a lot of money. Frank is very proud of what Joey accomplished.

• • •

Frank had always been attracted to Italian girls. He believed that they had old-fashioned values, so they'd be more devoted to their husbands than American women.

One night while he was making the rounds of the Chicago saloons, he met Marie, of Sicilian ancestry, and Frank liked her right away. She said she didn't know how to drive, so he made a date to teach her. From there, things got serious. Frank brought her home to meet his mother and she seemed to like Marie.

One day Marie called Frank and asked him to come to her house. When he got there, he found that she and her mother were arguing. Marie packed her clothes and loaded her suitcase into Frank's car. He took her to his house, but because he lived with his mother, she slept in a separate bedroom.

Josephine Cullotta never warmed up to Marie, though. There was something about her she couldn't put her finger on, and she warned her son to be careful.

In spite of his mother's reservations, Frank married Marie. She wanted a big wedding; he invited more than 200 people, rented a large banquet hall, and ordered filet mignon as the main course. The reception cost him about six grand. The party went okay, but the newlyweds got into an argument as soon as the couple got home from the reception. Frank wanted to have sex. Marie wanted to count the wedding-gift money.

"Put that stuff away until tomorrow and let's go to bed," he said, as Marie started to open the gift envelopes.

"No. I want to see how much is here."

"The boost [gift money] will be there in the morning. Forget about it now and come to bed."

"No. I'm going to count it now."

After some heated words, the disagreement ended in a stalemate. They eventually went to bed together, but they weren't on speaking terms. Marie didn't get to count the boost and Frank didn't get laid.

Frank believes the problem was that Marie was a nice girl and didn't really know what he did for a living. As she met his friends and learned more about him, she was overwhelmed. The first time he suspected that he'd made a mistake was when he brought home a load of hot clothes to the house after he and his crew had burglarized a shop specializing in top-of-the-line women's fashions. When they got the stuff to Frank's garage, they put everything on racks and inventoried it. Frank's accomplices picked out a couple of things for their wives. After they left he told Marie she could take a few items too. She started looking everything over, picking and pulling. She didn't understand the protocol thieves followed. Frank told her to slow down, that she was taking more than she was supposed to.

He explained the way things worked. "In my business, loyalty and honesty toward your crew are crucial. We all have to depend on each other. I can't cheat my people. I've got to treat them right and take care of them. You can't take any more of the merchandise than what my crew did. That's the way it has to be."

Marie didn't seem to like what she'd heard. She pouted for a while, but left the merchandise alone.

Another incident occurred after the robbery of a fur salesman. Frank and his men followed the salesman all the way to Wisconsin, waiting for a chance to rob him. About 3 a.m. the salesman finally pulled into a motel. As soon as he parked, two of the robbers jumped him, pushed him out of the driver's seat, and got into his car. With the work car following, they drove out to a secluded area and dumped the salesman in a field. Then they transferred all the furs to their car and headed for home.

After unloading the furs in Frank's garage, the other guys picked out a jacket each for their wives and left. Frank looked around and Marie was standing there, ready to take her share. She took two mink coats, one more than she was entitled to. This time he didn't argue with her; he said it was okay, even though it wasn't. When he fenced the merchandise, he paid his men extra money to make up for Marie's excess.

The last straw came when Marie got into an argument with Frank's brother. This was after he'd asked her to pick his clothes up from the cleaners and she hadn't done it, so he was already mad at her. Frank started to argue with her. "Goddamn it! You didn't even pick up my fuckin' clothes and now you're calling my brother names?"

Marie was defiant. "So I didn't get your clothes. Big deal."

One word led to another and Marie tried to slap him. Frank picked her up and threw her on top of the table. The table broke and Marie ran into the bedroom with Frank in pursuit. He swung at her, missed, and his fist went through the closet door.

When things settled down, he told Marie, "You know, this just isn't working out. I think it would be best for both of us if we split up."

Marie agreed. She left with her clothes—armloads of garments and furs—and the $10,000 diamond ring Frank had bought her. As she walked out the door, he wondered why he hadn't listened to his mother.

• • •

Being a rising star in the crime arena brought Frank into the law-enforcement spotlight. He recalls that the notoriety was not only an annoyance, it carried a financial cost as well. At least once a week he was pulled over and questioned. He found that nine out of ten times, he could bribe the cops. He believed that in most cases, a little extra cash was all they were looking for anyway. Usually fifty or a hundred bucks would work. Sometimes, if he was short on money or just didn't feel like paying, he'd give them the dodge. But then he'd have to keep out of that jurisdiction for a few days and the cops wanted even more money the next time they caught up with him. Sometimes he was locked up overnight; other times they kept him for forty-eight hours.

During one arrest Frank was in a particularly defiant mood and refused to let them take his mug shot. He told the officers to go fuck themselves, pulled down his pants, and mooned them. Reinforcements were called in and Frank was handcuffed and punched around.

"Listen you prick, you're going to the lockup until we get that picture," one of the cops said. "If we have to frame you for something to keep you locked up, we'll do it."

They got their mug shot.

Some of the cops, especially the detectives, liked to play hardball. Frank always figured the ones who gave him a beating while they had him cuffed were cowards. He had little respect for them and challenged them to take off the cuffs to see how tough they were. He felt the ones who didn't rough you up were trouble. They were the ones who got you by using their minds, not their fists. They were the ones who would build a case against you that could put you away for years. They were the really dangerous ones.

· · ·

In the late 1960s, the Chicago Police Department created a special unit to confront the crews of professional burglars and robbers overrunning the streets of Chicago at that time. The new outfit was called the Criminal Intelligence Unit, or CIU. An officer named Bill Hanhardt was in charge of it; Jack Hinchy was second in command. These cops were sharp, and if Frank hadn't known better, he'd have thought they were burglars or robbers themselves. They thought just like he did and continuously nipped at his heels.

Hanhardt was a quiet guy who did his talking with his eyes. Frank was in his office a few times and Hanhardt asked him questions about things he'd done that nobody knew about. But the head of the CIU knew. Frank had no idea how he knew, but he did. He found it kind of scary that Hanhardt had so many things figured out.

On the other hand, Hinchy, in Frank's opinion, was a maniac. He used to threaten Frank by saying, "Cullotta, some day I'm going to catch you walking out of a joint you just robbed. I'm going to be right there. And I'm going to blow your fucking head off."

Frank just smirked at him, which made him all the madder.

Frank, his car-bombing friend Bushelhead, and another guy named Vince got word from Frank's dispatcher friend about a truckload of televisions and made the snatch. They drove the rig to a big junkyard the gang used. The plan was to leave the rig and come back in a couple of days to move the load. They didn't know it then, but the CIU was on them the whole time. When they returned, the cops were waiting.

Frank was up on the trailer when the yelling started. Then he heard gunshots. He tried to jump to a fence behind the trailer, but didn't make it. A cop ordered him to the ground with his hands on top of his head. Then he hollered to the other cops, "Don't shoot! Don't shoot! I'm back here and I've got Cullotta on the ground. Don't shoot!"

Frank doesn't know if it was intentional or not, but he thinks that cop saved him from taking a bullet. If he'd tried to run, he believes he would have been killed. Bushelhead was shot in the arm and the ass and was taken to the hospital. Frank and Vince went to jail and were bonded out the next day.

On a side note, Frank's observation that the CIU cops thought just like crooks proved to be accurate in the case of Bill Hanhardt. On October 25, 2001, the former CIU boss pled guilty to overseeing a ring of jewelry robbers and having a decades-long relationship with organized crime.

In April 2002, John Kass of the *Chicago Tribune* spoke with Frank about Hanhardt. Frank said he wasn't surprised to learn about Hanhardt's double life. He told Kass that he became suspicious of the cop at the time of the jewelry-store robbery in the Maller Building on Wabash Avenue. Frank said that the day after that score, Hanhardt pulled him in and said he never figured Frank to be in on the job. Hanhardt laughed about it and let him go. Frank told Kass, "The only people who knew [about his involvement] were Tony and one other guy on the score. How could Hanhardt know so quick?" Frank said he posed that question to Tony. "The look Tony gave me made it perfectly clear to me that they [the Outfit] had him. Years later Tony told us, 'That's our guy. We got him.' I was no angel, but [Hanhardt] was no better," Frank concluded.

In Frank's mind, he may have been an outlaw, but at least he was honest about who and what he was. He has absolutely no use for crooked cops. Under the color of law, they break every rule in the book. In his opinion, they're even worse than the criminals they pursue.

The 77-year-old Hanhardt is currently serving his sentence at the Federal Correctional Institution in Waseca, Minnesota. His projected release date is January 13, 2012.

• • •

The truck hijacking for which Frank, Bushelhead, and Vince were arrested turned into a federal rap, because the stolen televisions had been an interstate shipment. That meant FBI agents, as well as the local lawmen, were now interested in Frank and his gang. They were still out on bail from that when they pulled another caper.

The three stole about 3,600 Sunbeam electric can openers and stashed them on a farm they owned in Elgin, Illinois, about

45 miles from Chicago. They leased the house on the property to a couple of girls. A night or two after the heist, they went back to move the merchandise. Vince and Frank were inside the barn when they heard a noise coming from the direction of the house. Frank took a look and saw two or three guys with shotguns coming toward the barn. He yelled to Vince, "The goddamn cops are on us! We've got to get the fuck out of here!"

As the thieves fled, Frank was running so fast that when he bumped into a horse, he knocked it over! He made it outside, but the cops were everywhere; there was no escape. The two were taken to the state police station in Niles and charged with possession of the stolen can openers. They posted bond and were let go.

They went to their bondsman's office and reviewed all the paperwork. The bondsman thought the defendants had a better chance to get a favorable verdict if they could get the case moved from Niles Township to Chicago. He said he had connections there and for the right amount of money he could help them. The bondsman wanted five grand to get things started. It was a big chance to take, but Frank gave him the money.

When they went to court, an FBI agent was there as an interested observer. It turned out the cops had erred on the search warrant. They hadn't asked the girls leasing the farmhouse for permission to come on the property. The judge ruled the warrant was invalid and threw out the whole case. As Frank was leaving the courtroom, he made a huge mistake. He laughed in the FBI agent's face and said, "Gotcha."

The agent stared back at him and said coolly, "We'll see about that."

Within thirty days of Frank uttering that one word, the heat was on. It was apparent the law wanted Frank, Bushelhead, and Vince real bad. Every place he and his associates owned or hung out, including their homes, was raided in a search for evidence of burglaries or robberies. Frank was out of town when the raids were conducted, but he got word that the cops were looking for him. He immediately contacted the same bondsman, the one with all the connections.

"I heard about the searches," the bondsman said, "but they aren't the real problem. I know that all three of you are going to be charged with the armed robbery of a supermarket in Belvedere, Illinois."

"That's a lot of bullshit. I've never been to Belvedere. I don't even know where the fucking place is."

"That may be, but right now you've got two choices: Turn yourself in or leave the country."

Figuring the Belvedere rap would be easy to beat, Frank turned himself in. He, Vince, and Bushelhead were put in a lineup. All three were positively identified as having pulled the job. A schoolteacher, the store-owner's daughter, and another witness made the identification. The case wasn't bullshit any longer. If convicted, they were facing some serious prison time.

When Frank and his crew did the Dad's Root Beer home invasion and robbery, someone else took the fall. Now he found himself in a similar situation, charged with a crime that he swears to this day he didn't commit. Frank had a number of other cases still pending, but this latest one was the most problematic and frustrating. With the help of their lawyers, Frank and his friends scrambled to extricate themselves from what they considered to be a gross injustice.

They fought this case for about a year. In an effort to create an alibi, the friendly bondsman used his clout to get an Oak Park cop to help out. The officer backdated a citation showing that he was writing Frank a speeding ticket five minutes before the robbery in Belvedere took place. During the jury trial, the fake ticket was introduced into evidence. It didn't do any good; nothing did any good. All three defendants were found guilty and sentenced to 15 years each in the state penitentiary. They were immediately incarcerated and there were no appeal bonds.

In addition to his 15-year stretch, Frank still had two hijacking cases pending against him. Compounding his woes, he was indicted for robbing the Brinks truck at the church rectory, after two of his accomplices in that caper rolled and became government informants.

Frank discussed the situation with his African-American lawyer. "We're in a lot of trouble on that federal hijacking charge," the attorney said. "A black man and a dago haven't got a chance in the federal system. I'm not telling you to cop out; I'll fight all the way. I'm just telling you what we're facing."

"Go for it then," Frank said. "We'll fight every one of these goddamn cases."

They did, starting with the state charges, and lost them all.

For years, Frank had had myriad charges against him reduced or dismissed and his one major conviction was reversed on appeal. Now it appeared the chickens were coming home to roost. But considering what he was facing in the way of jail time, the veteran thief believes he didn't come out too bad.

He was sentenced to a total of 16 years for the two truck hijackings and copped a plea on the Brinks job, getting four more

Dennis Griffin and Frank Cullotta

years. Adding in the 15 for the bogus robbery conviction, he was looking at up to 35 years. But he got the time cut more than in half by getting all the sentences lumped together and having them run concurrently.

That was the good news. The bad news was that the federal charge for hijacking the interstate shipment of televisions was still unresolved. A guilty verdict in that case could negate the relatively good disposition he'd received at the state level.

So, as the 29-year-old headed off to serve up to 15 years in state prison in 1968, there was no guarantee that would be all the time he'd have to spend behind bars.

In and Out of Prison

Frank, Bushelhead, and Vince entered Stateville prison in Joliet, Illinois, on September 13, 1968. Frank found the conditions there to be much harsher than the Cook County Jail or the House of Corrections, where he'd previously done time. To survive in that environment required mental and physical toughness. Having some equally hard-nosed allies didn't hurt.

The inmate population in Stateville was predominantly black. There were fistfights, stabbings, and rapes. It was a very hard place for white inmates to get along in, especially if they had to go it alone. Fortunately for Frank, several Italians in the prison stuck together and looked out for each other. But for the other white guys, it was a terrible place. With Frank's extensive criminal background, one could argue that he deserved to be there. But being incarcerated for something he hadn't done caused him to become a very bitter man.

The main black gang in Stateville was the Blackstone Rangers.

Formed in the early 1960s, the gang was named after its home turf, the impoverished Woodlawn neighborhood on Chicago's South Side. Many of the Rangers were cold-blooded killers. They murdered rival gang members or anyone else they had a mind to, whether they were on the streets or inside the prison. They were a dangerous group to be on the wrong side of, but could be powerful allies if they liked you. And Frank was already on good terms with one of their incarcerated members.

Frank had met a man known as Thunder while both were being held in the Cook County Jail. He knew that Thunder was a Ranger and that the gang had power and a lot of members. Nearly every correctional facility in Illinois—local, state, and federal—held a number of the gangsters at any given time. With that in mind, Frank included Thunder in some of the perks he received because of his relationship with the jail warden, things such as better food and extra phone calls. He didn't have to do it, but he considered it good business. In Stateville, that investment paid dividends. With Thunder's endorsement, Frank became a friend of the gang.

Inmates were able to work in the prison. Vince went to the barbershop and Bushelhead worked in the receiving-area clothing room, outfitting new inmates. Frank hoped to get into a program that would teach him more about electronics, but there wasn't an opening for him. That resulted in an initial assignment to the coal pile.

Stateville's boilers burned coal. The fuel was delivered to the prison by rail and dumped alongside the tracks. Inmate work crews then moved the coal to the boiler rooms using shovels and wheel-barrows. It was dirty backbreaking work. Frank felt it qualified as hard labor.

After about three months on the coal pile, Frank transferred to the barbershop as a clerk. His job there was to give tests to inmates who wanted to become barbers after they got out. He didn't particularly care for those duties, but he made the best of the situation. For a carton of smokes, he made sure any would-be barber got a passing score.

. . .

As Frank bided his time waiting for a better job opportunity, he found that he sorely missed many of the things he'd taken for granted on the outside. Freedom itself was a terrible thing to lose for an extended period of time. To him, if you didn't have your freedom, you didn't have anything. Everything was regimented. You got up, went to bed, ate your meals, and took a shower when you were told to, not when you felt like it.

Items such as soap and toilet paper that didn't seem like a big deal on the outside were suddenly important. A decent writing pen, a good pair of socks or underwear, were precious possessions. And money was a hell of a thing to be short of. Cigarettes and food could be used as trading material, but good old cash was the best bargaining tool of all.

Inmates were allowed one visit per month. Frank's relatives, especially his mother, were his main visitors. But if one of his friends wanted to see him, she'd stay away and let the friend visit instead. Although Frank exchanged letters with several girls he knew, none of them ever came to the prison.

Messages to Frank from his criminal associates still on the streets were received through his family and legit friends during regular phone calls, or delivered by visitors. The information relay system in the prison was so efficient that inmates often knew what was happening on the outside before the people on the streets knew it.

Although Frank certainly didn't like prison, he never thought about escape. As the time passed, he even decided that he'd try going straight when he got out. The reason for this decision wasn't because he'd been rehabilitated, far from it. When it came to rehabilitation, Frank thought incarceration was a waste of time. If anything, prison made him tougher and angrier toward the system. And it wasn't because he'd experienced a moral awakening, either.

The reason he was willing to turn his back on a life of crime was because of his mother. He'd been in scrape after scrape since he was a kid, which put her through hell. He'd let her down for most of his life, but she never abandoned him, never gave up on him. As she grew older, he wanted to repay her loyalty by not having her read in the paper that he'd been arrested, by not having to visit him in prison or some other detention center. The only way he could do that for her was by cleaning up his act. She deserved it and he was willing to try.

• • •

Frank was able to leave the prison from time to time in order to attend the proceedings in the federal hijacking case against him. The federal trial went no better for him than his encounters with state prosecutors, though. He was convicted and faced a maximum penalty of 10 years. On March 27, 1969, Frank appeared before Judge Hubert Will in the United States District Court, Northern

District of Illinois, Eastern Division, to learn his fate. Before pronouncing the sentence, Judge Will explained the rationale for the decision he was about to hand down. His comments serve to sum up Frank's life to that point.

"I find myself considerably distressed by the length of the prior arrest record, though the convictions are not ... well, there is a year in the House of Correction in 1956 when Mr. Cullotta was, I guess, seventeen, another year in the House of Correction in 1960 when he was twenty. There are arrests every year, one or more. Some years he was more prolifically arrested than others; '62, '63, '64, '65, '66, '67. There are other convictions, a fine in one instance. Most of them are either no disposition shown or he was released."

As Judge Will spoke, Frank could see the writing on the wall. He was sure he'd be given another 10 years. The only thing that mattered now was whether the new sentence would run concurrent with his state time or be a consecutive term tacked on at the end. But the judge wasn't quite ready to make his announcement. He had a few more things to say first.

"I am reluctant to say that somebody's business or profession is crime, but that is likely the case based on his prior performance, unless something drastic happens. I look at the prior employment record and there is no verifiable gainful employment, for example. I look at the prior criminal record and it is substantial. I wonder what it takes to persuade Frank John Cullotta that the way he has lived in the past is not good for him, much less the community or society.

"Obviously, all these arrests have not done it. Even the one-year sentences haven't done it. I now find myself with, I think, only one alternative. It will protect the community for some considerable period of time, even if it doesn't accomplish rehabilitation. I am going to remand Mr. Cullotta to the custody of the Attorney General of the United States for a period of ten years."

There was no surprise there. It was the judge's next words that would make all the difference in the world to Frank. He tensed as the judge continued.

"That sentence to run concurrently with the sentence he is now serving imposed by the Circuit Court of Boone County."

Frank left the courtroom in much better shape than when he'd entered it. Although he had another conviction on his record, the judge's decision to run the new sentence in conjunction with his state term meant he wouldn't have to spend any additional time in prison. He would, however, have to serve a portion of his incarceration in a federal facility.

Frank was transported back to Stateville right after the hearing to begin serving out the rest of his sentences.

• • •

As luck would have it, a couple of Frank's old nemeses were in the prison at the same time: none other than ex-cop Tom Durso, the Robbery Detail detective who had once used cattle prods on Frank, and his buddy Mike Gargano. They'd been convicted of killing a drug dealer they were shaking down and sentenced to a couple hundred years each. Gargano wasn't a bad guy and Frank gave him a pass. But Durso was the same kind of asshole inside as he'd been as a cop.

One day Frank saw him walking down a corridor; nobody else was around and security cameras were not yet in use. Frank picked up a stool and waited for Durso to pass his hiding place.

The former tormentor of Chicago's thieves never knew what hit him. As the stool crashed into Durso's skull, he fell to the floor in a fetal position. Frank stood over his victim, taunting him. "Do you remember me, you cocksucker? Do you remember me now? This time we're on equal terms, you piece of shit."

Durso spent some time in the hospital, but he didn't identify Frank as his assailant. Neither did he attempt to retaliate. If anything happened to Frank, the Blackstone Rangers would have killed him and Durso knew it.

• • •

After about a year working in the barbershop, Frank heard about an opportunity that he thought would improve his lot: An opening came up in the psychiatric ward for the criminally insane. This unit was located in the front end of the prison, out of general population. Prisoners assigned to jobs in the front were on the honor system. One black inmate and eight white inmates were assigned to work in the psych ward. They had their own TV, exercise room, and kitchen. They got better food and clothes and had a lot more freedom.

Frank met with Vince and Bushelhead and let them in on what he was considering. "I found out there's an opening in the psychiatric ward and I'm thinking about putting in for it."

"You're out of your fucking mind," Bushelhead said.

Vince agreed. "Everybody hates the guys who work there. They call them the goon squad. If you work in the unit and go back in population, you'll end up with a fuckin' shiv in your back."

"I don't give a fuck what anybody thinks of me," Frank said. "Besides, if I get that job, I have no intention of coming back in population."

Frank submitted for the psych-ward opening and was interviewed by a captain. After the interview the officer gave Frank his decision. "Cullotta, you're just a wiseguy dago. If I give you that job, you'll spend all your time plotting and scheming. The answer is no. You're staying in population where you belong."

If Frank was nothing else, he was resourceful. Determined to circumvent the captain, he did some research on the captain's boss, the warden. It turned out that the warden had started his law-enforcement career as a street cop. As such, he might be susceptible to the request of another lawman. Frank sent word of his predicament to an old police-department contact: CIU boss Bill Hanhardt. The cop contacted the warden. In a short time the captain received orders to assign Frank to the psych unit.

The inmates housed in the psych ward included those who had committed heinous crimes—like chopping people up—and other crazies. The child molesters were in there for their own protection; they would probably be killed if they were in the general population. One of the things the inmates assigned to work in the ward were responsible for was suicide prevention; there were four hangings while Frank was there. They also gave out medications and, when necessary, went into the cells in general population to restrain inmates who were acting up and remove them to the ward. That's where the name goon squad came from.

It wasn't uncommon for the patients to rip their sinks off the walls and their toilets from the floor. They also urinated and defecated all over their cells. On those occasions the goon squad went into action. Carrying shields to protect themselves from thrown excrement or other material, they rolled in on the culprit. The offender was often beaten, sometimes severely. The guards didn't seem to care. For the most part they were afraid of the crazies, and didn't really give a damn what happened to baby rapers and other sub-human prisoners. Working in the psych unit wasn't for the fainthearted, but Frank was up to it and thought it was a good job overall.

The last time Frank saw Sam DeStefano was while he was on the goon squad. He'd never cared for Mad Sam, so he didn't go out of his way for him when he showed up in the psych ward to have some work done on the veins in his legs. He noticed one thing, though: Sam wasn't the same tough guy inside that he was on the street. Without his weapons or gang, he'd lost his swagger. But Sam wasn't the only one. That happened to a lot of guys when they got inside those walls.

The assignment also gave Frank the opening to cement his relationship with the Blackstone Rangers. Gang members came in for treatment from time to time and Frank always took good care of them while they were there. When they got back in population, they in turn took care of his friends. It was a one-hand-washes-the-other situation.

Another advantage was that Frank liked most of his inmate coworkers, one of whom was Lawrence Neumann. Neumann was doing a 100-year-plus sentence for a triple murder in a Chicago tavern. In Illinois, no matter what his sentence, the convict appeared before the Illinois Parole Board in eleven years. At that time, Neumann had four more years to go before his parole hearing. The two men became friends and later joined forces in Las Vegas.

While Frank was working in the psych unit, an inmate phone room opened in the front end of the prison. All inmates were subsequently allowed to make one personal phone call a week. In addition to correctional staff, the phone room required inmate workers. Vince had already transferred from the main barbershop to the psych-unit barbershop. His duties were limited to cutting hair, so he wasn't part of the hated goon squad. At Frank's recommendation he applied for and got a clerk's position in the phone room.

This new job was a position of power for Vince. He was responsible for scheduling the phone calls and could make sure his friends got more than one call per week. Other inmates who wanted extra phone time had to pay Vince for that privilege. Some of the prisoners had cash, which Vince gladly accepted. But the most common method of payment was cigarettes, which could be smoked or bartered for other items.

Frank and Vince also cultivated a relationship with one of the guards assigned to the phone room. They had him visit their friends or relatives while off duty and pick up money and items of clothing or food that they wanted brought into the prison. The guard was compensated in cash, for both his courier services and for the contraband.

. . .

In 1972, Frank was paroled by the state, but was transferred to the medium-security federal prison in Terre Haute, Indiana, to serve that portion of his sentence. The difference between the two facilities was like night and day. Federal prisoners got to use regular silverware during their meals, instead of the one big spoon he'd had to eat with at Stateville. And they had plastic plates rather than metal. He even got to sit at a regular table in the dining hall instead of the long metal jobs in the state facility.

When a new prisoner arrived at Terre Haute, he was initially housed in a reception area for processing. From there he was assigned to a dormitory. After that, with good conduct, he could earn his way into a cell and the privacy it afforded. But Frank knew the inmate who was in charge of housing assignments, so he was able to skip the dormitory and go directly from processing to his own cell.

The goal of any inmate was to get transferred from the main prison to the work farm. This was a minimum-security area, where the prisoner could work outdoors and enjoy even better food and accommodations.

After six months, Frank was assigned to the farm and worked in the fields baling hay. It was a good deal, except for one guard who seemed to enjoy harassing the inmates. He was a little guy, but nitpicking seemed to make him feel like a big man.

Frank came up with a plan to bring attention to the inmates' displeasure with the guard without anyone having to come forward to file a formal complaint. He arranged for a can of black spray paint to be smuggled in from the outside. One night, he snuck out the window of his room and painted a list of grievances against the guard on the outer wall of a trailer in the yard used as an office. When his work was discovered the next morning, all hell broke loose and an investigation was launched. Authorities were unable to identify the author of the message, but the problem guard was transferred to another facility.

Frank's next step toward freedom came about 18 months after his transfer to the farm. His parole hearing was coming up and if things went well, he'd go from the prison to a halfway house, then back on the streets. Naturally, he was anxious to have his hearing and learn the results. But the formal notification wouldn't be generated right away. That meant he'd have to sweat it out until the paperwork was finished and delivered to him. Or did it? Frank figured that rather than spend the time waiting to receive word of the decision, it would be best to listen in on the deliberations that went on after the hearing ended. So he decided to bug the hearing room.

Each administrative area of the prison had an inmate janitor assigned to it. Frank arranged for a radio transmitter to be smuggled in by a visitor. The center of a book was hollowed out, with the transmitter concealed in the empty space. The book was given to the janitor, who placed it on a bookshelf in the hearing room. Although the farm was too far away to pick up the signal, Frank's cohorts in the cell house 50 feet away from the hearing room received the transmission over their FM radio. A couple of hours after the hearing, Frank knew he had made parole.

While in the halfway house, Frank temporarily became involved with his second wife, Marie, again. He wasn't allowed to have a car at the time, but Marie was a manager at a large Ford dealership and she let him use a brand new Thunderbird that was registered in her name. They had another falling out, however, and Marie wanted the car back. Frank made a proposal to her: the Thunderbird for the $10,000 ring she took with her when they first split up. Both were satisfied with the agreement.

In 1974, after serving a total of six years, Frank was paroled from the halfway house. He was again a free man.

The Straight Life Fails

When Frank was released on parole, he was 36 years old. He fully intended to give up his life of crime and become a productive member of society. In spite of his good intentions, however, he soon found out that going straight wasn't as easy as he'd thought.

In order to qualify for parole, an inmate had to have a job lined up. Frank's mother was able to help her son meet that requirement. The owner of the restaurant where she worked also owned a dental lab. Frank had absolutely no qualifications to make dentures, but Josephine arranged for him to be hired at the lab. The deal called for Frank to show up at the lab each Friday to collect his paycheck, creating a paper trail showing him as an employee. He cashed the check, then returned the money to the owner. The parole people were satisfied, it didn't cost Josephine's boss any money, and Frank had lots of free time to pursue other endeavors. The arrangement lasted until Frank opened a business of his own about a year later.

Without a real job to tie him down, Frank looked around for a good business opportunity. He found a deal that seemed perfect for him. An acquaintance owned some property near Wrigley Field and wanted him to go partners in a restaurant. They built an upscale establishment right across from the ballpark. It was totally legit and Frank worked in the place day and night. But when the cops found out he was one of the owners, they started hanging around the place and harassing him. Making themselves visible around the restaurant at all hours discouraged customers from stopping in. Almost every night some windows were broken out. It got to be very depressing for Frank. He thought his hatred of the system and the desire to be like his father were under control, but they were beginning to resurface.

Business dropped off and the vandalism continued. Fed up, Frank sold his share in the restaurant to his partner. He took out enough money to buy into a lounge out in Schiller Park. He kept on one of the former owners, whose name was on the liquor license. Frank did some remodeling and changed the name of the place to Spanky's. Even though his disgust with the system was bubbling over, he planned to run the place legit. Then the cops found him again and the harassment resumed.

Frank's brother Joey was working for him part-time as a doorman. One night when Frank came in, he learned there'd been an altercation. "I had a little trouble with some kids earlier," Joey said. "I ran them out, but one of their fathers is connected."

"Was anybody hurt?"

"No, nothing like that. I just made them leave."

It didn't sound serious and Frank forgot about it. But half an hour later an Outfit guy named Louie the Mooch came into the bar;

Mooch worked for Outfit boss Joe Aiuppa. He said, "Frankie, what the fuck did you hit my son for?"

"What the hell are you talking about? I haven't hit anybody and I didn't even know you had a son."

"I'm talking about my stepson. He said you roughed him up and threw him out."

"He's mistaken, Louie. I just got here a little while ago and I haven't had a beef with anybody."

Louie called his stepson in. He looked at Frank and said, "Yeah, he's the guy."

"You're full of shit. I've never seen you before," Frank insisted.

The Mooch had come into the bar with an attitude and now he was even madder. "Nobody smacks my kid around. You're gonna pay for that."

"I told you I never saw the kid before. Now get the fuck out of my place, both of you."

"We'll leave," Mooch said, "but this isn't the end of it. I'm gonna get you whacked, you cocksucker!"

Frank figured Louie would take his complaint straight to Aiuppa, so the next day he called Tony Spilotro for advice. Tony, while Frank was in prison, had moved to Las Vegas to keep an eye on the Outfit's casino interests. Tony told him, "Contact Joey Lombardo and tell him what happened. I'll call him myself, too."

Frank went over to Lombardo's brother's restaurant, Rocky's Steakhouse, on North Avenue. He asked Rocky to contact Joe and tell him he needed to speak with him. As the two men were talking, the door opened and Louie the Mooch walked in. Frank figured he was also there to reach out to Joey Lombardo.

When Louie spotted Frank, he threw a punch. Frank blocked it, grabbed Louie's arm and neck, and rammed him into the wall.

"You're a dead man!" Louie hollered.

At that point Rocky Lombardo had seen and heard enough. "Listen, the both of you!" he yelled. "I don't allow fighting in my goddamn place! You know Jackie Cerone [Outfit underboss] is my partner here. Jackie don't want any bullshit in here either. Settle your beef somewhere else."

Frank knew he'd better leave before he ended up with even more trouble. He told Rocky he'd go to his brother Joey's barbershop and wait for Joe Lombardo's call.

Lombardo called two hours later and invited Frank to meet him at a tavern. Frank took his brother along with him. When they got to the bar, a bunch of guys, Louie the Mooch included, were outside having a cookout. Lombardo called Frank aside and questioned him about the incident with Louie's stepson. He asked Frank if he'd hit the kid and Frank said no.

Just then Louie walked over. "You're a goddamn liar!" he hollered and took a swing. Frank ducked the punch and smacked Louie in the head. Before he could do any more, Lombardo grabbed his arm. "Don't fucking hit him," Lombardo ordered.

Frank couldn't believe it. Everything inside him said to give Louie a good beating and Lombardo was telling him not to retaliate. Louie came at him again. Frank threw Louie on the ground and sat on him. Lombardo kicked a brick over to Louie. He grabbed it and hit Frank in the head three or four times. While Frank was getting his head bashed in, a bunch of other guys held his brother to keep him out of the fight.

Frank had taken all he was going to, Lombardo or no Lombardo. The mob big shot must have sensed that Frank was ready to

Dennis Griffin and Frank Cullotta

blow and called for a halt in the action. "Are you satisfied, Louie?" Lombardo asked.

"Yeah, I'm done with him," the brick-wielder said.

After Louie took off, Frank was given a towel to wipe the blood from his face. He asked Lombardo, "Why the fuck did I have to take a beating from a prick like Louie?"

"I had to do it this way," Lombardo explained. "Louie came to me and said he wanted to use a baseball bat on you; I wouldn't let him. He said he'd wait until Joe [Aiuppa] got back from vacation and get the okay from him. I didn't want that to happen, so I made this compromise to get it over with now. Louie has no more beef; it's over. Put it on the shelf today. You might be able to take it back off later."

Although he wasn't happy about what had happened, Frank accepted the fact that Lombardo's decision had probably been the right one under the circumstances. In the world of organized crime, that was the kind of logic used to settle grievances. Had Aiuppa been in town, Louie might have been given more leeway in how he got his revenge.

• • •

Being harassed by the law, then being victimized in an unwarranted Outfit assault, didn't help Frank's attitude. Even so, he tried to stay on the straight and narrow. But then a situation developed that drove him over the edge and back to his criminal ways: He found out that a contractor was building another disco just two blocks from his place.

Had he been thinking clearly, Frank might have realized that the competition could be a good thing. Instead, he looked at it as something that would bring his whole world crashing down. He couldn't let the new joint open.

When the building was nearly completed, Frank went into action. First, he put a combination of gas and diesel fuel into a five-gallon plastic container. Then he got a canister of dynamite, a cap, wick, and timer and headed for the new lounge. Placing everything in the center of the building, he set the timer and left. Half an hour later the potential competition was flattened.

It didn't help, though. Frank's business continued to fall off. After being in business for about a year, he sold the place for what he'd paid for it. He'd tried the legit route for almost two years and it hadn't worked out. It was time to get back to doing something he was good at.

• • •

Frank was ready to return to stealing for a living. But before resuming burglaries and robberies, he needed to update his procedures. His first priority was to figure a way to neutralize alarm systems.

He got hold of alarm-system schematics from a guy who was in the industry. He learned how the alarms were wired into the businesses and police stations. A friend helped him develop a way to bypass the alarm wiring without interrupting the flow of electricity. Through trial and error, they came up with something that worked. Since there wouldn't be a power outage, the alarm company or police station wouldn't be warned of the burglary. That would give the burglars all the time they needed to work on the vault or safe.

It took nearly six months of preparation, but Frank finally had a crew together and was stealing again. Using the new technology, they pulled off a bunch of burglaries, hitting all different kinds of stores. One jewelry store job netted $150,000.

They also scored a bank vault once. The job took a month to plan. The crooks penetrated a vacant building next door to the bank, then dug under the foundation and right up under the vault. They drilled through the bank's concrete floor and once inside, they went after the safety-deposit boxes, drilling out the locks and emptying the contents into bags. The take was over $300,000.

The only trouble was that a score that large required a kickback to the Outfit. It happened that one of the crew was an Outfit guy, so there was no way around paying the tribute. By the time everybody got their cut, Frank only ended up with around $30,000. Still, that was a good haul for a single job.

Frank split with that crew after the jewelry-store burglary. Without him, they went on to pull another major jewelry score. But soon after that job, Outfit hit men tracked them down. When they caught up with the crooks, the hit men cut themselves in on the score, telling them, "You've got a partner."

The thieves weren't happy, but they had little choice other than to comply. Not long after that, some of the crew started coming up missing and were later found murdered.

Frank doesn't know for sure, but the story on the street was that these same crooks had burglarized Tony Accardo's house. That was a big mistake, for which they paid the ultimate price.

. . .

When Frank was paroled from prison in 1974, his friends threw a coming-out party for him in Chicago. Tony Spilotro came in from Las Vegas to help celebrate his long-time pal's return to freedom. During the festivities, Tony invited Frank to join him in Sin City. Planning on going straight at that time, Frank declined the offer.

However, nearly five years later, things were much different in Frank's life. There was so much heat on him in Chicago that the cops were always either arresting or just plain harassing him. Often they put their hands right in his pocket, helping themselves to whatever they found there. The Outfit, meanwhile, had its hand in his other pocket. Everyone wanted a piece of his action. For Frank it was a choice of paying off, getting arrested, or taking a bullet in the head.

The next time Tony called, Frank was more than receptive. "Frankie, I've got a lot going and I need you out here real bad," Tony said.

Frank didn't hesitate. "I'm on my way."

Joseph Cullotta, Frank's father, eight years before Frank was born (1930).

Joe Cullotta holds Frank as a baby next to Josephine and Jean Cullotta.

Frank at a birthday party; his hand is in a cast from a fight with a boy who made fun of his eyeglasses.

Crash kil_ _eeder after 70-mph chase

The identity of a man killed in a car crash that ended a wild chase by Oak Park police remained a mystery today.

The man, described as wild eyed and frightened, died in the wreckage of his car after it collided head-on with another auto near 2100 N. Harlem, Elmwood Park.

Oak Park Policemen Harry Glos and Milton _____ ____ go on the trail of the speeding car at Marion and Paulina, in Oak Park. They curbed it shortly, but when they tried to question the driver, he sped away almost running down Mollenhauer.

The policemen returned to the chase at 70 miles an hour. The fugitive drove recklessly, periling traffic while the policemen fired eight shots, three of which hit the car, in an unsuccessful attempt to halt him.

Finally, the man's car sideswiped

a railway bus and then smashed headon into an auto driven by William B. Strauss, 28, 2822 Maplewood.

Strauss was taken to Oak Park _____ _____ __ and facial lacerations. The fugitive died as he was lifted from the wreck.

Police traced his 1934 Ford license to a John Sarno, 2038 Mohawk. The name of Sarno was found on the door. But at that address a woman said she never had heard of Sarno and ripped the name from the door.

The dead man, who appeared to be about 27, carried no identification. In his car were several cases of various brands of cleansing compounds.

Left: Newspaper clip concerning the car crash that killed Joe Cullotta, Frank's father.

Below: A line-up photo taken in 1959 of Frank (left) and his friend Tom Leahy.

Frank and his third new Cadillac in 1961.

Left: Frank in his cell in Terre Haute.

Even at the federal pen at Terre Haute, Frank needed a special license to drive a truck.

Left: Snapshot taken in the visiting room/dining hall of Terre Haute Federal Penitentiary of Frank's family and his friend Mikey's (Bushelhead).

Above: The matchbook cover passed at his release party; the dates signify his time incarcerated.

Left: Frank's mother Josephine and Frank at his surprise homecoming party after being released from the Terre Haute federal lockup in 1974.

Above: The four Cullottas taken in Chicago in 1974: (from right) Frank, his older sister Jean, his mother Josephine, and his younger brother Joe Jr.

Above (left to right): John Spilotro, Frank, Marie, and Marie's sister at Frank and Marie's wedding reception in Chicago in 1967.

Michael Spilotro and his wife at Frank and Marie's wedding.

Above: The exterior of the Upper Crust pizza place in Las Vegas with girlfriend and soon-to-be-bride Eileen.

Right: Partner in crime Leo Guardino and his wife Vie in the dining room of the Upper Crust.

Another mug shot of Frank taken in Las Vegas in 1980.

Above: Meeting of the Chicago Outfit, circa 1970s. From left to right (front row)—Anthony "Joe Batters" Accardo, Joseph "Black Joe" Amato, Joseph "Little Caesar" DiVarco, James "Turk" Torello; (back row)—Joseph "Doves" Aiuppa, Martin Accardo, Vincent Solano, Alfred Pilotto, Jackie Cerone, Joseph "The Clown" Lombardo (courtesy of Gene Smith).

Left: Former site of Bertha's Gifts & Home Furnishings, 896 East Sahara, 1981 (courtesy of Dennis N. Griffin).

Above: 2004 prison photo of Lawerence Neumann (courtesy of Illinois Dept. of Corrections).

Left: Bertha's burglars, July 4, 1981. From left to right: Ernest Davino, Lawrence Neumann, Wayne Matecki, Leo Guardino, Joe Blasko, and Frank Cullotta (courtesy of Gene Smith).

Left to right: Special Agent Mark Kaspar, Tony Spilotro, Special Agent Dennis Arnoldy, and Supervisory Special Agent Charlie Parsons (courtesy of *Las Vegas Review Journal*).

Above: Tony Spilotro's 1983 mug shots (courtesy of Gene Smith).

Left: Herb Blitzstein, Tony Spilotro's trusted lieutenant (courtesy of LVMPD).

Far Right: Kent Clifford, Commander of the LVMPD Intelligence Bureau under Sheriff McCarthy (courtesy of Kent Clifford).

Right: Sgt. Gene Smith of the LVMPD, circa 1975 (courtesy of Gene Smith).

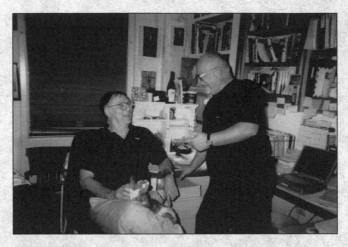

Frank and Nick Pileggi in Pileggi's office in New York City.

FBI agent Dennis Arnoldy, who debriefed and protected Frank for so long that the two became friends (courtesy of Dennis Arnoldy).

07/01/24

Denny Griffin and Frankie Cullotta (courtesy of Dennis N. Griffin).

Part Two

Las Vegas

Together Again

While Frank Cullotta was in prison, Tony Spilotro moved to Las Vegas. The Outfit had interests in several casinos there and Tony's old pal Lefty Rosenthal was overseeing their gambling operations. But with so much money involved, an enforcer was needed to assist Lefty as necessary. With his reputation as a whatever-it-takes type of guy, Spilotro was a logical choice for the job. So in 1971, Tony, his wife Nancy, and their adopted son Vincent headed for the gambling and entertainment oasis in Southern Nevada.

Soon after settling into town, Tony made his debut as a businessman. His first venture was opening a jewelry and gift shop at the Circus Circus Hotel and Casino. Concessions in major casinos were generally hard to come by, especially for people with known ties to organized crime. According to Nevada gaming regulations, any casino doing business with such people could lose its license. Nevertheless, Circus Circus owner Jay Sarno chose to ignore the rules and let the mob-connected Spilotro open his shop. The fact that Sarno had obtained around $20 million in Teamster loans may very well have influenced his decision.

Las Vegas was also ideal for an experienced loanshark like Tony. The casinos paid low wages, which many employees couldn't stretch from paycheck to paycheck. It was a golden opportunity for someone with money to lend and the ability to get it back.

In August 1972, Tony was indicted for the 1963 murder of Leo Foreman. He was arrested and lodged in the Clark County Jail. Spilotro wasn't the only person charged in Foreman's murder. In Chicago, the DeStefano brothers, Mad Sam and Mario, were named as co-defendants.

Tony received troubling news when he learned that Mad Sam, out of Stateville prison after serving a five-year sentence on a conspiracy conviction, was planning to act as his own attorney. Even worse, Sam had been diagnosed with terminal cancer. Rumor had it that he was contemplating making a deal with prosecutors so he wouldn't have to die in prison. There was no doubt that any such arrangement would require Sam to give up Tony and Mario.

Tony took matters into his own hands and went to Outfit boss Tony Accardo. Five weeks before the trial, a person or persons unknown fired two shotgun blasts into Mad Sam's chest. In June 1973, Tony was acquitted of the Foreman charges. He was off the hook in Chicago, at least for the time being. But Tony's presence in Vegas was far from unnoticed.

In Tony's first three years in Vegas, more gangland-style murders were committed there than in the previous 25 years combined. A casino executive and his wife were gunned down in front of their home, another casino executive was murdered in a parking lot, a prominent lawyer was blown up in his Cadillac, a loanshark victim

Dennis Griffin and Frank Cullotta

went missing, and another casino boss was beaten and crippled for life. A witness against Spilotro in a fraud case in Chicago was murdered. Two Caesars Palace employees, one a pit boss, were killed gangland style in Las Vegas. And a San Diego real estate investor with points in several mob-run casinos was murdered with a .22 pistol, Spilotro's weapon of choice.

It didn't matter whether or not Spilotro was directly responsible for the violence. People, including the cops, believed he was, and as his reputation for viciousness grew, so did his boldness.

Not only was Tony Spilotro becoming more powerful. His organization was growing as well. By 1975, Tony's entourage had increased dramatically, with the arrival of his brother John and an influx of bookies, loansharks, burglars, and other heavies from Chicago. He moved his operations from Circus Circus to the Dunes, then the Las Vegas Country Club, and finally another jewelry store, the Gold Rush. The two-story building located at 228 West Sahara, just off the Strip, had a front door that could be operated by a buzzer located behind the counter; a private security company regularly swept the building for electronic bugs and monitored the alarm system. The second floor housed communications equipment, including two radio transmitters and receivers and five scanners that monitored police and FBI activities. Gang members with binoculars were sometimes stationed on the roof or parked on the street looking for signs of law-enforcement surveillance operations. It was the perfect set-up to accommodate the growing inventory of loot from Spilotro's thriving burglary ring.

Tony, his brother John, and Herbert "Fat Herbie" Blitzstein, a 300-pound convicted bookie from Chicago, operated the store itself. A loaded 9mm semi-automatic pistol and a .45 revolver were kept behind the counter, should anyone be foolish enough to try to rob the robbers. And Tony even had two cops, a detective and a sergeant in the police department's anti-crime unit, working for him from the inside.

Although he never officially attained "Don" status, the attention Tony Spilotro received from the law was nearly the same as that bestowed on higher-ranking mobsters. In spite of being almost continuously under investigation and a suspect in some 25 murders and countless other felonies, Tony conducted his affairs in Las Vegas for more than a decade without being convicted of even a minor offense. Part of the reason for that impressive run could be his skills as a criminal; another likely factor was that his reputation and willingness to use violence made witnesses against him scarce.

• • •

The FBI had been investigating Spilotro and his gang for years and by March 1978, they'd developed sufficient probable cause to obtain warrants authorizing them to monitor the activities of the mobsters through the use of wiretaps and electronic eavesdropping. In addition, the feds had managed to infiltrate the Spilotro operation via an undercover agent.

By the middle of June, after 79 days of wiretaps, eight thousand conversations had been recorded on 298 tapes. The FBI had amassed enough evidence to obtain search warrants for 83 locations. On June 19, the warrants were executed simultaneously, one of them at the Gold Rush. Some four thousand pieces of jewelry were seized from the store, of which 1,400 were later identified as being stolen.

Dennis Griffin and Frank Cullotta

The feds had collected a lot of items that might have led to convictions and prison time for Tony and his boys. That was not to be, though. A U.S. magistrate later ruled that the raiding agents had gone far beyond the scope authorized in the search warrants and that nearly all the evidence gathered was inadmissible. Chalk up another victory for Spilotro. But a downside arrived later in the year: In October, Tony's name was added to Nevada's Black Book, barring him from all casinos.

. . .

In addition to his many criminal activities, Tony became involved in another thing he shouldn't have: He began having an affair with Geri Rosenthal, Lefty's wife.

The once-close relationship between the two men had been on the skids for a while. Lefty was having licensing problems with the Nevada Gaming Control Board and placed part of the blame on Spilotro's presence. And then Geri admitted to her husband that she was having an affair with Tony. Lefty was certainly angry and hurt, but he was also scared. He made Geri promise not to tell Spilotro that she had confessed. There was no telling what the bosses in Chicago would do if they discovered their Las Vegas enforcer had become involved with their embattled inside-man's wife. Lefty reasoned that Tony would be afraid that he, the aggrieved husband, might complain to Chicago. Knowing that people who posed a threat to Tony tended to have a brief life expectancy, he told Geri that if the volatile Spilotro learned Lefty knew the truth, he'd probably kill them both.

Tony's first seven years in Las Vegas were eventful, to say the least. He was firmly entrenched as the King of the Strip and his tentacles reached far and wide. Money was coming in from a variety of illegal sources. Allegations of criminal acts rolled off him like water off a duck's back. The federal and local agencies investigating him had problems of their own, based on some of their own operatives being loyal or at least friendly to organized crime, and they didn't trust each other on the organizational level. The law seemingly was unable to lay a glove on him. It was true that his relationship with Lefty Rosenthal had gone sour, but the one with his former friend's wife was perking along and, to his knowledge, wasn't known to the oddsmaker. All seemed to be good in his realm.

When Tony reached out to Frank Cullotta to join him in Las Vegas, he was more than likely feeling somewhat invincible. Asking a man like Frank—a master thief and killer who had proved his trustworthiness over the years—to join his team was a logical move.

What Tony may not have realized was that his victories over the law had only been the initial skirmishes. The battle was far from over; in fact, it was only beginning. Things were happening in the law-enforcement arena that soon began to turn the tide. The FBI was making personnel moves and preparing to launch a full-court press to take Tony down. And in November 1978, Clark County voters made a change at the top of their police department, electing a reform candidate who had vowed to put Tony and his gang in jail or run them out of town.

Whether it was knowingly or unknowingly, Tony invited Frank into a war that was just heating up.

. . .

When Frank arrived in Las Vegas in early 1979, one of his first stops was at the Gold Rush, Tony Spilotro's store and headquarters. After touching base with Tony, Frank rented a condo at a place called the Marie Antoinette, at 205 East Harmon Avenue. It was a beautiful place and Frank's unit was located right by the pool. Everything was furnished except for the television.

After getting settled in, Frank met Tony for dinner to discuss what his function was going to be.

"I want you to be my eyes, ears, and muscle," Tony said.

"It sounds like I'm going to be pretty busy," Frank smiled. "Seriously, though, I'll probably need some help to keep up with things. What do you think?"

"Sure, bring in whoever you want."

Frank got to work lining up his crew. One of the first men to join him was Leo Guardino, a Chicago burglar who was already living in Las Vegas. Guardino was trying to go legit, but was having trouble landing a decent job. When Frank reached out to him, he was more than ready to listen to his proposal.

When they got together Frank made his pitch. "I'm working for Tony Spilotro and I'm putting a crew together. You interested?"

"What's the setup?"

"We'll do our own scores and any that Tony tells us about. All we have to do is kick back some of the money from our jobs to Tony and fulfill our other obligations to him."

"What kind of obligations?"

Frank shrugged. "That depends. He'll probably want us to muscle people once in a while. Maybe shake down drug dealers and renegade bookies, things like that."

"I don't mind a little rough stuff, but I'm not a killer. I don't want to get into that kind of shit."

"Don't worry about it; you won't have to do anything you don't want to do. I'll have some other guys around to handle anything like that," Frank assured him.

That seemed to satisfy Guardino, but he had another question. "Tony's an Outfit guy. What about them?"

"Tony will determine how much money has to be sent to Chicago. We're going to make a lot of money for ourselves, too; you can count on it. On top of that we'll have carte blanche at some of the casinos. Shows and meals and stuff will all be comped. We'll be living the good life."

Guardino liked the deal and went for it.

The next man to join the team was Ernie Davino. Frank had never met him before, but he came highly recommended as a thief and was also living locally.

Next, Frank's thoughts turned to his former co-worker from Stateville's psych ward, Larry Neumann. After serving only 11 years, the murderer had somehow managed to get out on parole while Frank was still in Chicago. Even though Neumann's father had died and left him a lot of money in a trust fund, he preferred the criminal life. He and Frank partnered on a couple of jobs before Frank left town and they remained in contact after Frank moved to Vegas. Because Neumann wasn't known as a thief, only a killer, Frank figured maybe he could use him in Sin City someday.

With Frank gone, Neumann was doing jobs in Chicago with a man named Wayne Matecki; they were both the kind who had to stay active. During one of their phone calls, Neumann asked Frank if he knew of any good scores in Chicago that he and Matecki could handle, then bring the merchandise to Frank in Vegas. As it happened, Frank was aware of a robbery that had a lot of potential and told Neumann about it. He didn't realize at the time that he was condemning the victim to death.

· · ·

The score Frank turned Neumann and Matecki onto was the robbery of a jeweler. Frank had information that the jeweler likely had between $150,000 and $200,000 worth of merchandise on hand at any given time.

The jeweler's name was Bob Brown. He was a friend of Allen Dorfman, who was involved in arranging Teamster loans to the Outfit. Neumann and Matecki prepared a plan for the job. It turned out that Matecki knew Brown and wouldn't be able to do the robbery himself, but he thought he could enter the store under the pretext that he was looking to buy a ring. After Matecki got inside, Larry could come in and stick the place up. Neumann called Frank and told him what he and Matecki had in mind. Frank agreed that it sounded like a plan that would work.

The two Chicagoans did the robbery and 36 hours later Neumann was at Frank's door in Vegas. He was carrying an attaché case. "It looks like everything went well," Frank said.

Neumann patted the case and said, "We got the money, but we changed the plan a little."

Frank didn't like the sound of that. "What kind of change?"

"I had to kill him."

"You killed Brown?"

"I didn't intend to when I got there. But it was in the back of my mind that the Outfit might figure out that Wayne was in on the robbery and come after him. When I got in the store, I said fuck it. I put my gun down and grabbed a machete that was hanging on the wall. I started stabbing him and Wayne broke a vase over his head."

Frank couldn't believe that a simple robbery had turned into a murder. He wasn't happy about it, but he had to be careful what he said. Neumann was a stone-cold killer and he wasn't afraid of anyone. If Frank said too much, he could end up dead, too. Frank sold the merchandise to a fence in Las Vegas. By the time he paid all the overhead the split was $25,000 each. It was hardly worth anyone's life.

Neumann returned to Chicago, but within thirty days he moved to Las Vegas.

·   ·   ·

There can be little doubt that Larry Neumann was extremely dangerous. He chose a life of crime not out of necessity, but because he enjoyed it. Stealing may have been fun for him, but he seemed to derive the most pleasure from killing people. He murdered when murder wasn't necessary. For example, the three people he shotgunned in the Chicago tavern were reportedly killed because he thought he'd been short-changed in the amount of two dollars. Also in Frank's opinion, there had been no reason to kill jeweler Bob Brown. And there were other examples of Neumann's penchant for homicide.

One time Neumann, Guardino, and Frank were sitting in Frank's restaurant when Neumann got up to take a phone call.

When he came back, he said, "Some guy got in a beef with my ex-wife in a lounge back in Chicago. The motherfucker grabbed her by the throat."

"Was she hurt?" Frank asked.

"No, she's okay."

"Hey, she's not hurt and you aren't even married to her any more. Don't get so upset," Frank told him.

Those words fell on deaf ears. Neumann said, "What he did was a sign of disrespect to me. I've got to go back and kill the bastard."

For the next hour and a half, Frank talked to Neumann, trying to convince him not to do anything. When the conversation was finished, Frank believed that he'd succeeded.

About ten days later, Neumann said he had to go to Chicago for a few days. Frank had a caper in the works for which he planned to use a kid named Tommy as an alibi. He figured if Tommy went out of town for a while, there'd be less chance anyone would connect them, so he asked Neumann if he'd take Tommy with him. As a side benefit, having the kid around would probably discourage Neumann from doing anything foolish regarding the supposed assault on his ex-wife.

Neumann and Tommy left for Chicago and the next day Frank received a call from a friend about a double killing in McHenry County, Neumann's home turf. According to the caller, a guy and his girlfriend were shot in the head while sitting in a lounge. Frank called Tommy to find out if he knew anything about the murders, but the kid didn't want to say anything on the phone.

As promised, Neumann was back the following week and he met with Frank. "Larry, did you kill those people in the bar?" Frank asked.

"Yeah. He was the son of a bitch that choked my ex-wife."

"You promised me you were going to let that go."

"I thought about what you said, but I couldn't control myself. I found out the tavern this guy was in and went there; I left Tommy outside in the car. I asked the guy why he grabbed my ex-wife's neck. He was feeding me a line of shit and I was getting more and more pissed off. I pulled my gun and shot him in the forehead. And then I shot the broad."

"But the girl had nothing to do with it. And I hear she had a couple of kids."

"Then the kids are probably better off without her."

Neumann's homicidal tendencies weren't lost on Tony Spilotro either. Spilotro, considered by some to be the most dangerous man in Las Vegas at the time, once spoke about Neumann to Frank. He said, "Jesus! Whatever you do, don't ever unleash that bastard on me."

• • •

Shortly after Frank recruited Leo Guardino, the two did three residential burglaries. Using $65,000 of the proceeds from those thefts, they opened up an Italian restaurant called the Upper Crust at 4110 South Maryland Parkway. Adjoining the restaurant was the My Place Lounge. Both businesses became hangouts for Tony Spilotro's gang and other Las Vegas wiseguys.

When Frank first opened the Upper Crust, he met a man named Nick Rossi (not his real last name). He was a long-time Las Vegan who knew a lot of people and had lots of contacts. A short time later Nick stopped in the restaurant and mentioned to Frank that he had a daughter, Eileen. She was 34 years old and had two children—Kimberly and Kent—from a previous marriage. He said she was an honest and loyal girl who'd make a good employee.

Frank subsequently spoke with Eileen. After a couple of meetings, he was satisfied that she was trustworthy and wouldn't steal from him. He put her to work in the restaurant; they were married on Jan. 1, 1980. She proved to be a loyal employee, wife, and confidant. His money and his secrets were safe with her. But Eileen was also very jealous, and with good reason. After they were married, she watched Frank like a hawk.

. . .

Within a year of moving to Las Vegas, Frank Cullotta was settled in. He was married, owned a restaurant, and had a crew of burglars, robbers, arsonists, and killers. Although Tony Spilotro was the overall boss, Frank did his own recruiting and planned the scores. His crew consisted of five guys. Leo Guardino and Ernie Davino specialized in burglaries. Larry Neumann, Wayne Matecki, and Jimmy Patrazzo would do it all, including armed robbery and murder. Except for Davino, Frank knew them all from Chicago. Matecki and Patrazzo were the only two who didn't live in Las Vegas. Matecki had no criminal record at all and Patrazzo was unknown in Nevada. That meant they were clean faces and didn't have to worry about being fingered in a photo lineup. Anytime Frank needed them, they'd fly into town to do the score. Afterward they'd drive to an airport in California or Arizona and fly back to Chicago. That way, if the cops had witnesses check the Vegas airport's security tapes after a job, they wouldn't be spotted.

Burglaries were their forte and they did three or four house break-ins a week. Many of those homes were alarmed and Frank had to figure out ways to get into the houses. Some alarms weren't wired into police or central security stations, so he could disable the ringers or bells. Others could be circumvented by making holes in the walls or the roofs of the residences to get inside. That M.O. led to them being dubbed the Hole in the Wall Gang (HITWG). Initially, Frank was afraid of copycats. He was concerned that if other thieves began pulling jobs using the hole-in-the-wall method, his crew would be charged with every burglary in the city if they ever got caught. But his guys didn't seem to care, so neither did he.

A few alarm systems were harder to beat. He couldn't just pull the ringers off the wall, or if they had motion detectors, a hole in the roof wouldn't work. He needed inside information.

Pulling a page out of his Chicago playbook, Frank sought the help of insurance agents. For a percentage of the score, he got all the information he needed to do the job: a list and location of valuables and how the house was alarmed.

Frank didn't consider the people whose homes were burglarized as victims. His gang never stole from anyone who was really poor. They always made sure their information was accurate and the people they were going to rob were well-to-do. The targets all had good insurance and usually ended up better off after the burglary. He thought that in reality he was doing them a favor.

Not everyone in his crew felt the same, though. Although Frank had put together a gang of professional crooks, one of them had a hang-up that was somewhat comical. During a burglary, Leo Guardino couldn't stand to see a picture of the people he was stealing from. He didn't want to know who they were or what they looked like. If he saw a photo in the room, he turned it upside down.

. . .

Leo Guardino was a good thief, but he wasn't prone to violence, as he admitted up front to Frank. However, on one occasion, rather bizarre circumstances drove the mild-mannered burglar to pull the trigger.

A hotel bellman told Frank that he knew two guys and a girl who were big-time dope dealers. They had a safe in their house full of coke and cash. As usual, the robbers took two cars to the job. They used Caddys or Lincolns so they wouldn't look out of place in the upscale neighborhoods they worked in. As in Chicago, the work cars were registered under fictitious names.

In anticipation of having to haul a safe, Frank drove a big Lincoln to the robbery scene. He stayed outside in the Lincoln while another driver cruised around in a legitimately licensed Caddy. Guardino, Davino, and a third guy did the robbery. Soon, Frank heard what sounded like a gunshot come from the house; minutes later he got a call on his walkie-talkie to make the pick-up. The guys brought out the safe and they took off.

While they were driving, Frank inquired about the gunshot-like noise. "What the fuck was that pop I heard? It sounded like a shot."

Guardino answered. "When we crashed through the sliding glass doors, the two guys were sitting at a table in the kitchen in their shorts, and the broad was in the bathroom. The two men ran; I chased one of them into the bedroom. He got up on the bed and started jumping up and down. I asked him where the safe was. The son of a bitch pulled out his prick and told me to suck it. Can you imagine? I shot the asshole in the leg. He got off the bed and on the floor. I asked him again about the safe. This time he told me which closet it was in. We tied them all up and grabbed the safe."

That safe had $30,000 worth of coke and $15,000 in cash in it. The bellman got his ten percent and Tony got a cut equal to the rest of the gang. As for the guy who got wise with Guardino, he would have been better off had he kept his pecker in his shorts.

• • •

In Las Vegas, other mainstays from his Chicago days sometimes proved not so successful—Sears, for one. Wayne Matecki hid inside the Vegas store until after closing. Then he rounded up all the furs and jewelry, put everything into the store's own clothing bags, brought them to a window, and crashed out. It was a bad score, though. Most of the merchandise was junk and brought in little money. It probably didn't do much more than pay for Matecki's week in Vegas.

Quickly, however, Frank adjusted to the southern Nevada lifestyle and as always, he opened the door for whatever opportunities knocked. Janet, a hooker he knew, called to say she was with a man in a casino. "We've been gambling all night and this guy has an attaché case loaded with money. Do you think we should rob him?"

"Damn right. Take the guy to a room somewhere. After he goes to sleep, give me a call and I'll come over."

Janet and her customer wound up in a high-rise not far from the Marie Antoinette. She called Frank with the address and room number. She let him in the room and showed him the case. As she was getting dressed the guy woke up and saw Frank standing by the bed holding his attaché case. He started to say something and Frank whacked him in the head three or four times with his own money, then he and Janet ran out. There was $20,000 in the case and they split it down the middle.

• • •

When Frank arrived in Vegas, only a few casinos had sports books. Most of the wagering on sporting events was done through illegal bookies and a large number of them were operating in the city. In some cases they were freelancers, not affiliated with any particular crime family. As independents, they cut into the business of mob-controlled book joints and didn't pay tribute to the Midwest crime bosses. These individuals were a source of irritation to the Outfit and their man on the scene, Tony Spilotro. Tony didn't allow such affronts to continue unchallenged. He assigned Frank to straighten out the offenders.

Tony called Frank and said, "There's a bookmaker named Sarge I want you to grab. This cocksucker's a renegade and we've got to bring him in line. Tell the prick that if he wants to continue bookmaking, he better start kicking in some money. If he gives you any static, tell him he'd better pay by tomorrow. Bring somebody with you that will scare him. Bring Lurch." Lurch was a nickname for Larry Neumann. The killer was over six feet tall and muscular. In Frank's opinion, Neumann could scare a hungry bulldog off a meat truck.

Neumann, Davino, and Frank went to see Sarge. Lurch did the talking and scared the bookie to the point of panic.

The next day Tony expressed his pleasure. "You guys put the fear of God into him and he came to me asking for protection. Now I own him. I can gamble into that cocksucker for free now. Got it?"

A few days after that, Tony told Frank about another bookie he wanted the boys to see. Dominic was from Boston and lived in one of the country clubs. Neumann grabbed the bookmaker by the lapels, pulled him close, and said, "Listen, you little grease-ball cocksucker. I know what you're doing out here. I know you're bookmaking. We want a piece of your action. Do you understand?"

Obviously scared, Dominic started rattling off the names of people he knew in Boston.

Lurch cut him short. "I don't give a fuck who you're with. You're gonna do what we tell you or you're dead. We'll be back tomorrow for our first payment of fifteen thousand. Do you understand what I'm telling you?"

Dominic did a little moaning, but he said okay.

Frank contacted Tony and told him what happened. The Ant loved that kind of stuff. He said, "I already got a call from this guy's boss in Boston. He asked me to do him a favor and look out for his man. I told him no problem. He's going to send Dominic money for me, to show his appreciation."

Dominic caused no further problems and he paid protection money to Tony on a regular basis. Everybody was happy.

• • •

It turned out that Nick Rossi, Eileen's father, was able to provide Frank with more than a mate. He also proved to be a good tipster. One of his leads involved a black man named Tony.

Tony ran an escort service and had a lot of white women working for him. He'd also operated a jewelry store that had recently gone out of business. Nick found out that the entire remaining inventory from the jewelry store was being kept in Tony's house. Frank and his crew sat on the place and waited for Tony to leave. When they were sure the house was empty, Davino, Guardino, and a burglar named Pete went inside while Frank stayed with the work car. They found a floor safe in the house and boxes and boxes of jewelry in the garage.

The score was huge. Each of the burglars ended up with $80,000. Nick got his ten percent.

• • •

Frank and his crew robbed drug dealers outright, but they also used another way to get money out of them. It was called a shakedown.

Frank got a call from Tony that he wanted to meet at the Upper Crust. When they talked, Tony explained the plan. "There's a big-time drug dealer in town from Chicago named Jack. I want you to put the muscle on him. Grab him. Tell him you're from Chicago and were sent out here to talk to him. Tell him he's a fucking cocksucker with no business selling coke out here. Then let him know the guys in Chicago want him to pay them five hundred grand and go out of business. See what he has to say and let me know."

Frank found Jack, who cried, "I can't come up with that kind of money. Fifty, maybe, but not five hundred."

Frank was unsympathetic. "I didn't set the price. Chicago did. I'll tell them what you said and get back to you."

"You've got to help me," Jack pleaded. "Make them understand I'm not fucking around with them; I just don't have that kind of money."

"Like I said, I'll tell them."

Frank left the shaken drug dealer and talked with Tony Spilotro the next day. Tony got a big kick out of Frank's description of his meeting with Jack. Then he said, "Tell him Chicago wants three hundred thousand, or else."

"Jesus, Tony, he said he hasn't got that kind of money and I believe him. He was too fucking scared to lie. You might be able to get a hundred out of him, but not three hundred."

Tony didn't want to hear it. "Bullshit. You tell him just what I told you."

Frank did as ordered, but the hard-nosed approach drove Jack into a panic and he dropped out of sight. When Tony heard the news, he flew into a rage. "Find that cocksucker and break his fucking head!"

Frank found Jack again. He and Ernie Davino drove to Jack's place, tied him up, and found the safe. It held about $35,000 in cash, a bunch of jewelry, a pistol, some coke, and other valuables.

$\cdot\ \ \cdot\ \ \cdot$

The problematic parts of the Las Vegas experience caught up to Frank soon enough.

Although he was married to Eileen, he saw other women as well. There were also many beautiful women at Frank's fingertips. It wasn't because of his looks; it was the money and power he had behind him. The ladies were infatuated with Outfit-connected guys and he even had groupies following him around.

The lifestyle Frank was leading caused him to do something he came to regret. He'd never in his life used drugs, but starting sometime in 1980 he began using cocaine.

His motivation was that he thought if he had cocaine, he'd be even more popular with the women. Initially, he just provided the white powder. It was a commodity he got for free by robbing drug dealers, so it was no big thing. But then he started using. He sat down with his girlfriends and snorted a line or two. Starting out with one gram a day, he soon progressed to four.

Frank came to love coke. It was the first thing he did in the morning and if and when he slept, it was the last thing he did at night. And then it started getting bad; he was always looking for cocaine. He knew that he was totally addicted. If he hadn't been getting it for nothing, he probably would have ended up like the other junkies, robbing anybody he could and snatching purses. He was on it for almost a year and blames no one but himself. But Frank was saved from his drug dependency by one thing: sex. His ever-increasing drug use was affecting his sex life and he decided to do something about it.

Frank went to see a doctor who was on juice with him for six grand. That meant the physician was paying $600 a week in interest. When he took Frank's blood pressure, the doctor said it was so high he was surprised his patient hadn't had a stroke. He asked Frank if he was taking any drugs and Frank told him about the cocaine. The doctor said he needed to give it up or face dire consequences.

Frank was fortunate in that he was able to quit drugs cold turkey. Within 30 days his sex drive and blood pressure returned to normal.

To show his appreciation, Frank cut the doctor's juice in half. But not long afterward he sold the doctor's account to one of his crew for the original principal of six thousand and the interest went back up. He believed that throwing some easy money at his men helped to keep them happy.

· · ·

Over the years, Frank and his associates had used explosives many times to blow up cars and buildings. His self-taught expertise led him back to Chicago and a nice payday.

An old friend of Frank's in the Windy City called him about coming to Chicago to do a dynamite job. "Do you remember that black minister, the one that owned a grocery store?" the friend asked.

"Yeah, what about him?"

"He and some of your Blackstone Ranger buddies you met in Stateville want you to do a job for them. I told them I'd get in touch with you."

"Any idea what they want me to do?"

"Apparently, the minister's store is losing a lot of money and he wants to get rid of the place. They know you can flatten it and make it look like an accidental explosion."

It sounded like a simple job and Frank was interested. He agreed, but with a caveat. "Tell them I'm on for it, but I've got to get the okay from Tony first."

Needing to get Tony's permission for anything he wanted to do beyond the regular burglaries and robberies annoyed Frank. Getting approval meant Tony would want a cut of the action for himself, and possibly for the Outfit. Frank didn't like being under that kind of control or having to make extra payouts. Failing to get the okay to handle outside contract work could get him in a lot of trouble, though. So he followed protocol, got Tony's blessing, and flew to Chicago. His brother arranged a rental car for him.

Frank met up with one of the Blackstone Rangers and was taken to see the minister. He was a little Bible-toting guy who apparently wasn't as religious as he appeared. As Frank's friend had reported, the minister's grocery store was losing money and he'd fallen on hard times. The reverend wanted to get out from under it and was willing to pay a good price to get the job done. He offered Frank $10,000 up front and an equal amount when the job was completed.

Frank rounded up his materials and went to do the job. He was more worried about getting through that black neighborhood at night without being mugged or killed than he was about the cops catching him. Fortunately for him, it was a winter night and he was able to wear a ski mask, gloves, and hood without looking suspicious. Frank set everything up, then hit the freeway. After the bomb detonated, he doubled back. When the smoke cleared, he saw the building had totally collapsed.

The minister was ecstatic when Frank met with him the next day. He said, "You all did a good job, brother, a good job." The explosion was blamed on a gas leak. Frank collected the other half of his fee and the minister subsequently received a big insurance check.

When Frank got back to Vegas with the $20,000, Tony wanted his cut. Frank didn't think he deserved anything, but he paid him five grand anyway. He also stroked his crew with a grand each. He felt that just like factory workers, getting a little bonus from the boss made them feel good.

• • •

Frank was in the Jubilation, a lounge at Harmon Avenue and Koval Lane, one night when he was introduced to Sherwin "Jerry" Lisner. He disliked Lisner from the start and considered him a flamboyant braggart and a scheming little weasel; his reputation on the street was as a scam artist. To Frank, Lisner wasn't a real crook, only a wannabe. Personal feelings aside, he kept an open mind regarding possible future business deals.

Lisner soon contacted Frank and asked him to come in on a scam he wanted to work on a man in Florida. "This guy's got a lot of money," Lisner said. "I'm sure we can take him in a money-laundering deal."

Frank was curious. "What kind of money are we talking?"

"I think we can get a hundred and seventy-five thousand out of him."

"How are you going to do it?"

"Here's the setup. I'll tell him I've got some money, about four hundred thousand, that I want to wash, because the serial numbers are in sequence. I'll say I'm willing to swap my cash for a hundred and seventy-five thousand in clean money. Once the guy bites, we'll pull the scam. I know how to do it and I've got a brother-in-law that's a cop in Washington, D.C., who'll work with us."

Frank digested the information for a few moments. "How do I fit in?"

"You'd help me set it up and then come with me to D.C. to exchange the money. We'll fix up an attaché case with a row of hundred-dollar bills on top of stacks of singles. You give the guy a quick peek in the case and it'll look like it holds a lot more money than it does. You'll swap cases and we'll leave with the hundred and seventy-five grand. As the other guy is walking away with the case he got from us, my brother-in-law will arrest him. He'll confiscate the money, then turn him loose. The victim will be thankful he didn't go to jail. We end up with both cases and the sucker will never even realize what happened. We'll all be clean."

Frank liked Lisner's idea to prepare a case of flash money to deceive the victim. He doubted Lisner had $400,000 to put up for show; he certainly didn't have that kind of money himself. And even if he'd had the cash, he wouldn't have put it at risk. Also, Frank knew from experience that things didn't always go as planned. If an honest cop, or a crooked cop not in on the deal, somehow ended up in possession of the bait case, all the money in it would be lost. If the target insisted on counting the money before switching cases, the best thing would be to simply rob him. Setting up the dummy case was the only way to go. But questions remained. "I still don't see what you need me for. Why not just do it yourself?"

"This guy in Florida is slightly connected and I know you're with Tony Spilotro. Having you involved will give me some credibility and make it more likely he'll go for the deal."

"What makes you think I'm tied in with Tony?"

"That's what I hear."

Frank decided to stall. "Let me think it over and I'll get back to you."

Frank went to Tony and filled him in on Lisner's pitch. "Sounds a little corny, doesn't it?" Tony said. "On the other hand, some people are so greedy they'd go for a deal like that. But us? As much as I love money, we're a little sharper than them guys. We wouldn't go for a deal like that. We'd know right away this guy was trying to fuck us. Here's what I want you to do. Go back and tell him you thought it over and it sounds like a good idea. Whatever you do, don't tell him you talked with me about it. Tell him you want seventy-five-thousand dollars, because you have to take care of your people. He can have the hundred and take care of his people. If he don't want to go for that, tell him to go fuck himself."

Frank got back to Lisner and told him he was in. He then explained the money situation. Lisner put up an argument initially, but backed off. He said the target, also named Jerry, planned to come to town in a couple of days and would be staying at Caesars Palace. "Why don't we meet in his room and work out the details?" Lisner suggested.

"I'll have to pass on that. You never know when a room might be bugged."

"Yeah, I hadn't thought of that. How about the Jubilation?"

"That sounds better. We'll meet there."

Florida Jerry was from New York, the kind who talked out of the side of his mouth. He asked Frank where the $400,000 he wanted to exchange came from. "I can't tell you," Frank said. "But it hasn't been reported as missing yet, so I want to move it as soon as I can. If you want to make the deal, fine. If not, we'll find somebody else."

"I'll have to talk this over with my father and get back to you," Florida Jerry said. "I'll let Lisner know what we decide."

"Do what you gotta do. But I want to get this done within a week," Frank said.

Florida Jerry agreed to the proposal and the next week, Lisner and Frank were in D.C. They stayed at a big hotel for almost $300 a night waiting for Florida Jerry to arrive. On the second day there,

Lisner called Florida to find out what was going on. Florida Jerry was apparently having second thoughts. He gave Lisner the run-around, wanting to put up less money. Lisner went back and forth with him. Frank finally told Lisner, "Tell him we'll do it the way he wants. We're not going to give him any money anyway, so what difference does it make?"

Even after they agreed to his terms, Florida Jerry still wouldn't go for the deal. Frank got him on the phone and told him to go fuck himself. Then he and Lisner flew back to Vegas.

Frank wasn't happy and Lisner must have sensed it. While they were on the plane, Lisner cried on his shoulder. "I'm real sorry about this thing blowing up on us. I thought for sure we had him."

Frank masked his anger. "Time is money and we blew a lot of both. But shit happens, so forget about it."

"I'll tell you what. I've got a Quaalude deal in the works. I can cut you in on that and you'll at least get your money back."

"I don't handle drugs," Frank said.

Lisner persisted, "There are a lot of outs for them and you won't have to touch them yourself. I'll get you five thousand Quaaludes for five grand. You'll be able to sell them for ten, doubling your money."

That sounded good to Frank, so he said okay. The next day he had the Quaaludes and told Tony about them. "Get rid of them fuckin' things quick. I don't want any drugs around," Tony said.

Frank sold the Quaaludes to a local kid for $10,000, gave Tony half, and kept the other half for himself. Because Frank had no use for Lisner and didn't consider him to be a business partner, he decided to stiff him. He told Lisner he had to dump the drugs because the cops were on him. Lisner probably didn't believe him and re-sented not getting paid. But there wasn't much he could do about it, at least not then.

• • •

Frank's duties working for Tony Spilotro included helping con-nected guys, moving to Las Vegas from Chicago, find employment. He also made sure visiting wiseguys had a good time.

Tony had been black-balled from the casinos; he couldn't step foot into one without risking arrest. Acting in his stead, Frank took over the responsibility of getting new arrivals from Chicago jobs in the Outfit-controlled joints. He didn't take care of just anybody from Chicago, though. They had to either be Outfit guys or their friends or relatives. He told them which dealer school to go to and when they finished their training, he sent them downtown to the Fremont to apply. Working through the casino manager, Frank's referrals were hired and dealt at the Fremont until they became proficient, then many of them transferred to the Stardust on the Las Vegas Strip. Neither Frank nor Tony charged for this assis-tance; it was done strictly as favors.

In addition to connected guys moving to Vegas, many of them went there for vacation. In those cases Frank got them comped into the Stardust through the casino manager. These wiseguys did a lot of gambling and most of the time would drop $20,000 or so during their stay, so the casino wasn't really giving up anything. The visitors were well taken care of and went back to Chicago feel-ing like big shots.

Dennis Griffin and Frank Cullotta

• • •

Two of the Outfit-controlled casinos at that time were the Stardust on the Las Vegas Strip and Fremont in Glitter Gulch downtown, and Frank's connection to Tony Spilotro earned him a great deal of clout in both. He could get anything he wanted in either place, but he preferred to hang out at the Stardust. When he married Eileen, they had their reception there in one of the ballrooms. Everything was comped. Frank didn't ask for it; Lou Salerno, the casino manager, did it on his own.

However, Frank did have one rather awkward moment at the Stardust. The problem arose because of a burglar from Chicago named Joey whom Frank was associating with. Although Joey's brother was a made man with the Outfit, Tony didn't care for him, so Frank never brought him around the Upper Crust or My Place. The only thing about Joey that Frank didn't like was that he sold drugs.

In addition to stealing and distributing narcotics, Joey was a gambler. One day he, Frank, and Ernie Davino were shooting craps at the Stardust and lost $26,000.They left there and went to the Thunderbird. Joey and Frank each drew a $5,000 marker and the three men headed for the crap tables. Davino was a notoriously unlucky gambler, so he was the designated shooter, making minimum pass line bets. Joey and Frank, playing against him on the don't pass, won $21,000. Then they went next door to the Sahara and won some more. They got all their money back.

The experience prompted the pair to come up with a scheme involving markers that they used in several casinos. The way it worked was that Joey and Frank got some of their friends in Chicago to open bank accounts showing balances of $10,000 or $20,000. Using the friends' names, Frank and Joey got lines of credit at the casinos and drew markers in the amount of the bank accounts in Chicago. As soon as their casino credit was approved, they notified the guys in Chicago, who closed their accounts, taking their money out of risk. Working four casinos at a time gave them each at least $40,000 of casino money to play with. If Frank and Joey won, they won big, because they didn't have a dime invested. If they lost, the casinos got stiffed. They didn't dare hit Outfit joints like the Stardust, Fremont, and Hacienda. It was a good scam, but it had a fairly short life.

But then Joey put Frank in an embarrassing situation by cheating at the Stardust. It wasn't really the fact that he cheated; it was that he got caught by Stardust management. Because it was known that Frank and Joey were pretty close, Cullotta was asked to straighten things out. And with the Stardust being Outfit-connected, Frank had no choice but to tell Tony about it. The Ant wanted everyone brought in and questioned. But Joey got scared and ran off to Chicago. Then one of the Stardust pit bosses admitted to Frank that he was in on the cheat with Joey and another guy.

The players were now all identified. The next question was what Spilotro would do about it. Other people had suffered grievously for lesser offenses. But because of his brother's status in the Outfit, Joey got a pass; his co-cheat was warned and banned from Outfit properties. Frank arranged for the pit boss to be fired, but got him another job at a nickel-and-dime joint. In the world of Tony Spilotro and the Outfit where transgressions often proved fatal, this was a mild rebuke. Not everyone who ran afoul of Tony was so lucky.

Dennis Griffin and Frank Cullotta

. . .

Although the Stardust was one of Frank's favorite hangouts, he got to Las Vegas too late to experience Lefty Rosenthal's management style. Lefty had lost his lengthy battle with the Nevada gaming regulators and had been replaced as casino boss by Al Sachs of Detroit. But Rosenthal was still in town and maintained some clout with the Chicago bosses and Frank learned quickly that the relationship between Lefty and Tony had deteriorated to a dangerous point.

When Frank arrived in Las Vegas, Tony told him to keep away from Rosenthal, but Lefty used to hang out at some of the same spots the gangsters did, so they were often in the same place at the same time. Lefty was one of the most arrogant men Frank had ever met. The oddsmaker acted like he thought he was God. He had an entourage of guys and women following him around like he was an emperor. The attention Rosenthal received got under Tony's skin big time.

One night Tony and Frank were in the Jubilation having a few drinks. Lefty walked in with six showgirls and a couple of his male stooges. Lefty looked in their direction, but didn't acknowledge them. Tony said, "Look at that Jew cocksucker. You'd think he'd at least wave at me, or wink, or something. He don't do shit. Look at him; who the fuck does he think he is, this guy? Believe me, Frankie, he's got me so fucking mad that if he didn't have the juice he's got, I'd have corked him a long time ago."

Frank never fully understood the rift between Tony and Lefty until he found out Tony had been having an affair with Geri Rosenthal. It was a fact that seemed to be known by everyone but him.

Even the local cops and the FBI were aware of it. But Frank didn't find out until the day Geri stopped at the Upper Crust looking for Tony.

She seemed upset and said, "Where's Tony? I've got to talk to him right away."

Frank told her a semi-lie. "He's not here right now. I can try to find him for you if you'd like."

"Please. It's very important."

Frank went next door to the My Place, where Tony was hanging out. "Geri Rosenthal's in the restaurant looking for you."

"What the fuck does she want?"

"I don't know. She only said it's real important that she talk with you."

Ernie Davino was also in the bar. Tony told him to move Geri's car behind the restaurant. Tony then went to get Geri and brought her back to the lounge. Half an hour later she left.

Afterward Tony came into the Upper Crust shaking his head. He said to Frank, "Boy, have I fucked up. I've been banging this broad and I shouldn't have. You know how it is; the dick gets hard and the mind goes soft. I have no respect for that Jew and that made it a little easier. But now they're arguing and she admitted she already told him about us. If this ever gets back to Chicago, I'll have nothing but headaches."

As Frank listened to Tony's admission, he smelled trouble. He wasn't surprised about the affair; he knew that Tony lacked control when it came to women. But he was concerned about how the Outfit would react if they heard about it.

It didn't take him long to find out.

Every so often Frank went back to Chicago to deliver the

Dennis Griffin and Frank Cullotta

money Tony was sending the bosses. On one trip after finding out about Lefty's wife, he made a delivery to Joe Ferriola, one of the big shots. Ferriola had a question for him. "Frankie, you've gotta level with me. Is the little guy fucking the Jew's wife?"

"No way. I know Tony and Lefty ain't gettin' along, but as far as I know Tony's not fucking Lefty's old lady," Frank said quickly and with a straight face.

"I believe you, Frankie. You know we've got a lot of money riding out there and we can't have some cunt fucking everything up just because some guy gets a hard-on. If that happens, a lot of people will be mad, including me."

"You've got nothing to worry about," Frank assured him. "Tony's not doin' anything wrong."

That night Frank was in a restaurant with Larry Neumann, who was in Chicago on other business, and Wayne Matecki. Outfit underboss Jackie Cerone happened to be in the same place. He came over to their table to talk. "How's Tony doing out there?" he asked.

"He's doing a good job; everything's fine," Frank answered.

"I'm glad to hear that. Give him a message from me. Tell him not to fuck up and to keep his nose clean," Cerone said, then walked away.

Larry Neumann wasn't impressed with Cerone or his message to Tony. "That bastard," he fumed. "Do you realize how easy it would be to take him out? We could take out this whole fucking joint."

"Take it easy, Larry. That's not going to happen," Frank said. He made it a point never to talk down to the volatile Neumann. Each recognized the other man's capacity for violence, and they treated one another with respect.

When Frank got back to Vegas, he told Tony what Ferriola asked him. Concerned, Tony asked, "What did you tell him?"

Frank teased his friend. "I told him you've been banging the broad." Both men laughed.

Then Frank turned serious. After delivering Cerone's message he said, "I'll tell you something. If those guys in Chicago ever find out I lied to them, they'll dig two graves in the desert. One for you and one for me."

The Law

9

While Tony Spilotro and Frank Cullotta were running the street rackets in Las Vegas, two law-enforcement agencies were gearing up to take them down.

The task of catching the lawbreakers fell primarily on the shoulders of the FBI and the Las Vegas Metropolitan Police Department, commonly referred to as Metro. Each agency had its own investigative responsibilities and both had recently suffered from scandal. Some FBI agents had been on the dole, taking complimentary meals and shows from the casinos they were supposed to be keeping an eye on. And Metro detectives had been caught passing information to the mobsters. But by the time Frank Cullotta got to Sin City, the law-enforcement ship was being righted.

The Spilotro gang counted a number of skilled and tough criminals among its members. These were men capable of doing whatever it took to protect their interests and expand their illegal enterprises. But even though they had to play by different rules, the lawmen who opposed them were no slouches when it came to dedication and toughness.

. . .

The feds were interested in Las Vegas organized crime from two perspectives: the skimming of money from casinos, and street crimes that violated federal laws. Several FBI offices across the country were involved in the skim investigations. The street crimes were more of an effort by the local office.

Starting in the late 1970s, the Las Vegas FBI office underwent a major reorganization as a result of allegations of improper or unethical practices. One of the first new agents to arrive in Vegas was Emmett Michaels in 1977. He was appointed supervisor of the Surveillance Squad, a part of the Special Operations Group. His unit was responsible for conducting surveillance, including the installation and monitoring of authorized wiretaps and electronic eavesdropping equipment. Early on, Michaels found the working relationship between the FBI and its local counterparts to be unproductive. This lack of trust was obvious on a night in 1978 when Michaels and a team of agents bugged Spilotro's Gold Rush store.

About 10 agents were involved. Because Metro had a reputation for being corrupt, the FBI didn't tell them they were planning to place bugs in Spilotro's store and tap the phones. Michaels and three other agents were up on the telephone poles when the store's alarm system activated. A Metro car showed up and the officer got out to investigate. The four G-men dangled from those poles, holding their breath and hoping the cop didn't look up. He didn't; he left a few minutes later without detecting any of the agents. Had

Metro caught them in the act, Michaels believed the incident would have been embarrassing at best. At worst, word may have gotten back to Spilotro.

In 1979, Charlie Parsons came on the scene as the supervisor of the Organized Crime Squad. He was subsequently transferred to the Los Angeles field office and became the special agent in charge (SAC) of that office.

Two more major players were assigned to Las Vegas in 1980: Dennis Arnoldy in August and Lynn Ferrin in September. Arnoldy was made co-case agent for the Spilotro investigations. When his partner transferred to other duties, he became the sole case agent. Ferrin was named the case agent for the investigations that addressed the mob's casino-skimming operations.

Also in 1980, Joseph Yablonsky was transferred to Las Vegas from Cincinnati as the new Special Agent in Charge. Yablonsky had a proven track record of developing cases against organized-crime figures and was handpicked for the Sin City assignment by FBI Director William Webster. During his three-year term, Yablonsky oversaw an operation consisting of 140 employees, 82 of whom were special agents and five were supervisors, and a $5 million annual budget.

The mission of these men and their colleagues was to remove the influence and corruption of organized crime from the streets and casinos of Las Vegas. To help meet those goals, the lawmen received some additional assistance from the government.

The Organized Crime Strike Force of the Department of Justice—a program established by Attorney General Robert Kennedy in the early 1960s for the sole purpose of fighting organized crime—provided resident Special Attorneys to coordinate investigative efforts between federal agencies, obtain necessary warrants, evaluate evidence, and prosecute cases in the courts. The unit had a maximum of three attorneys assigned to Las Vegas at any one time.

Stanley Hunterton was one of those lawyers. Hunterton grew up in New York and after completing law school in 1975, he joined the Strike Force. Initially assigned to the Detroit office, in 1978 he was sent to Las Vegas. He, too, noticed that the relationship between the FBI and the local police was strained when he first arrived in Las Vegas.

That lack of confidence in Metro kept the two agencies from having an institutional association at the time. But starting in 1979, the Department of Justice lawyers and the FBI began to develop several relationships with Metro personnel on a personal level. It wasn't long before the Las Vegas agents and Metro detectives began to share information and cooperate in their investigations.

• • •

In November 1978, a reform candidate for Clark County Sheriff, John McCarthy, was elected. During his campaign he promised to clean up corruption within the department and declare war on organized crime; he vowed that if elected, Tony Spilotro and his gang would either go to jail or be run out of town. McCarthy, who had commanded Metro's vice, narcotics, and juvenile bureaus prior to being elected, began to fulfill those promises even before he took office in January 1979. His first step in that regard was to appoint veteran detective Kent Clifford to take over the Intelligence Bureau. Clifford's assignment included making sure his detectives were free of mob connections and developing a strategy to combat Tony Spilotro.

Clifford was a decorated Vietnam combat veteran and had worked in the vice and narcotics units of the Las Vegas Police Department and Metro. He acted with the urgency McCarthy demanded. Within a few weeks of assuming the new position, Clifford announced that the Intelligence Bureau was clean, ready to resume normal relationships with other law-enforcement agencies.

Clifford's next priority was to develop a plan to confront Tony Spilotro and his men. Although his prior duties hadn't involved Spilotro, Clifford was well aware of the gangster's presence and reputation. He wasn't impressed, however, and never held Tony in very high esteem. In one newspaper interview he said: "Tony Spilotro was a cold- blooded killer. You could see it when you looked into his eyes. He was capable of being extremely vicious and violent." And then he added: "He was just a soldier, a punk. That's all he ever was."

Clifford put an aggressive strategy in place to go after Tony, attacking both overtly and covertly. Five officers were assigned full-time to the Spilotro investigation and could be supplemented by additional personnel as needed. They kept pressure on Tony and his associates by implementing round-the-clock surveillance, often making no effort at concealment. The targets knew the cops were there, watching their every move, even following them into restaurants and taking seats at adjoining tables.

In addition, the tailing cops were told to aggressively enforce traffic laws. When a subject was pulled over for a motor-vehicle violation, he was arrested and had his car towed. This tactic disrupted their activities, costing them time and money and causing annoyance. It also allowed the cops to get positive identifications on the players and possibly pick up some good information.

Although this strategy invited allegations of police harassment, Clifford believed it was necessary and appropriate. He explained his reasoning this way. "We were up against people who weren't required to play by any rules; we were. Everything we did was legal, but sometimes we went right up to the edge. The goal was to put Tony in prison or drive him out of town. Also, there was a possibility that by keeping the media's attention focused on him, along with his own huge ego, his bosses in Chicago might eventually get fed up with him."

So, as Tony and Frank pillaged and plundered, the law was ready to launch an all-out effort against them.

Dennis Griffin and Frank Cullotta

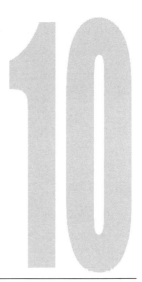

The Beat Goes On

Jerry Lisner was arrested by the FBI on July 11, 1979, and charged with interstate transportation of stolen property, aiding and abetting, grand larceny, and conspiracy. Free on $75,000 bail, he was scheduled to go on trial October 29 in U.S. District Court in Washington, D.C.

In the late summer of that year, Lisner came back into Frank's life. His reemergence posed potential problems for Frank and Tony, but the repercussions were much worse for Lisner himself.

It started when Frank got a call from a friend who owned a restaurant in town; he said they needed to meet. The friend brought another man along with him, a lawyer. "Do you know a guy named Jerry Lisner?" the lawyer asked Frank.

"Yeah. Why?"

"Lisner's in trouble with the feds and he's playing ball to get himself a deal. He's been in front of a grand jury in Washington and he's been cooperating with them. I found out that he's mentioned you and Tony Spilotro. I don't know you or this Tony guy, but I thought you ought to know."

Frank thanked the informant, then got hold of Tony.

"I don't like it, Frankie," Tony said. "If this shit is true, it looks like they're trying to indict one or both of us."

"What do you want to do?"

After a brief hesitation, Tony said, "For right now, nothing. I want to check into this thing myself and I'll get back to you."

A few days later, Frank heard from Tony. He'd confirmed what the lawyer had said, plus a little more. "Listen to me," Tony said. "This fucking Lisner is cooperating with the grand jury in Washington. He's giving testimony about you and your affiliation with me. And he's talking about that deal in Washington [the money-laundering scam] you tried to pull. Subpoenas are going to be issued."

Tony's information couldn't have been more solid. The very next day the FBI served Frank with a subpoena to appear before the grand jury in Washington. After the feds left, Frank called Tony. "What should I do, Tony? Should I make up a bullshit story? Should I take the Fifth [exercise his right against self-incrimination] and force them to offer me immunity?"

"Get a lawyer out of D.C. and make up a story." Then he added ominously, "We'll deal with Lisner later."

Frank went to Washington and retained a lawyer. After discussing his testimony with the lawyer, Frank was interviewed by a United States Attorney and some FBI agents. They gave him a grilling, but he stuck to his made-up story. He testified the same way when he went before the grand jury.

When Frank got back to Vegas, he told Larry Neumann what was going on. "Let's kill the fucker right now," Lurch said.

Dennis Griffin and Frank Cullotta

"We can't just go around whacking people without permission. I've got to find out what Tony wants to do first. And if he wants Lisner hit, he'll have to clear it with Chicago. While we're waiting, try to get close to Lisner's wife at the Aladdin. See what you can learn from her. If we want to feed any bullshit to Jerry, we'll do it through her."

Neumann did as instructed and became buddies with the Lisners, but he didn't like them. He told Frank that when it was time to hit Lisner, he wanted to do the job. "I want to kill both of them, though. He's got it coming and she's a no-good fucking bitch. She's got to go too."

Tony finally made up his mind about Lisner and when he did, he was emphatic. He told Frank, "I want him fucking whacked. And if *you* don't do it, *I* will."

"Take it easy, Tony. I'll handle it."

"I just want to make sure you understand that I want that cocksucker taken care of. I got the okay from Chicago and it's gotta be done."

"It'll be done. Should I take Larry with me?"

"No, leave him out of it. Have Wayne [Matecki] come in from Chicago." Whatever reason Tony had for rejecting Neumann's participation, it probably saved Jeannie Lisner's life.

"Okay. I'll contact Wayne. Anything else?"

"Yeah, get hold of Lisner. Meet him for a few drinks or something, so he gets comfortable with you being around him."

Frank contacted Lisner and invited him and his wife to meet him at the My Place Lounge. They had a good time, laughing and joking. Tony Spilotro stopped by, making the couple even more at ease. Tony turned on the charm and by the time the Lisners left, they seemed to be feeling pretty secure. The plan could now advance to the next stage.

Frank drove to Los Angeles and flew from the Burbank airport to Chicago. He made contact with Matecki and briefed him on the plan to murder Lisner. Matecki packed his bag and the two caught a plane back to Burbank, then drove to Vegas. Frank already had a work car stashed in the underground parking garage of his condo. The two killers assembled the rest of the necessary equipment: a .22 pistol, a police radio, and walkie-talkies. Everything was ready.

On October 10, 1979, Frank called Lisner. "Jerry, I need to discuss something with you, but I don't want to do it on the phone. Can we get together tonight?"

"Sure. Why don't you stop by my house and we'll talk."

"Good. This is private, though, so —"

Lisner cut Frank off. "Jeannie has to work. I'll be alone, so you don't have to worry."

"Thanks, Jerry. I'll be over."

After dark Frank and Matecki put their radios and walkie-talkies in the work car and headed for the Lisner house at 2303 Rawhide Avenue. Frank concealed the murder weapon in his waistband. When they arrived, Frank told Matecki to wait in the car while he went to the door and rang the bell. Lisner responded and let him in. They stood in the hallway for a few seconds making small talk. Then Frank used a ruse to get Lisner away from the door. "What was that?" Frank said suddenly.

"What was what?"

"I heard a noise." Frank pointed down the hallway. "I thought you were alone."

"Nobody's here but me. Come on, let's take a look."

Frank followed his victim into the living room. The hit man couldn't wear gloves without looking suspicious to Lisner, so he was very careful not to touch anything that could retain his fingerprints.

"See, nobody's here but you and me," Lisner announced.

"Maybe the noise came from outside," Frank suggested.

Lisner led the way toward the rear of the house to check the backyard. As they passed through the dining room Frank pulled his gun. He fired two rounds into the back of Lisner's head from point-blank range. And then the situation became surreal. Instead of going down, Lisner turned around and said, "What the ... Why?" Then he started to run through the house toward the garage.

Frank caught up with him and emptied the rest of the bullets into his head. Lisner fell, but he was still alive, still moving. Frank had trouble believing what was happening. He got on top of the wounded man and held him down. Out of ammunition, his eyes searched for an alternate weapon. He saw a knife on a counter next to the door leading to the garage and made a grab for it; it was just out of his reach. Next he spotted an electric water cooler that was within his grasp. He ripped the cord out of the cooler to strangle his victim with, but when he wrapped it around Lisner's neck, the cord broke.

Getting frustrated, Frank got up and dragged Lisner into the den. The man was still conscious and aware of what was going on. "My wife knows you're here! She's going to know you did this!" he screamed at Frank.

By that time Matecki had become concerned and came into the house; he was carrying an extra magazine of ammo with him. Frank reloaded the pistol and put pillows from a couch over Lisner's head to muffle the gunshots. Frank then emptied the pistol into Lisner's head again. It had taken ten rounds, but Lisner was finally dead. The killers dragged him outside to the pool and dumped him in. The body floated for a few seconds, then sank to the bottom.

Frank and Matecki went back into the house; there was blood everywhere. They wiped everything off, then checked the house for any security cameras or recorders. There weren't any. They also looked for any papers or address books that might have had Frank or Tony's name in them. They didn't find any of those either.

After completing their search, the pair drove back to Frank's place. They showered, scrubbed their hands with kitchen cleanser, and cut the clothes they had been wearing into little pieces. Then they drove the work car into the desert, scattering the dismantled gun and scraps of clothing. Finally, they parked the work car and Frank used his personal vehicle to drive his accomplice to McCarran Airport. Matecki was on a plane back to Chicago that same night.

The hit was big news all over town. The next night Frank met Tony at My Place; they talked in the parking lot. "I've got a couple of questions about Lisner," Tony said. "We'll talk about him now, but never again after tonight. Understand?"

"Sure. Go ahead."

"How come you guys dumped him in the pool?"

"We wanted to get rid of some of the blood and any prints we might have left on his clothes."

"That was a bit theatrical, wasn't it?"

Frank shrugged. "We did what we figured we had to do."

"How come you had to fire so many shots?"

"I was hitting him right in the fuckin' head every time. But that small caliber didn't work well, didn't do the job."

The two men didn't discuss Lisner again.

Initially, the Lisner killing seemed to have been a total success. According to press reports, Metro was in the dark as to who killed Lisner or why. But the cops had their suspicions. They knew about the dead man's legal problems. They knew about his cooperation with authorities. They knew who benefited from his demise. It didn't take long for Frank to realize the law had an interest in him in regard to the murder. And because Lisner had been both a federal witness and defendant, the FBI was also able to get involved.

• • •

Shortly after the killing, Frank sold the work car to Herbie Blitzstein, the former Chicago bookie who helped operate Spilotro's Gold Rush store. Blitzstein was working with the burglar Pete. Frank didn't care for Pete at all. He wouldn't follow orders and wasn't kicking back the money he was supposed to. But Tony liked him and asked Frank to take him on some scores.

Frank protested. "Jesus, Tony. There's something about that guy that bothers me. I'd just as soon not have him involved."

"Frankie, I've got my reasons. Just do what I ask, huh?"

So, in spite of his misgivings, Frank let Pete hang around and took him on some jobs. But that wasn't the worst of it. Later on, Pete began bringing around another thief, Sal Romano.

Romano was a burglar from Chicago and was familiar with Tony Spilotro, Frank Cullotta, and most of their crew. In the late 1970s, however, he came to the attention of agent Donn Sickles, who was working organized-crime cases out of the FBI's Phoenix, Arizona, office.

Sickles' office received a Teletype from the Chicago field office about a burglar who was believed to have moved from there to Tucson. His name was Sal Romano and he had the reputation of being a pretty good alarm and lock guy. After receiving the information, Sickles and another agent named Bill Christensen began checking on Romano to find out where he was and what he was doing.

One of the things they did was contact the Tucson Police Department to see if they'd experienced any recent burglaries matching Romano's modus operandi. Sure enough, some coin-operated laundries were getting knocked off and Romano looked like a good fit. The police initiated a video surveillance and Romano was caught on tape doing a laundry burglary. The cops let Sickles know when they were going to make the arrest and he went to the station to see if Romano would be willing to talk with him, specifically if he might be interested in working a deal to stay out of jail.

Sickles and his partner got to speak with Romano and the burglar was willing to cooperate. He told them about burglaries he'd done in various places, including some with Tony Spilotro's people in Las Vegas. He also said that a lot of the goods stolen in Vegas were fenced in Tucson. Romano was released without being charged, but he had to produce credible information in order to stay free. Based on what he told them, the agents were able to retrieve some of the items stolen in Las Vegas from the fences in Tucson.

Romano wasn't asked to target any specific person or group, but the agents kept him on a short leash and always knew where he was. When the informant decided to go to Las Vegas and pal around with some of Spilotro's associates, the Phoenix agents contacted Dennis Arnoldy and Joe Gersky at the Las Vegas field office and told them what was going on. That was the beginning of the excellent cooperation and coordination among various field offices and agents in handling Romano and the information he provided.

• • •

Frank's Upper Crust was located in a strip mall. The FBI was interested in learning what went on in the back room of the restaurant, so they applied to a federal judge for a warrant to install eavesdropping equipment to find out. It wasn't an easy placement for the G-men. The fact that the adjoining and affiliated My Place was open around the clock further complicated the job. Agents ended up accessing the roof and installing a camera and microphone down an airshaft. It was ticklish and time-consuming, but they got it done without being detected. That was the good news. The bad news for the law was that the bug was discovered less than 24 hours later.

Things began to go downhill for the agents when Leo Guardino went into a back room to take a snooze before Frank picked him up to go on a burglary. He climbed on top of a chest-type freezer and before he closed his eyes, he saw something shiny in the ceiling. He pushed up a ceiling tile and found the bug. Then he picked up a phone and called Frank at home. Without going into detail, Guardino summoned his partner to the restaurant.

When Frank arrived, Guardino motioned him into the back room. Using hand signals he directed Frank's attention to the eavesdropping equipment. The two men left the room to discuss what to do.

Next to My Place Lounge in the shopping center were a clothing store and a real-estate office. Only a small firewall separated the stores. A crawl space above the ceilings ran through all the stores. Because it was a Sunday, the real-estate office and the clothing store were closed. Guardino was dispatched to go into the crawl space above the ceiling and follow the wire to the monitoring equipment. He returned from his mission and reported he'd traced the line to the real-estate office.

This time both Guardino and Frank went into the ceiling and dropped down into the real-estate office. Frank ripped the wires out of the equipment there, then crawled back to the restaurant, removing the camera and microphone as he descended from the ceiling.

Frank next went to My Place and called Tony. "Bring that camera to my house. We'll check it and find out who it belongs to," Tony said.

When Frank got to Tony's, he found Joe Blasko there. Blasko was an ex-cop; while he was on the force, Tony recruited him to provide information on police activities. When he was caught on FBI wiretaps passing sensitive data to the mobsters, he was fired. Afterward he continued to advise Tony on police-related matters. Frank considered him to be Tony's stooge, and the Ant threw him a bone every once in a while to keep him happy.

Blasko checked the camera and found a metal tag that had been painted over. He removed the paint with alcohol and it said "Property of the U.S. Government."

Tony was angry. "The fuckin' FBI," he fumed.

"What are we going to do now?" Frank asked.

Tony pointed at the camera. "I know a Jew who can use shit like that. I'll give it to him. Then we'll sit back and see how the G is going to handle this."

Dennis Griffin and Frank Cullotta

• • •

Not long after the transmissions from the Upper Crust stopped, agents Charlie Parsons and Emmett Michaels met at their office to discuss their options. They came to the conclusion that the bugging equipment was government property and had been legally installed. Under those circumstances they saw no reason why they shouldn't go to the restaurant and get their property back. They decided to call on Frank the next day.

• • •

Frank spent the rest of Sunday at the restaurant waiting for the G to do something, but nothing happened. On Monday morning he and Eileen got the restaurant ready for business. He told her to be very careful about what she said and that the phones might be tapped. Then he looked out the window and saw a sea of suits; he was sure they were FBI. Five or six agents came inside. Two of them went to the pay phone and the others sat at separate tables. Frank took a seat at a table with Ernie Davino. In his pocket he had the FBI's microphone that he'd ripped out of the ceiling the previous day. In case he was about to get searched, he removed it and set it in an ashtray. The ever-reliable Eileen noticed the move, came over, and took the ashtray. She removed the mike, went next door to My Place, and flushed it. The suits didn't pay any attention to her.

Frank walked up to one of the men and asked, "Are you with the FBI?"

The man laughed. "Me with the FBI? No way."

"I know you guys have to identify yourselves if you're asked."

"Sorry. You're mistaken," the man said.

Frank knew it was a lie, but decided not to challenge him any further and returned to his seat. The agents hung around a few more minutes and then left.

Charlie Parsons returned in about an hour with Emmett Michaels. Parsons asked Frank outside to talk. He said, "We want our camera back."

Frank said, "I don't have your fucking camera."

"We know damn well you've got it. If you don't give it back, we'll ride you day and night."

"You can go fuck yourself. I wouldn't give you the camera back now even if I did have it."

"Contact your lawyer and have him give me a call," Parsons said. He and Michaels left, but they weren't happy.

Frank contacted Tony and told him about the FBI's visit. Tony tried to reach his lawyer, Oscar Goodman, but Goodman was out of town and couldn't fly back. So he called Dominic Gentile, a lawyer originally from Chicago. Frank also got in touch with his own lawyer, John Momot. Gentile was dispatched to handle the FBI. The lawyer contacted Charlie Parsons and arranged a meeting at the Upper Crust that night. Frank, Tony, Gentile, Parsons, and Michaels all got together to talk.

While Parsons was pleading his case that the camera was government property and had been placed pursuant to court order, Tony was standing with his hand stuck inside his shirt. Michaels said to him, "You look like a little Caesar standing there like that."

Tony didn't find the agent's comment amusing. "Fuck you, you bald-headed motherfucker."

Michaels and Tony eyed each other like a mongoose and a cobra as the tension built. Knowing any further comments could escalate into a physical confrontation, Frank intervened. He said to the agents, "Look, this is my place and your beef is with me. If you've got anything to say, say it to me, not Tony." That defused the situation and there was no further interaction between Michaels and Spilotro.

After some negotiating, the agents said that if they got their camera back, that would be the end of it. Gentile called Frank and Tony aside to talk it over. Frank wanted to play hardball, but Tony figured if the camera was returned, the feds would back off a little. Frank reluctantly went along with him. Frank told Parsons he'd get his camera back, but that the mike was probably somewhere in Lake Mead.

That night Frank picked up the camera from Tony's friend and got it to Parsons. It wasn't until later that he figured out how the agents determined where to plant their bug.

• • •

Around the same time the FBI placed their surveillance devices in the Upper Crust, Metro detectives got in the bugging business as well. Their target was the vehicle operated by Ernie Davino, an old restored Caddy Frank had sold him.

Frank found out about it three days after giving Charlie Parsons his camera back. He was in the restaurant when he received a phone call from a man he didn't know. He didn't recognize the guy's voice and the caller wouldn't give his name. He said, "Right now your man has a transmitter on his car. I'm listening to a police radio and can hear what they're saying. They're following this guy Ernie Davino around."

Ernie was getting ready to drive to Chicago to deliver some merchandise and was out getting an oil change when Frank tried to get hold of him. As soon as Ernie got home Frank went over to talk with him.

"I got word the cops are on you," Frank said.

"You might be right. I've been noticing some cars that always seem to be around me."

"There's one way to find out for sure," Frank said.

They went out to Davino's car and found a tracking device under the right fender. Walking away from the car Frank told Davino, "We should probably pull the goddamn transmitter. But in case the cops did anything wrong here, I want to check with John Momot first."

Davino agreed. "Good idea. Maybe he'll be able to back those bastards off a little."

They left Davino's car parked and drove Frank's vehicle to the restaurant. When they walked in, Eileen said a man had brought in some audiotapes. She didn't know who the guy was, but it seemed likely it was Frank's mystery caller from earlier.

The tapes were recordings of Metro's surveillance of Ernie Davino. The two men listened to the radio transmissions as the cops followed Davino around. When his car was being serviced, one of the cops said, "Holy Christ! The car's up on the rack and they're changing the oil. I hope they don't see that transmitter."

Another cop said, "Yeah. If they do I'll drive in there and rip it out of their fucking hands."

Frank called Tony and told him about the bug. "The G and now

Metro," Tony said in disgust. "Those cocksuckers are on us big time. Who's this fuckin' guy that tipped you?"

"I told you I don't know. I'm just glad he got hold of me, whoever he is."

Tony was silent for a few seconds. Then said, "You guys are causing all this goddamn heat. You'd better cool it or they'll be up our ass every fuckin' minute."

Frank resented the implication that the bugging incidents were the fault of him and his crew. Here was Tony, the guy running the whole show, acting like he had nothing to do with anything. But it was obvious to Frank that Tony was getting nervous and when Tony got nervous, he got mean. "Look, Tony, we're keeping as low a profile as we can and still take care of business. We're not spending lots of money or buying lots of stuff. They think we're doing all these scores, but they can't prove anything. That's why they're on us; they're trying to find out what we've got going."

Frank contacted John Momot. He and Davino met the attorney at a service station. The Caddy was put up on a hoist and Momot took a picture of the transmitter. Then Frank pulled the device off the car and gave it to the lawyer. Momot said it could come in handy later on to make a case for police harassment.

• • •

Metro detectives were also very curious about what took place at the Upper Crust. Officers assigned to the Spilotro investigation regularly conducted surveillance of the eatery. Two of those detectives were David Groover and Sergeant Gene Smith. On the evening of June 9, 1980, the pair was in their unmarked police vehicle parked nearby when a car with Illinois license plates pulled in.

Tony Spilotro and Frank Cullotta were sitting at a table outside the restaurant. The operator of the vehicle went inside, apparently to order a pizza to go, then came back out and joined Frank and Tony at their table. They talked for several minutes until the new guy's pizza was ready. At that point he got back in the Lincoln and drove away.

The detectives weren't sure who this new player was, but it was obvious he was acquainted with Tony and Frank. Smith and Groover decided to follow the Lincoln to see what information they could gather about who the driver was and what he was up to.

As soon as the car pulled out onto Flamingo Road, the driver started speeding, doing 80 or better, and driving recklessly. With Groover behind the wheel, the detectives kept pace with the Lincoln, but made no effort to stop it at that time. Eventually, they figured there was enough probable cause on the traffic violations to pull the car over and check out the operator.

At that time, Groover and Smith didn't know that the driver of the Lincoln was Frank Bluestein, a 35-year-old maitre d' at the Hacienda Hotel & Casino, one of the properties controlled by the Chicago Outfit. Also known as Frank Blue, his father, Steve Bluestein, was an official in the local Culinary Union and had been subject to a 1978 search warrant as part of the FBI's investigation of Tony Spilotro.

The officers pulled over the Lincoln and Groover approached the vehicle. The driver lowered his window. Suddenly Smith hollered, "Watch out, Dave! He's got a gun!"

Groover returned to the police car and stationed himself behind the driver's door. Both officers yelled at the driver that they were cops and to put down his gun. Bluestein never said a word, but instead of getting rid of the weapon, he turned slightly in his seat, opened his door, and started to get out of the car. The gun was still in his hand and, according to police, aimed toward Smith. Believing the man was about to shoot, the officers opened fire.

The shots rang out at approximately 11:45 p.m. and several of the rounds struck Bluestein. He was rushed to a nearby hospital where he died a couple of hours later. A .22 handgun that had allegedly been in Bluestein's possession was recovered at the scene.

. . .

Frank and Tony were well aware that Groover and Smith were watching them as they sat outside the restaurant that night. In fact, they made gestures at the cops to make sure the officers knew they'd been detected. It was a game they played all the time. The baiting was interrupted when Frank Bluestein pulled up and got out of the Lincoln. Bluestein was acquainted with the gangsters through his father, Steve. He'd moved into town from Chicago a few months earlier and was working in the showroom of the Hacienda.

After exchanging pleasantries, Frank said to him, "I see you've still got Illinois plates on your car. Are you going to get a Nevada registration?"

"Someday I will. I just haven't had the time yet."

"You'd better get it done pretty soon," Frank advised. "These fuckin' cops here are real cowboys. Any time they see a car with Illinois plates, they think you're a gangster from Chicago."

"You know, I think somebody's been following me around," Bluestein said.

"It's probably the goddamn cops," Frank told him.

"No, I don't think so; I think it's somebody looking to rob me. Anyway, I've got a gun in the car. If anybody tries anything, I'll be able to take care of myself."

"Do yourself a favor. Get rid of that fucking gun. I'm telling you, these fucking cops are nuts. If they think you've got a gun, they'll shoot you," Frank warned.

When Bluestein's pizza was ready, he got up to leave. "Get rid of that piece and get the right plates on your car," Frank told him again as Bluestein walked away.

About twenty minutes later, Eileen came out of the restaurant and told Tony he had an important phone call. Tony went inside and came back out with a shocked look on his face. He said, "That was Herb Blitzstein on the phone; they just killed Frankie Blue."

Frank was stunned. "Who killed him?"

"The fucking cops," Tony said. "I'm going over there to find out what happened."

"Do you want me to come with you?"

"No, Frankie. Stay here and I'll be back as soon as I can."

An hour later Tony returned with Herb Blitzstein and Steve Bluestein, and he was in a foul mood. "The cops claim they tried to get Frankie to get out of his car and that he reached for a gun. That was when they opened up on him," Tony said. "It was Smith and Groover and they put a lot of bullets into him."

Frank recognized the names of the two cops as the same ones who'd been tailing him and Tony earlier that evening. He considered Smith to be a trigger-happy maniac. Bluestein had admitted having a gun in his car, but Frank wondered whether or not he'd actually pulled it.

Tony said, "We gotta do something with these fucking coppers. I know if we whack one of them, we'll have to fight the Army, Navy, and Marine Corps. You just can't win against these cocksuckers. I gotta figure out a way we can get them corked without it coming back to us. I've gotta think about this, the bastards.'"

While Tony was considering how to punish the police, the Bluestein family went on the offensive. They alleged that the gun the police found in Frank's car the night of the shooting had been a plant, intended to mask what was really a police execution. However, at the coroner's inquest two weeks later, evidence was introduced that the weapon in question had been purchased in Chicago by Frank's brother, Ron Bluestein. That information effectively knocked down the planted-gun accusation and the shooting was ruled a justified use of deadly force.

The legal system had spoken, and neither Tony nor the Bluesteins liked what was said.

. . .

Frank continued to tolerate Pete the burglar and Sal Romano, but his dislike and distrust of each man increased with the passage of time. Although he couldn't understand why, Tony Spilotro seemed to think they were both stand-up guys, and his was the opinion that mattered most.

One night Romano was in My Place with a girl. They were at the far end of the bar, talking and laughing with a couple of other women. Romano called Frank over and introduced him to his girlfriend. Frank said hello and they talked a little bit. Frank didn't find out until much too late that the girl was actually an FBI agent and Romano was wearing a wire in his cowboy boot.

Eileen got bad vibes from him too. "Is that Sal guy a friend of yours?" she asked later that night.

"No, I can't stand the son of a bitch. Why?"

"I heard him talking on the phone and something didn't sound right. I can't put my finger on it, but there's something about him I don't like."

Although Frank and Eileen turned out to be right in their feelings about Romano, at the time all they had were their suspicions.

• • •

On August 5, 1980, just weeks after Frank Bluestein was killed, Oscar Goodman filed a class-action lawsuit alleging police harassment of Tony Spilotro and his associates. Goodman asked the court to restrain Sheriff John McCarthy from continuing a program of harassment that had been ongoing since November 2, 1979.

In an article in the *Las Vegas Sun* on that date, Goodman is quoted as saying, "I believe the lawsuit will protect the citizens of the state of Nevada from false arrests, harassment, and possibly injury or death that has taken place in the past." Goodman charged that Bluestein's death was the direct result of police harassment. He added of the alleged police conduct, "I think it's un-American. These are really Gestapo-like tactics. It literally has become a police state in this community."

In the lawsuit itself, the lawyer said, "The object and purpose of this program is to make unlawful any unfounded investigatory detentions and arrests of Spilotro and any persons observed in his company or known to be an associate of Spilotro."

In addition to McCarthy, the suit named nine Metro intelligence officers, including Kent Clifford, and 20 unnamed officers as defendants.

The *Sun* article went on to report the specific charges leveled by Goodman. He said that since November 1979, the police had: kept Spilotro and nearly a dozen of his friends under intensive surveillance; stopped and interrogated Spilotro and his friends without lawful or reasonable ground under the false guise of making some police investigative inquiry; and made false accusations or alleged minor traffic violations as a pretext for jailing persons known to be associated with Spilotro.

Attacking the Sheriff directly, Goodman said, "[McCarthy] didn't care whose rights were being violated. He said it was legitimate police work."

The attorney said the killing of Bluestein was the "last straw" in leading to the filing of the lawsuit. In Goodman's opinion, Metro officers had conducted a high-speed chase of Bluestein, who had committed no violations of the law, and gunned him down while carrying out Metro's harassment policy against Spilotro.

. . .

Frank's dislike for Pete the burglar came to a head one night outside the Upper Crust when the two men got into a dispute about an alleged tip on a potential burglary target.

Pete and Joe Blasko stopped to see Frank at the restaurant. They asked him to come outside to talk. Pete said, "What happened to the tip I gave you about that Oriental rug place to rob?"

"I don't know about any tip," Frank said. "You never told me about it."

Standing off to the side, Blasko egged Pete on. "Don't let him shit you; he knows what you're talking about. He doesn't want to give you your cut."

"How about it?" Pete asked. "I gave you the tip and you're supposed to take care of me."

"You're a fucking liar," Frank said to Pete. "I don't know what you're talking about. And if you don't believe me, you can go fuck yourself."

Pete threw a punch at Frank and the two men started wrestling, with Blasko trying to pull them apart. Frank got one good punch in, then grabbed the metal lid to a trash can. Before he could crack Pete in the head with it, Blasko grabbed him and shoved him up against a wall. At that point Guardino and Davino came out of the restaurant and broke things up. Pete and Blasko left a couple of minutes later.

Frank was like a madman; he went looking for Tony. When he found him he said, "You've gotta let me whack this fuckin' Pete. He's a no-good lying cocksucker and he's gotta go."

"I'm sorry, Frankie. I know you're pissed off, but I've got to say no."

Like a good salesman, Frank wasn't ready to give up with the first refusal. "The bastard came to *my* goddamn place, called *me* a liar, and swung on me. You've told me that he's even held back money from his scores. Let me get rid of the motherfucker."

"I know the kid's no good, but I can't let you do it. Pete's the out-of-wedlock son of an Outfit big shot and he's under my protec-

Dennis Griffin and Frank Cullotta

tion. You've got to put it on the shelf."

Finally, Frank understood why Tony ordered him to let Pete hang around. He was Outfit-connected. But that didn't cut any ice with the enraged Frank. He tried one more time. "I can do it so Pete's old man won't know what happened to him."

"I'm sorry, Frankie. The answer is no."

Frank said okay, but it wasn't okay. For the first time he was going to defy Tony, he was so mad. He told Davino to stay close to Pete and Blasko, to be their friend. Tony had taught him, when setting up the Lisner hit, that if you get people to like you and be comfortable around you, it's easier to take them out when you need to.

Ernie did as he was told, but Blasko got suspicious and ran to Tony. He said he thought he and Pete were being set up. Tony assured him that he hadn't given the okay for anybody to be whacked.

After his talk with Blasko, Tony called Frank. "What the fuck are you trying to do? I told you to put this thing on the shelf, didn't I?"

Frank denied that he had anything up his sleeve. "Hey, I wanted to do it, but you said no. Those guys are just being paranoid."

"Okay, case closed. It's all over with," Tony said. "But I'll tell you what. Pete's becoming a real pain in the ass and I'm going to encourage him to move back to Chicago."

Reluctantly, Frank had no choice but to cancel his murder plans.

• • •

Not long after issuing the order that saved Pete's life, Tony called Frank. "Pete burglarized a radio store and he's got a lot of police radio stuff. He wants to give you a couple of walkie-talkies."

"Look, Tony, I don't like that fucking kid and I don't want anything from him."

"Come on, Frankie. He didn't realize how tight you were with me when you had that beef with him. Now he wants to make amends."

Frank relented. If taking those walkie-talkies would make everybody happy, he'd do it.

Pete called Frank later and brought the radios to him. "I hope there are no hard feelings," Pete said. "I'd like us to be friends."

"No, no hard feelings. Let's forget about it."

"You know, there's an awful lot of heat on me out here and I've decided to move back to Chicago. They're after you guys big time, too. Have you thought about going back?"

"I'm not in a position to leave; I've got too many obligations here," Frank said.

Pete left without telling Frank one very important thing: The radios were stolen in Chicago, not Las Vegas. That meant anyone caught in possession of them in a state other than Illinois would be subject to federal charges.

Even though Frank had only accepted the radios to placate Tony, they were good units and he decided to hang onto them for possible future use.

• • •

Tony also appeared to be somewhat lax about security when

Dennis Griffin and Frank Cullotta

it came to tolerating Sal Romano. Ignoring Frank's warnings, he didn't seem to be overly concerned about whether Romano had loose lips or was an out-and-out informant. Frank didn't know what to make of it, especially because Tony took extraordinary precautions to keep the Gold Rush and other places he frequented free of electronic listening devices. Tony's caution and, perhaps, his increasing paranoia, were also in evidence during a meeting at the house of his brother, John Spilotro. Frank, Tony, John, and Joe Blasko were there.

Tony said, "Why don't we all go into the Jacuzzi and talk?"

Frank laughed. "Are you nuts? I don't even have a swim suit with me."

"Don't worry. John's got suits for you and Joe," Tony said.

Blasko went in the bathroom first to change. Tony opened the door right after and walked in with the swimming trunks. He did the same thing when Frank went in. That's when Frank realized what was going on. Tony thought someone was giving information to the cops and he was checking his guests for wires. It also gave him an opportunity to search their clothes if he wanted.

Frank thought the Jacuzzi thing was actually a good idea, though. There weren't any transmitters in the water and the participants were able to talk freely. He wasn't offended. His only regret is that Tony never made Sal Romano strip.

•   •   •

In late 1980, Frank, Eileen, and her two children moved to another home. Their new place was much larger than their old digs and they found themselves short of furniture. Like his father before him, Frank figured there was no sense in paying for what you could get free. He got his furniture okay, but it turned out to be far from free. In fact, it ended up costing him dearly.

Knowing Frank was looking for furnishings, Ernie Davino came to his aid. He knew of a woman and her husband who were going to be out of town for two months. In fact, Davino's daughter was watching their house for them, so getting a key would be no problem. Frank had an associate rent a truck using a fake name, then went to the house and took everything. The stolen goods looked great in Frank's new place.

However, Davino made a big mistake when he told Jerry Rossi, Frank's brother-in-law, about the burglary. Jerry had another guy with him at the time who was an informant. He ran right to Metro and told them all about the score.

Metro raided Frank's house early on the morning of November 20, 1980. The police kicked the door down while he and Eileen were still in bed. They handcuffed them both, with Eileen in her nightgown and Frank in his shorts. They identified all the stolen furniture. And they found the walkie-talkies Pete had given Frank. A prosecutor named Don Campbell was present during the search; he held the radios up and said, "We've got you now. We've got you with these radios."

Frank didn't understand why such a big deal was being made about finding the radios; the furniture was worth a lot more. He asked Campbell what he was talking about.

Campbell explained. "These radios were stolen in Chicago and you've got them here. There's a federal law concerning the interstate transportation of stolen property, and you broke it."

Frank and Eileen were taken to jail. The charges against her were dropped and she was released. Frank spent half a day locked up before he bonded out. After he was released, he told Tony that he was sure the cops were looking for those walkie-talkies. He believed they knew he had them before they broke his door in. If they did, the information had to have come from Pete. And his brother-in-law's friend had provided the probable cause to get the search warrant. As far as he was concerned, the grin he saw on Don Campbell's face that night was a confirmation of his suspicions. Frank had to admit it had been a good setup.

.   .   .

Possession of the stolen walkie-talkies landed Frank back in the federal system. It didn't take prosecutors long to present his case to a grand jury. It was a proceeding that produced even more headaches for him.

The feds served Eileen with a subpoena. Although a wife doesn't have to testify against her husband, Frank hired attorney David Chesnoff to represent her. For himself, he used John Momot, with Oscar Goodman as an advisor. And then the government subpoenaed his 16-year-old stepdaughter. Whether they actually thought Kimberly had information or were simply trying to increase the pressure on Frank is unknown, but Kimberly said she wasn't going to talk with the grand jury; she had nothing to say. Frank retained Dominic Gentile to represent her. The creative Gentile decided to argue that his client didn't have to testify due to something he called family privilege. When that news hit the papers, the federal prosecutors were stunned. It was a privilege that didn't exist. However, the publicity cast the government lawyers in the role of bully, and Kimberly was never called to the stand.

The local case regarding the stolen furniture took a bad turn when the woman whose house was burglarized claimed she'd been threatened. According to her, a man approached her on the street and said she'd better not testify against Frank Cullotta or she'd be killed. The woman identified Jerry Rossi as the person who'd made the threat. The cops arrested Jerry and roughed him up in the process. When they cut him loose, he went right to Frank and told him the story. Frank figured they'd be after him next.

His hunch was right. Metro arrested him in the restaurant and booked him for intimidating a witness. He was taken before a judge who was friendly toward the cops. The judge scolded Frank in the courtroom, wanting to know who he thought he was to intimidate a witness. He revoked Frank's bond and sent him back to jail.

Moving quickly, Frank's lawyer arranged for him to go before a different judge a week later. Bail was granted, but it wasn't cheap. Frank had to post a $100,000 bond. His mounting legal problems were not only starting to drive him crazy, but they were wiping him out financially as well.

To escape the pressure temporarily, Frank took a trip to Chicago. While he was gone, Guardino and Davino continued to pull burglaries. Frank got word that even though he wasn't in town, the cops had come by his house to arrest him for one of those jobs. He contacted his lawyers in Vegas and asked them to check things out. They got back to him and said the cops were going to arrest him on the new charge, but a judge had promised he'd get a light bail, only $30,000 or so. He went back to Vegas, surrendered, and bonded out. Now he was loaded up with pending cases.

He was handling it, but it was beginning to get to him.

11

Warning Signs
and Murder Plots

During Frank's first couple of years in Las Vegas, resentments in his relationship with Tony Spilotro smoldered just below the surface. Tony's permission to do many of the things he wanted to do, Tony's cuts of scores in which he'd done nothing to earn the money, and Tony's rebuffs of his complaints about Pete and Sal Romano—these could be chalked up to differences of opinion or simply being the way things were done. However, as Frank's legal problems grew, he began to get the first inklings that there might be more serious problems between him and Tony.

Custom dictated that at the minimum, Tony, as the boss, put up Frank's bond money. And helping out with attorney's fees was also a common practice. But Tony was only taking; he wasn't contributing anything. Frank's crew was donating for these expenses, but not the Ant.

Frank never said anything about it, but the other guys noticed. Ernie Davino mentioned it to Frank one day. "How come Tony doesn't kick in any money for your bonds and lawyers?"

Although Frank wasn't satisfied with Tony's performance, he was still loyal to him. "If I were you, I'd mind my own business. You're damn lucky you can steal in Las Vegas."

"I know other guys stealing here that aren't kicking back to Tony. Why do we have to pay a guy who never does anything for us?"

Frank knew how to shut Davino up. "Do you want me to take your beef to Tony?"

"No, don't do that. Just think about what I said."

"Look, Ernie, I know where you're coming from. But you're better off to forget it."

• • •

After Ernie Davino complained to Frank about Tony, he began to make himself scarce. Frank couldn't reach him by phone and he stopped coming around the regular haunts. Frank assumed that Davino thought the heat was getting too intense and wanted to distance himself.

Tony, getting increasingly paranoid as the law's attention started to affect him, saw it differently. He suspected that Davino had become a police informant.

Frank found that hard to believe. After all, the cops had tailed Ernie and even bugged his car.

About a week after Davino dropped out of sight, Tony contacted Frank. "Have you seen anything of Ernie?"

"No, he still hasn't been around."

That seemed to convince Tony that Davino was a rat. "He's our fuckin' problem. He's talking to the cops."

"Are you sure?"

"Yeah, I'm sure. He's no good; take him out."

Frank didn't know whether or not Ernie was a snitch. But he had been making himself scarce lately, which could be a sign that he had something to hide. And Tony seemed confident that Ernie was an informant. Maybe it was better to be safe than sorry. He said, "Jesus, Tony, Ernie's avoiding me; I won't be able to get near him."

"Leo and Ernie are pretty tight. Have Leo set it up for you."

Frank talked with Guardino that night. Guardino didn't believe Davino was an informant and didn't want any part in setting up the hit. Frank respected his wishes and said he'd get somebody else to take care of Davino. He picked Larry Neumann.

Frank approached Neumann about doing the killing. "I'll be glad to do it; I never liked that asshole anyway. How do you want him killed?"

"It's your job and your call."

"Okay. I think I'll cut him into little pieces and throw him in Lake Mead."

Frank cringed. It was Lurch's hit and he was entitled to dispose of the body as he thought best. But to Frank, killing was one thing, while the kind of butchery Neumann had in mind was another. He didn't want to be personally involved in a slaughter. "Like I said, that's up to you. If you need some help, Jimmy Patrazzo is in town. Take him with you."

Neumann came up with a plan to call Ernie to go with him and Patrazzo to check out a score; when they got him to a vacant house, they'd kill him. But in order to dispose of Ernie's body, or whatever was left of it, Neumann needed a boat. He asked Frank to line one up for him. Frank said he'd see what he could do.

It turned out that Neumann wasn't able to make contact with Davino. Frank reported to Tony that the target was playing hard to get. Tony said, "I'll get in touch with the cocksucker. If I can get him to my house, I know I can make him feel comfortable and he'll start coming around again." Tony's plan worked. He lured Davino out and Ernie started making himself available.

When Frank saw Davino at the Upper Crust, he asked why he'd been avoiding him. "I figured you were pissed off at me over that furniture score. I know it's caused you a lot of grief," Davino said.

"Hey, it wasn't your fault; don't worry about it. I've missed you. Start coming around more often."

Frank told Neumann that Davino was starting to relax and he could probably get to him now. Neumann called his prey and made arrangements to meet a week later to check on the fictitious burglary. But before that meeting took place, Tony called off the hit. He said, "I found out Ernie's not the culprit. Pass on it."

Frank was happy about the reprieve, but Neumann was another story. When Frank told him the killing had been called off, he became angry. "I've got everything ready and I've already put five hundred bucks into it. Fuck Tony; Ernie's an asshole and I'm going to kill him anyway."

Frank had a long talk with Lurch and calmed him down. When he finished, he felt that Davino was safe. Of course, he'd felt the same way after he talked to Neumann about not killing the guy in Chicago who had the altercation with Neumann's ex-wife. When dealing with Lurch Neumann, there were no guarantees.

This time Lurch followed Frank's instructions. Ernie Davino lived to steal another day.

• • •

While Frank welcomed the news that Tony had withdrawn the contract on Ernie Davino, he was still in financial trouble due to his ever-increasing legal expenses. He needed money and he needed it soon. With Tony's continuing silence on the subject, Frank had to make a big score. And it was his father-in-law who came through.

Nick Rossi told Frank he had a tip on a job that could be worth $100,000 or more. It involved a book joint called the Rose Bowl, located on the Strip near the Aladdin. According to Rossi's information, a woman from the Rose Bowl made a money run from there to the owner's house in Chateau Vegas when the action for the day reached the six-figure mark. That meant that the heavy betting during football season was the best time for a robbery. As it happened, it was the tail end of the gridiron season. It was an opportunity Frank couldn't let pass.

He quickly put together a crew and plan. Jimmy Patrazzo was still in Vegas and with his clean face, he was the best candidate to grab the moneybag. Frank, Neumann, and Davino would each drive a work car. Rossi wanted his son Jerry used in some capacity, such as calling from the outside pay phone to let the robbers know when the money was ready to leave the bookie joint.

The robbery went down. Jerry called when the money was going out the door; Jimmy Patrazzo stuck a gun in the faces of the courier and a man who was walking her to her car. After taking the money, he ran through the parking lots and Davino picked him up on the Strip. Frank pulled up in back of them, while Neumann used his car to block off traffic in the Rose Bowl parking lot. It was a perfect score.

The money was taken to Nick Rossi's house for the split. The take was a little less than what had been hoped for, about $60,000. Nick got his ten percent and his son was given $1,500 for making the phone call. That night Patrazzo blew half of his cut gambling. Frank got him on a plane to Chicago the next day before he ended up completely broke.

Frank's share of the proceeds from that robbery was $10,000. It helped, but was nowhere near enough to offset what he had going out. He needed more scores and he needed them fast.

· · ·

Two weeks after the Rose Bowl job, Tony gave Frank an assignment. He said he'd received a call from a man named Paul, a Chicago thief and hit man. Paul was living in Scottsdale, Arizona, and had a big score lined up. The problem was that he wasn't exactly sure how to pull it off and asked for assistance. Tony, always ready to lend a hand if it meant a good payday, dispatched Frank and Larry Neumann to help out.

When they got to Scottsdale, Paul told them he and his crew were going to take down a jewelry-store owner, an Arab who had a big walk-in vault in his home. According to what he'd learned, the vault couldn't be peeled, drilled, or burned open; the Arab would have to open it up himself. That meant a home invasion, which was why Paul wanted Frank and Neumann there.

When the robbers arrived at the Arab's house, no one was home. They gained entry by making a hole in the wall, just like in Vegas. After waiting for two hours, the victims came back. The invaders, wearing hoods, took control of the couple at gunpoint. The wife was tied up and her husband opened the safe. There were no problems. Frank and Neumann went straight back to Vegas with all the merchandise. The next day they took everything to the Gold Rush. It was a good score, about $75,000.

. . .

Frank began to feel like the police pressure on him was easing up a bit. He believed that with so many cases going against him, the cops thought he was washed up. Though they backed off a little, the heat was by no means off. He decided to play it safe and not do too much in Vegas, but he needed money and had to stay active. That meant spending more time on the road. He and his crew pulled more robberies in Arizona, mostly in Scottsdale, then moved on to Palm Springs and Los Angeles. They always brought the cash or merchandise back to Vegas to dispose of.

Frank even got a call to do a job in Florida. He went via Chicago, where an Outfit guy gave him the details. A pawnshop owner in the Pompano Beach area had a line on some Jamaican dope dealers. The Jamaicans supposedly had about $500,000 in drugs and cash in their house. The tipster said they were ripe for a robbery.

Frank took a nervy kid from Chicago with him and drove to Florida. They met with the pawnshop owner, then checked into a hotel in Pompano Beach to wait for the call to pull the job. The tipster finally called and said the drug dealers had gone out of business. That score was off, but something else had come up: a home invasion. He said a friend of his was dating an old Jewish woman worth a ton of money.

Frank figured they could force their way into the old lady's house and have the run of the place, but she turned out to be one of the toughest victims he ever faced.

That night Frank and his partner stole a car, changed the plates, and got guns from the pawnshop. The tipster knew that the woman to be robbed had recently been involved in a hit-and-run accident. When the two thieves got to her house, Frank's partner flashed a fake badge at the woman and said, "I'm investigating the accident you were recently involved in. I need to come in and talk with you."

"If you want to talk with me, you have to go through my lawyer. Goodnight," she said and started to close the door.

"Wait a minute! We need to get this resolved tonight. Now let me and my partner come in to talk with you."

"Don't you understand English? I told you to talk with my lawyer. Get off my property or I'll report you to your department!"

Finally, the younger thief shoved her inside the doorway and he and Frank followed.

"Fuck you!" she hollered as she was pushed into the bathroom, then she started to scream at the top of her lungs.

The lady had a five-carat emerald ring on one finger and a four-carat cluster ring on another. The two thieves were trying to get those rings off her hand, but she was putting up a hell of a fight.

Then the old lady bit Frank's partner; he got mad and broke her finger. It wasn't pretty, but he managed to get one of her rings off.

The job had turned into a circus and Frank had heard and seen enough. He was pretty sure that with all the screaming going on, the whole neighborhood knew something was awry. He just wanted to get the hell out of there. The tipster's buddy was serving as the getaway car driver and was apparently pretty anxious to leave the area. Frank's partner jumped in the car, but before Frank could get inside the car started moving. Frank ran alongside and leaped in through a window.

The robbery netted only the one ring that was removed from the woman's broken finger. It was taken back to Chicago and fenced through Michael Spilotro, another of Tony's brothers, for $10,000. After paying the tipster, his partner, and travel expenses, Frank's cut was so puny, he didn't have to give anything to Tony.

. . .

As 1981 began, the police shooting of Frank Bluestein hadn't been avenged by the mobsters. It wasn't that Tony hadn't given the matter any thought; he hatched a plot to exact revenge against Groover and Smith for Bluestein's death. This idea involved a rather elaborate scheme that would allow the mobsters to escape responsibility for killing the cops by diverting the law's attention elsewhere.

He met with Frank and explained the plan. "Frankie, I think I know how we can whack those fucking cops that killed Frank Blue. Do you think your friends in the Blackstone Rangers would give us a hand?"

"Yeah. A lot of them are out of prison now and will give me any help I ask for."

"Good. Here's what I want you to do when I'm ready. Get hold of the Rangers and have some of them come here. We'll hit Smith and Groover, but we'll make sure the Rangers are seen in the area. The cops will figure the blacks whacked 'em and come down on them hard. When they go into the Westside looking for suspects, it'll be easy for your friends to start a little race war. The cops will have their hands full with the blacks and we'll be in the clear. What do you think?"

"It sounds okay to me. Just let me know when."

Frank doesn't know what happened, but he never heard any more about it.

A more serious threat against Groover and Smith allegedly originated in Chicago, not Las Vegas. Metro was informed by the FBI's Chicago office that they'd picked up credible information about contracts put out on the lives of David Groover and Gene Smith. A pair of hit men from Chicago were on their way to do the job.

For quite a while after the Bluestein shooting, a verbal battle had raged in the press between the department and the Bluestein family's lawyers. Several civil cases had also been filed and it seemed that was all that was going on. So the news of a hit was a real shock to the police department.

Kent Clifford, the boss of the two detectives, went berserk when he heard it. There were certain rules the opposing sides played by. One of them was that you didn't put contracts out on cops. He was certain that even if Tony didn't actually order the hits, he damn sure knew about them. Nothing like that was done in Las Vegas without Spilotro's knowledge and approval.

Gene Smith moved his family out of state for their protection; cops were assigned to stay at his house. Detectives were waiting for the alleged hit men when they arrived in town and checked in at the Fremont Hotel. They were under surveillance around the clock. One of the people they met with was Ron Bluestein, Frank Bluestein's brother. The supposed cop killers were in Vegas for about a week, but only came near Smith's place once. They stopped a couple of blocks away, then left the area. The cops eventually confronted them and had a little chat. The men headed back to Chicago shortly afterward.

The immediate threat was over, but the cops wondered if someone else would show up to make an attempt on the lives of the detectives. In Kent Clifford's mind, the only way to remove the danger once and for all was to have the contracts lifted. He also wanted to know whether Spilotro had authorized the hits on his own. There was only one way to find out for certain. In an unprecedented move, Clifford went to Chicago to have a face-to-face with Tony's superiors.

Clifford issued an ultimatum to the Outfit bosses: Lift the contracts on my cops, or else.

The top mobsters had a meeting and lifted the contracts. Informed of their decision, Clifford returned home.

Clifford arrived back in Las Vegas thinking that the resolution of the Groover and Smith matter would return things to normal. It did, but only temporarily. At around 10 p.m. on April 9, 1981, someone launched a shotgun attack on the home and vehicle of Tony Spilotro and the nearby house of his brother John. No one was hurt during the shootings, but both houses and their parked vehicles were damaged. At 10:47 p.m., John Spilotro reported the incident to the police. The subsequent investigation failed to identify the assailants.

The Spilotro side believed the police were behind the shootings. A newspaper story reported that a witness claimed to have seen Gene Smith in the vicinity of the Spilotro houses loading a shotgun. Metro denied the charges. The Spilotros demanded the Clark County District Attorney's office conduct an independent inquiry.

The results of that investigation failed to identify the shooter(s) and the police were cleared, but those results weren't acceptable to the Spilotro brothers. Tensions were running high.

The additional violence and war of words were the final straws for Kent Clifford. He called Oscar Goodman and asked to have a meeting with the Spilotros. The session was held soon afterward in the lawyer's office with the Spilotros, Goodman, and Clifford present. The conversation got pretty heated. But when Clifford left the meeting, all parties appeared to understand that the personal stuff was over.

• • •

On May 26, 1981, the police observed Larry Neumann seated in a parked vehicle in the vicinity of the Upper Crust. Interviewed by detectives, they determined that Neumann was an ex-felon who had failed to register with the police department upon his arrival in Las Vegas. After Neumann was taken into custody on that charge, his car was searched. Found in the glove box was a .380 Mauser semi-automatic pistol. A check of the weapon revealed it had been stolen in a burglary on April 9. As a result, Neumann was additionally charged with receiving stolen property and as an ex-felon in possession of a concealed weapon. Neumann's arrest would play an important role in events the following year.

• • •

Frank's financial problems continued to worsen. In addition to increased expenses, he was finding it more difficult to pull off local

Dennis Griffin and Frank Cullotta

scores, because of the mounting pressure from Metro and the FBI. But the lawmen weren't only slowing down Frank's income from criminal activity; they were also affecting the revenue from his legitimate restaurant business. On top of that, it seemed to Frank that every time he turned around, Sal Romano was lurking about.

The Upper Crust was no longer operating in the black. The cops and FBI were around constantly, harassing not only the gangsters but the customers, too, many of whom were celebrities. Frank wasn't taking in enough to cover payroll, so he had to make up the difference out of his pocket. There wasn't much choice but to put the place up for sale.

One day Sal Romano came in the restaurant while Guardino, Davino, and Frank were there. Guardino and Davino had a job to go on; Frank couldn't go along, so they decided to take Romano with them. The gang knew the G was on them day and night. Sometimes they saw them; most of the time they didn't. But they just knew they were there; they could sense it.

Romano was wired that day. The FBI wasn't supposed to allow informants to commit crimes, so when they heard the burglary being discussed, they had to do something to stop it. The surveilling agents suddenly became very visible, making sure they were spotted. It worked; there was no way Leo or Ernie would go on a job with the agents practically sitting in the back seat. The planned burglary was scrubbed.

Romano was always trying to get the other thieves to go to his condo to talk about scores. They went over to his place one day and took a lot of evasive measures to ditch the agents tailing them. It didn't make any difference, though, because Romano's apartment was completely wired, including a camera.

When they got to Romano's place, Frank took a look around. It didn't seem like someone's home; it wasn't cozy and didn't have the feel of being lived in. Only a few clothes were in the closet. Some of them supposedly belonged to Romano's girlfriend, who was actually an FBI agent. To explain away her absences from the apartment, the cover story was that she was an airline stewardess and frequently out of town. Frank's inspection of the premise caused him to become even more suspicious of Romano. He was very cautious about what he said, but Guardino and Davino weren't. The whole visit was recorded on audio and video.

When they left, Romano stayed behind. Back in the car, Frank mentioned his observations about the apartment. The other two laughed and said he was being paranoid. It seemed to Frank that other than his wife, everyone he talked to about Romano just shrugged it off. Nobody seemed to give a damn.

Dennis Griffin and Frank Cullotta

12

Bertha's

On July 4, 1981, the Hole in the Wall Gang went after a score estimated to be worth $1 million. What happened that day and the resulting aftermath became a turning point in the law's battle against Tony Spilotro, Frank Cullotta, and their gang. There are two distinct sides to this story: the cops and the robbers. The opposing forces planned their activities carefully, not wanting to leave anything to chance. But the law had one big advantage over the burglars: They had Sal Romano.

Bertha's Gifts & Home Furnishings, located at 896 East Sahara, was an upscale furniture and jewelry store. When Frank first arrived in Vegas in 1979, one of the guys he hung around with told him about the store and took him there to case it. It was family-owned and had been in business for more than 40 years. Frank's source told him that the store was loaded with jewelry and antiques; if the place could be hit, it would probably be worth seven figures.

Frank checked the store inside and out. He struck up a conversation with one of the sales clerks and got some information from her. He looked around for alarms and sensors and located the vault. After that he explored the outside of the building, then discussed the results of the survey with his associate.

Frank believed Bertha's was directly alarmed to the police station. His friend suggested pulling a big truck alongside the building and popping a hole in the wall next to the vault. Frank said it was a good idea, except that they'd be right off the main street and could easily be spotted by passing police cars or citizens. And if the wall next to the vault was made of steel, they'd have to cut through it. Using torches at night would be sure to draw attention. Frank needed to think about it some more.

In the meantime, he and the other guy had a falling out and he didn't do anything more about it. But the idea was always in the back of his mind. During the intervening two years, Frank developed a plan for attacking the store. When his financial situation turned critical, he decided it was time to take another look at Bertha's.

The store was alarmed, but that could be overcome by going in through the roof. From there, it was just a matter of dropping down through the false ceiling right on top of the vault. If the vault was encased in steel, it could be penetrated using torches; if it was in cinder block, it could be easily chopped through.

Frank discussed his idea with Tony. The Ant liked it and added a couple of things to the plan. "We'll fence everything through my brother Michael in Chicago; that way our money will be guaranteed. And I want to use Joe Blasko on the job."

Frank wasn't enthused about Blasko; he figured once a cop, always a cop. "Why Blasko?"

"The guy needs money and I'm tired of carrying him. We'll use him as a lookout and make him earn his keep."

They scheduled the burglary on the night of the Fourth of July, a Saturday. Not only would there be lots of noise with all the fireworks going off, but the cops would be busy handling traffic and fireworks calls. Because it was a long holiday weekend, they'd be able to drive the merchandise to Chicago and be back in Vegas before the crime was even discovered. In addition to him and Blasko, the crew would consist of Neumann, Guardino, Davino, and Matecki. Frank thought that other than Blasko, it was a good crew.

· · ·

With the details of the Bertha's job in place, it was a matter of waiting until the date for the burglary arrived. While counting down the days, Frank was sent to Chicago with some kickback money for the Outfit from Tony.

When he made his delivery to Joe Ferriola, they talked about all the heat being put on the gang in Vegas. The next words out of the bigshot's mouth were, "Who in the fuck is murdering all those people out there?" He mentioned a few names, including Jerry Lisner.

Frank denied that he or Tony had anything to do with the murders in question and the subject was dropped. He was bothered by the conversation, though. The man who asked him the question was the one to give Tony permission to murder Lisner. Now he was acting like he knew nothing about it and wanted to know who was responsible. After giving it more thought, Frank came to the conclusion that Tony had lied to him. He'd authorized the Lisner killing on his own and Chicago knew nothing about it. *What the fuck was going on? Why would Tony do something that stupid?* Frank asked himself. He didn't know the answers. But he did know that committing a hit without prior approval was the kind of thing that could get him and Tony both killed, and he didn't like it.

When Frank returned to Vegas, he didn't mention his concerns to Tony, but they did discuss other things. "I've got a job I might need to have done," Tony said. "I want you to prepare for it. Make sure Larry is ready to go and get one other guy. Who else can you get?"

"What's the job?"

"I might want to get rid of the Jew [Rosenthal]."

"For something like that, I can have Wayne come in from Chicago."

"I'm not sure right now I want to do this, so don't do anything until I tell you. I'm going to bring in a couple of other guys, one from California and the other from Arizona. They're going to dig a big hole in the desert. They'll cover it with plywood and dirt. You'll know where the hole is, because I'll take you there and show you. When I'm ready to get rid of the Jew, I'll tell you. Then you scoop him up from the street. Don't kill him on the street, Frankie. Kill him when you get to the grave we're going to dig. Then dump him in and cover him up. That will be the end of that."

Frank wasn't surprised. The relationship between Tony and Lefty had long since deteriorated past the point of no return. The only question was whether Tony would seek permission from Chicago to take Rosenthal out or make the decision on his own, as he had apparently done in the Lisner killing. In either case, Frank worked for Tony, not the Outfit. If the order to kill Rosenthal came, he'd carry it out and worry about the consequences later.

This plan, like Tony's plot to bring the Blackstone Rangers in

Dennis Griffin and Frank Cullotta

on the killing of Groover and Smith, never went any further. Frank didn't get much time to reflect on Tony's plans for murder, though. As the date for the Bertha's caper drew closer, he received some upsetting news.

• • •

This time Frank's information came from two sources he considered highly credible. He believed that what they told him was the smoking gun that would surely convince Tony Spilotro that having Sal Romano hanging around was risky business.

Two Chicago cops whom Frank had known for years and worked for Bill Hanhardt in the CIU were in Las Vegas on vacation and they stopped at the Upper Crust to see him. They asked if he knew Sal Romano; he said he did. One of the cops said, "We don't know about this guy. We busted him at O'Hare Airport with a load of furs he'd stolen here in Vegas. Because we had him for interstate transportation, we turned him over to the feds. Well, they haven't done anything with it. He hasn't even been indicted. We're looking at this Romano as maybe being an informant now. We're not sure, but it doesn't look right. We figured we'd pass this on to you while we were here."

Frank gave the cops $500 each and got their rooms comped. And then he told Tony what he'd learned. Tony said, "You gotta take this stuff at face value. How much can you trust these guys? They're cops!"

It was apparent to Frank that Tony had been completely taken in by Romano. And he found Tony's response short-sighted in the least, and suicidal at most. But there was worse to come.

• • •

Not long after talking with the Chicago cops, Frank got about the worst news he could imagine: Out of the blue Ernie Davino told him that he'd asked Sal Romano to come along on the Bertha's job. Frank was livid. "You had no goddamn business bringing him in! Tony and I make those decisions, not you."

"I only asked him because I figured he could help out with the alarms."

"We don't fucking need him. Everything's covered. I don't trust the son of a bitch and I don't want him in on the job."

Frank went to Tony and gave him the news. Spilotro wasn't happy about it either, but he said, "If Sal is bad like you think, the damage is already done; he knows. You might as well let him come along."

"I'd rather just pass on the whole thing."

"There's too much money involved and it's too close to back off now."

"Sal installed a burglar alarm in your house. I wouldn't doubt but that he bugged your place."

Tony dismissed the idea. "If he did, the cops would have arrested me by now. Sal did a nice job putting that system in for me, Frankie; he's a good man. You've just got a hard-on for him for some reason."

Frank didn't give in. "He's bad fucking news and I don't want any part of him."

Tony relented slightly. "Tell you what. Take him on the job, but have Larry watch him. Tell Larry that if Sal does anything funny, he should take him out."

So as the Fourth of July drew near, Frank found that his crew now consisted of himself and six other guys. Four of them he trusted. A fifth, Blasko, he didn't trust completely. And the sixth, Romano, he didn't trust at all.

. . .

In June, the thieves began to fine-tune their plan for Bertha's. Tony Spilotro obtained police radio equipment from Chicago and Frank lined up additional gear and a couple of vehicles to use.

One of Tony's devices unscrambled police calls and scrambled the gang's transmissions. Frank wanted to have a van available, but didn't want to rent one in his name in case things didn't work out. He knew a man who ran a steam-cleaning business and had a van with all his equipment inside and a big Superman logo on the outside. Frank made arrangements to use the van on the Fourth of July for a fee. Joe Blasko would set up in the van across from Bertha's with the police scanners, walkie-talkies, and a CB radio. Frank sent Larry to Chicago to get some acetylene tanks and torches. Getting stuff from out of town would make it tougher to trace than if it was obtained locally. Neumann stole what was needed and brought it back. The burglars had a ladder, picks, sledgehammers, and cutting tools, about everything they could possibly need. Finally, they scrounged up a station wagon to bring the equipment to the scene.

When the crew got together at an apartment one last time to go over the plan, Sal Romano was wired and the FBI was parked out on the street, listening to every word that was said.

• • •

With full knowledge of the Hole in the Wall Gang's plans, the lawmen of the FBI and Metro prepared their ambush. The team was headed on-scene by the FBI's Charlie Parsons and Joe Gersky and Metro's Gene Smith. Their bosses—Joe Yablonsky and Kent Clifford—were nearby and available if needed to make any command decisions.

Although the actual crime wouldn't take place until after dark, the lawmen were at work much earlier. Surveillance teams were active around Bertha's all day, monitoring activity and making sure they were thoroughly familiar with the area. They had to keep an eye on the bad guys as well, looking for any indication of a change in their plans or other last-minute situations.

With two different agencies participating in the operation, communications were critical. Their radios had to have a common frequency, one that wasn't known to the burglars. A secret frequency was obtained and divulged only to those with a need to know. At the same time they continued to use the regular frequencies, those likely to be monitored by the thieves, to disseminate bogus information as to the location and status of personnel. In the late afternoon, the balance of the agents and officers deployed to the field.

The main observation point overlooking the roof of Bertha's was from the top of a nearby five-story building. Charlie Parsons, Joe Gersky, and videotape personnel took up positions there. Gene Smith worked with the surveillance detail, riding with an FBI agent. The burglars were not to be arrested until they actually entered the building, making it a burglary rather than the lesser charge of an attempted crime.

Dennis Griffin and Frank Cullotta

The cops knew that the crooks planned to use at least four vehicles, three of them to conduct counter-surveillance activities and one to transport the three men who would go on the roof and do the break-in. Representing the gang's forces on the ground were Frank Cullotta driving a 1981 Buick, Larry Neumann in a late-model Cadillac, and an unknown individual—possibly Joe Blasko—in a white commercial van with the name of a cleaning business and a Superman logo on the side. Sal Romano would be functioning as a lookout, using either his own vehicle or riding with one of the others. The occupants of each vehicle would be equipped with two-way radios and police scanners. The actual burglars—Matecki, Guardino, and Davino—would arrive by station wagon and go on the roof to gain entry to the store. They would also have radios to keep in contact with the lookouts on the ground.

At around 7 p.m. the gang's counter-surveillance units began to appear. Cullotta and Neumann, with Romano in his car, repeatedly drove around the area, apparently checking for a police presence or anything that seemed suspicious. In turn, they were being tailed by cops and agents. The white van took up a position in the driveway to the Commercial Center shopping plaza, across the street from Bertha's. From this vantage point the operator had an unimpeded view of the store. As the man in the van watched, he was under constant surveillance himself.

While this game of cat-and-mouse continued, the whole operation almost came to an abrupt end. Gene Smith and the FBI agent were stopped at a traffic light when a car pulled up next to them. Out of the corner of his eye, Smith saw that the driver of the other car was none other than Frank Cullotta. The cop—who was well-known to Cullotta—went to the floor of the vehicle as fast as he could. The light changed and Cullotta pulled away. It's almost a certainty that had Smith been spotted in the area, the burglars would have scrubbed their plans.

At approximately 9 p.m. a station wagon bearing Matecki, Guardino, and Davino arrived and parked behind a Chinese restaurant located at 1000 East Sahara. A police surveillance vehicle parked nearby went unnoticed by the burglars. The three men exited their vehicle and unloaded tools and equipment, including a ladder. They next proceeded to the east side of Bertha's and gained access to the roof, hauling their gear up with them.

From the roof a few buildings away, the videotape was rolling.

Plugging into electric outlets located in the air-conditioning units, the burglars went about their business, using power and hand tools to penetrate the store's roof. Everything was going smoothly for both sides. Other than Lt. Smith's close call with Cullotta, the only thing that had gone wrong for the law so far was that a member of the surveillance team had to be treated for dehydration.

Agent Dennis Arnoldy was in charge of a four-man team, two FBI and two Metro, responsible for arresting the thieves on the roof. They relaxed as best they could in the back of a pickup truck in the parking lot of the Sahara Hotel & Casino, located on the Las Vegas Strip a few blocks from Bertha's.

Arnoldy and his team weren't expecting their prey or the lookouts to be armed. These were veteran criminals who knew that if they were caught with guns, the charges against them and the potential penalties would be more serious. The lawmen certainly hoped that would be the case and that the arrests would be made without bloodshed.

As the burglars progressed in their efforts to get through the roof, Arnoldy and his men made their way to the scene. Using a ladder, they too got onto the roof. An impressive fireworks display exploded in the sky over Las Vegas as the lawmen secreted themselves behind vents and air-conditioning units to wait for the predetermined arrest signal to be broadcast.

At that point a minor snag developed. When the burglars broke through, they realized they hadn't hit their target: the store's safe. Recovering quickly, they soon made another entry in the right place. At approximately 10:40 p.m., Leo Guardino dropped through the opening and into the store, carrying the tools necessary to break into the safe.

The act of burglary was complete.

Arnoldy, shotgun at the ready, directed his team into action. When Davino and Matecki detected the lawmen approaching, they scurried to the front of the building and possible escape to the street below. But when they looked down they saw more agents and officers on the sidewalk pointing weapons in their direction. Knowing the game was up, they surrendered without incident. A few seconds later Guardino's head popped up through the hole in the roof and he was taken into custody.

At street level, other agents and cops were already busy apprehending the lookouts. Neumann and Cullotta were nabbed a short distance from Bertha's. Agent Gary Magnesen and two Metro officers arrested Joe Blasko.

One of the Metro officers was in uniform and driving a black-and-white. As planned, the marked car came up on the van from the rear with its lights flashing and headlights illuminating the van's interior. Another detective, armed with a shotgun, and Magnesen with a pistol approached the van from the front and ordered the occupant out. Up until that point, it was thought that Blasko was inside the van, but no one knew for sure. In fact, some of the Metro cops didn't want to believe that their former colleague had really gone to the other side. When Blasko emerged from the vehicle, the veil of uncertainty was gone.

No weapons were found on Blasko or any of the other arrestees.

When agents and officers entered the store, they found that the burglars' second hole in the roof had been accurate, located directly over the safe. Burglary tools were found nearby and several holes had already been drilled into the safe in an effort to open it. Leo Guardino had been a busy man during his short time inside the building.

Joe Yablonsky and Kent Clifford held a press conference shortly after the arrests were made. They told reporters that Frank Cullotta, age 43, Joe Blasko, age 45, Leo Guardino, age 47, and Ernest Davino, age 34, all of Las Vegas, were in custody. Also arrested were Lawrence Neumann, age 53, of McHenry, Illinois, and Wayne Matecki, age 30, of Northridge, Illinois. The six men were charged with burglary, conspiracy to commit burglary, attempted grand larceny, and possession of burglary tools. They were all lodged in the Clark County Jail.

When reporters asked how the lawmen happened to be in the area at the time of the burglary, Yablonsky and Clifford turned vague. In fact, they lied outright when they denied that the arrests were the result of an informant's tip. The reporters also weren't told that Sal Romano, an expert at disabling alarm systems and an FBI informant, was working as a part of the gang's counter-surveillance team. When the signal was broadcast to arrest the burglars,

Romano was immediately removed from the area and placed in the Witness Protection Program. His role in the Bertha's operation wasn't made known to the general public until much later.

In many respects, the Bertha's bust was a great victory for both the FBI and Metro. For one, it proved that the two major law-enforcement agencies had overcome their prior differences and could work together. For another, it was instrumental in getting one of the key criminal players to switch sides and become a government witness, sending shockwaves from Las Vegas to Chicago and beyond.

. . .

Although the involvement of Sal Romano in the Bertha's job had dampened Frank's enthusiasm for the score, he put his concerns aside and went along on the heist. It turned out to be a night he will never forget.

The crew split up into two groups. Blasko, Neumann, and Cullotta were responsible for monitoring police activity and keeping an eye out for anything suspicious. Blasko was in the van parked in the entrance to the Commercial Center shopping mall opposite Bertha's. Neumann and Cullotta cruised the area in their cars. Romano was told to ride with Neumann. When he wanted to know why he couldn't be alone, Neumann told him there was no need for him to be anywhere but with him; they would listen to the police calls on the radio. Neumann was prepared to take Romano out of the area and kill him if he pulled anything funny. Guardino, Matecki, and Davino drove the station wagon and were assigned to do the actual burglary.

Frank was driving a new Buick Riviera with a CB radio built in. Neumann and Romano were in Neumann's Caddy. Frank and Lurch had good communications and thought Romano was more or less neutralized.

The burglars unloaded their station wagon and got all their equipment up on the roof. When they were almost ready to break through, Romano was sent to move the station wagon closer to the store. He reported back to Neumann by walkie-talkie that the wagon wouldn't start and he was unable to move it. Frank stopped by the allegedly disabled station wagon to see what the problem was. He turned the key and it started right up. He radioed Neumann, "There's nothing wrong with this goddamn car. Where's Sal?"

"I don't know; he's not with me."

Frank's instincts told him trouble was brewing. "Find the son of a bitch!"

Right about then the burglars radioed that they had gotten through and were inside the store. "I can see the vault. It's only cinder block; we're in," Guardino gloated.

As Frank listened to Guardino's good news, he checked his rear-view mirror and found a van right on his tail. He drove into a shopping center parking lot with a lot of people around and the van pulled him over. The occupants of the van jumped out, hollering "FBI!" and "Metro!" They got Frank out of his car and told him to put his hands on the hood and not to move. They searched him and his car. After that he was handcuffed, put in the van, and read his rights. As they left the parking lot for Bertha's, Frank heard a radio transmission that Blasko had been captured, along with all the radio equipment. When they pulled up in front of the store, he saw Guardino, Matecki, and Davino face down on the concrete with their hands cuffed behind their backs. Neumann had been picked up, too. Everybody was accounted for. Except Sal Romano.

. . .

Almost as soon as the burglars were booked into the jail, Frank started searching for Sal Romano. He wasn't in the lockup; nobody had seen him and nobody knew where he was. Somebody said Romano must have gotten away.

"Bullshit," Frank said. "He's a fucking informant and he set us up."

Joe Blasko didn't believe it. "Tony would never have let that happen."

Frank said, "I never trusted that bastard and I told Tony about it several times. But Tony knew it all, and here we are."

The arrestees were put in cells side by side, so they were still able to talk. But because of concerns that the cells were bugged, they were careful about what they said. Blasko complained that he couldn't stay in jail. He said he had obligations and asked Frank to get him bonded out first. Frank agreed and assumed Tony was already working on it. He wasn't.

Frank called the Upper Crust and talked to Nick Rossi. His father-in-law said Romano had phoned wanting to know if he was the only one who escaped. When Rossi asked how he had managed to get away, Romano hung up on him.

Frank used one of the phone calls he was allowed to call the gang's regular bondsman and find out why he wasn't there getting the guys out. The answer was simple: Frank's call was the first he'd heard about the arrests. Tony hadn't contacted him. When the bondsman got to the jail, he got the crew out one at a time, Blasko first. Finally, everyone was out but Frank. The bondsman said he wasn't getting out; the judge had revoked his earlier bond. Frank's lawyers went into high gear and got a hearing before a different judge. He released Frank on yet another $100,000 bond. In the end, Frank put up all the bail money for the entire crew. Tony hadn't contributed anything and things were getting lean on Frank's end. He had to live, too, and had his own family to take care of.

Once he was out of jail, Frank discussed his ever-increasing legal problems with Tony. "Why don't you change lawyers and hire Oscar [Goodman]?" Tony suggested. "He's a lot sharper than Momot."

"Why, just to prolong the inevitable?"

"Well, he can prolong things, but he can win cases, too."

"What cases has he ever won for you?"

Tony became angry. "Look, do you want to listen to me or be a fucking know-it-all?"

Frank relented and met with Goodman; the lawyer wanted $10,000 to represent him. Frank gave him the money, but Tony continued his pattern of keeping his own cash in his pocket. Goodman delivered for Frank in the form of getting him continuances, lots of them.

. . .

The media covered the Bertha's story aggressively for the first several days after the burglary, pressing their law-enforcement sources for additional information. They were particularly interested in the arrest of ex-cop Joe Blasko and alleged ties to Tony Spilotro.

Dennis Griffin and Frank Cullotta

On July 6, the *Las Vegas Review-Journal* ran a front-page story about the arrests. The headline read, "Mob-linked ex-cop held in burglary try." The article reported that the six men arrested were believed to be members of the Hole in the Wall Gang. According to the reporter's police sources, the gang was responsible for $1 million in local thefts since 1979. All the suspects reportedly were connected to a Chicago organized-crime family.

A story appeared the next day in which it was divulged that the burglary arrests were part of an FBI mob probe. This article stated that unnamed law-enforcement authorities firmly believed the burglars were underlings to Tony Spilotro, who was the subject of an ongoing federal racketeering investigation. It was also mentioned that federal racketeering indictments might be sought against the thieves.

· · ·

While Frank was out on bail, Tony Spilotro told him that two men needed to be killed: Joe Blasko and Sal Romano.

"The big guy [Joe Blasko] is getting me nervous," Tony said.

"Why? What's he doing?"

"He's sort of insinuating that I didn't listen to you guys about Romano. Couldn't I feel a problem coming on with the guy? And why did I let him in on the score? Stuff like that. I'm afraid the motherfucker is going to roll on me, Frankie. I want you to get rid of him."

As far as Frank was concerned, that was a job that should have been done a long time before then. Tony subsequently backed off on the hit, saying Blasko was behaving himself and to let it go.

Tony still had killing on his mind, however. The next thing he wanted Frank to do was whack Sal Romano.

"I'd love to kill that son of a bitch, Tony. But how in the fuck are we going to get to him? He's in Witness Protection being guarded by the U.S. Marshals."

"I don't know where they've got Sal stashed, but they'll have to bring him into town to testify, and when they do we can get him."

"I still don't see how we're going to know where he is."

"I know the guy that caters food to the marshals when they're protecting someone. When they bring Sal here, they'll have to feed him. I'll be able to find out where the food is delivered to and then we can whack him."

"But he'll have a lot of guys around guarding him. What about them?"

Tony said, "You gotta do what you gotta do if you want to stay free. Hit them, all of them. That's it, an open-and-shut case."

This plan never got past the talking stage either. Tony was making plans to have a lot of people killed, but seemed unable to issue the final orders. Frank saw this as a sign that Tony was losing it. He was under tremendous pressure from the law and Chicago wasn't pleased about all the media attention he was getting. Frank was convinced that Tony had become paranoid to the point that he didn't trust anybody.

As Frank pondered Tony's behavior, he asked himself: *Does he still trust me?*

• • •

All the stress Tony was under may have been slowly driving

him crazy, but in spite of that he continued to play out the role in public. The women still flocked to him and when they went out to dinner, an entourage of groupies, wiseguy wannabes, and sometimes entertainment celebrities followed along. And nobody could pick up the dinner check but Tony.

The Ant also remained the guy people came to if they wanted something done. In a restaurant one night, somebody complained to Tony about a dealer at the Fremont. After dinner Frank, Neumann, and Guardino were sent to the casino to deal with the culprit. They broke his ribs and blackened an eye, then told him if there had to be a next time, it would be worse. The dealer straightened out and caused no further problems.

. . .

Still free on bond, Frank and his family moved back to Chicago to escape his troubles in Las Vegas. Before leaving, he and Guardino sold the Upper Crust. The constant presence of agents and cops had caused business to drop off dramatically and the restaurant was operating in the red every month. They had bought it for $65,000, but only got $15,000 for it when it sold.

Frank made his move during the winter and it was bone-chillingly cold in the Midwest. Things didn't work out too well for him and he managed to make just enough to pay the heating-oil bill and his lawyer's fees. The Outfit guys he talked with complained about what was going on in Vegas, including the unauthorized hits. It was pretty obvious to him that they weren't happy. He now knew for certain Tony had deceived him and continued to be bothered by it.

Frank's trial for possessing the stolen furniture was coming up in Vegas and with things in the doldrums in Chicago, he moved back to Sin City.

When he made his decision to return, he wasn't aware of how much his relationship with Tony Spilotro had deteriorated. He'd soon find out.

. . .

Frank was scheduled to go on trial in April 1982. Not long before the court date, Eileen became suspicious of Tony Spilotro. It got her thinking that perhaps in Tony's eyes, Frank had become expendable.

When the couple returned to Las Vegas, they moved into an apartment next door to Eileen's father. In early April, Frank received a 1 a.m. phone call from Tony. He asked Frank to meet him in the parking lot of My Place. It wasn't unusual for Tony to want to meet at odd hours, so Frank didn't think much about it at the time.

During their get-together they discussed Frank's upcoming trial and a couple of other things, none of which were urgent. Tony went inside the bar four or five times to use the pay phone. Other than that, it was a routine session.

When Frank got home, Eileen was upset. She said, "What's the matter with that guy? Can't he sleep? Why does he bother you all hours of the day and night? He calls and you run; this is ridiculous!"

"That's none of your business; don't worry about it," he said.

Frank got in bed and before his head hit the pillow he heard gunshots. He pushed Eileen out of bed and onto the floor, then covered her with his own body. When the shots stopped, he went outside to look around. He saw two things: a guy lying in the doorway of the apartment next to his with blood gushing from a wound in his leg, and a van speeding away. He went back inside and told Eileen that it looked like the guy next door had been shot, probably due to a drug deal that went sour.

Eileen didn't buy that explanation. "Your friend calls you and you go out to meet him. You get home and aren't in bed two seconds and somebody gets shot next door. Right next door, Frank! Come on! Don't you think maybe your friend Tony is trying to kill you?"

Frank laughed. First Tony was becoming paranoid, and now Eileen. "You're fuckin' crazy. You know that, don't you?"

"Laugh all you want, but I've got a feeling Tony wants you dead. I can understand that you're blinded by your friendship for him. But think about what I'm telling you, please."

"Sure, I'll think about it," he promised.

Frank had to admit to himself that Tony got under his skin now and then and had lied to him. Tony had also made some questionable decisions lately, like getting taken in by Romano and ordering the Lisner hit without Chicago's approval. Tony was going through some tough times; so was Frank. But they'd been friends for years and they still were. He'd never turn on Tony and was sure Tony felt the same. He dismissed Eileen's concerns as resentment over his friendship with Tony.

The phone rang again about an hour later. It was Tony wanting to know what Frank was doing and if he could come out for another meeting at the bar. After Frank hung up he said, "That was Tony. I'm going back out for a while."

"Frank, he was checking to see if you were dead or alive. Can't you see that? You make sure you tell Tony that I know about the meeting and if anything happens to you, I'll know who was responsible."

For the second time that night Frank laughed at his wife, then left again for My Place. When he met with Tony, he mentioned the shooting at his apartment building. "Well, imagine that," Tony deadpanned.

. . .

On April 20, 1982, Frank Cullotta was convicted of possession of stolen property, in the case of emptying the absent couple's home to furnish his own. Because of his prior felony convictions, he was facing a potential sentence of life in prison. A number of unresolved charges were hanging over his head as well. In addition, Tony Spilotro had been noticeably slow in lending a helping hand as Frank's legal problems grew. He was even less enthusiastic after the conviction of his right-hand man.

Frank had gone into the courtroom with a bad feeling about the outcome, but he did have one ace up his sleeve. During the defense portion of the case, he had his lawyer, John Momot, put on a surprise witness: Eileen's cousin. He testified that he received the stolen furniture and gave it to Frank and Eileen. In theory, if Frank didn't know the furnishings were hot, he'd be innocent of the charge. The jury was apparently unconvinced. They were out for only five hours before returning the guilty verdict.

The judge was a pro-prosecution type who kept a 45-caliber handgun between his legs during court. After the verdict, he wouldn't set an appeal bond and Frank was taken straight to jail.

On one hand, Frank felt like a deflated balloon. On the other, it seemed like a great weight was off his back. Much of the uncertainty in his life had been lifted. Even though he still had other charges hanging over him, he was at peace, in a way. And in that frame of mind, he started thinking. He thought about Tony, about the shooting at the apartment next door, and about Jerry Lisner. He thought about the Outfit guys he talked with when he was back in Chicago, how messed up everything had been in Vegas for a long time, and how it kept getting worse.

Frank called a lawyer to appeal his conviction. The attorney said he'd appeal, but only if Frank came up with $10,000. Frank said he was almost broke and told the lawyer that he'd have to get the money from Tony. When the lawyer got back to Frank, he said Tony was avoiding him and not returning his calls. The attorney finally caught up with him, but Tony would only kick in six thousand; Eileen had to come up with the other four.

Frank started thinking some more. He'd been doing all the giving and Tony had been doing the taking. Getting any money out of him for bonds or lawyers was like pulling teeth. He now knew that something was seriously wrong in his world. And he didn't like it one bit. For the first time since hooking up with Tony in Vegas, Frank Cullotta started thinking for himself.

And then Eileen told him that Herb Blitzstein wanted her to give him back her gold cross. Frank had gotten it from the Gold Rush and given it to her as a present. And now, with Frank behind bars and fighting for his life, Blitzstein wanted the damn thing back. Frank was furious. With all Tony's money, including hundreds of thousands that Frank had handed over, now they wanted his wife's gold cross? Frank asked himself: *Are they setting me up? Will they be glad to get rid of me?*

With the money situation becoming critical, Frank told Eileen to ask Tony for a job. Tony told her, "Gee, I don't know what I can do for you right now." He offered to see if he could get her a job at a restaurant about thirty miles outside of town. This further incensed Frank. Here was the guy who ran Las Vegas and that was the best he could do?

The more he thought about it, the more Frank began to believe Tony was trying to set him up. Spilotro was the King of the Strip, the mob's man in Vegas. He had the world by the balls, but had gone and fucked it all up. It made sense that he'd be looking for a fall guy to lay everything off on. Frank could imagine the word getting back to Chicago: Cullotta is out of control and doing his own thing. He's the one hitting people without getting approval.

Maybe that was why Tony hadn't helped Frank with his bonds and legal fees. He'd already decided to throw him to the wolves.

As he searched his memory, he realized the signs had been there all along. Eileen had seen them; he'd chosen to ignore them. But no longer. He was now a believer in his wife's intuition. And if he and Eileen were right, he was in a tough goddamn spot.

. . .

Frank and Tony weren't the only ones with contacts in Chicago. The FBI also had their sources of information and they learned that Frank and Eileen's fears were real; a contract on Frank had, in fact, been authorized.

On April 30 the FBI's Chicago agents informed their Las Ve-

Dennis Griffin and Frank Cullotta

gas colleagues that the Outfit had approved a contract on Frank Cullotta. The FBI had a policy that if they became aware someone's life was in danger, they had to inform that person, regardless of who he was or what they thought of him. Charlie Parsons called the gangster's lawyer. He told him he had some very important information regarding his client and asked for a meeting at the jail that afternoon.

When Parsons got to the jail, he told Frank and the lawyer that it had been a long week and he'd be brief. And then he made his announcement. "We've received credible information that the Chicago Outfit has authorized a contract on Frank." He left immediately afterward. His matter-of-fact delivery was intentional, designed to get Frank's attention.

For Frank, the agent's visit served as confirmation of what, in his heart, he already knew. He thought long and hard about his situation over the weekend. By Monday morning, he'd made his decision. He called the FBI office and spoke with Parsons. "This is Frank Cullotta. I want to talk with you."

"Don't say anything on the phone," Parsons said. "I'll be there in five minutes."

With that phone call, Frank Cullotta's life took yet another turn, one he never thought possible. The man whom the cops were never able to intimidate or beat information out of was about to become a cooperating government witness.

Part Three

Witness Protection and Beyond

Switching Sides

Obtaining the cooperation of an insider can be a huge boon to law-enforcement officers and prosecutors. Such witnesses can also be worth little or nothing. Their value depends on many things, including how much they know, what they're willing to tell, their honesty and credibility in regard to the information they provide, and what the government must give them in return for their assistance.

Charlie Parsons knew all of that when he received the call from Frank Cullotta on the morning of May 3, 1982. Cullotta was certainly in a position to know a lot. But how much would he be willing to tell and how candid would he be? Those questions and many others needed to be answered before Frank's potential benefit to the government could be determined.

The first step in evaluating the possible new ally was to have a face-to-face meeting and get some cards on the table. Parsons hung up the phone and headed for the jail.

. . .

For Frank, what he'd made up his mind to do ran contrary to the way he'd led his life for more than 30 years, since his days as a schoolboy tough guy and petty thief. The law had always been his enemy. The code of honor he lived by required loyalty to his crew. And he never, no matter what, gave his friends up to the cops. Suddenly, he found himself ready to do a complete reversal. His circumstances, however, dictated that course of action as a method of survival for himself and his family. There were no other realistic options. As Frank awaited the arrival of Charlie Parsons, he knew the immediate road ahead would neither be easy nor pleasant for him.

When Parsons got to the jail, he told Frank he wasn't going to read him his rights. He said he wasn't sure if Frank really knew anything and wanted to begin with an off-the-record conversation. First they talked about Frank's lawyer situation. Parsons recommended that Frank drop John Momot and retain a public defender who would have no ties to other organized-crime figures. After that Parsons pulled out a yellow legal pad and started asking questions. Frank spoke and Parsons wrote. Finally, they discussed the Witness Protection Program.

"I've got to be honest with you, Frank. Most people who go into it don't like it, but participation in the program is entirely up to you," the agent said.

Frank shrugged. "I know how these people think and work. They're going to want to kill me, and if they can't do that they'll try to intimidate me. I want me and my family to go into that program."

This session was just the beginning. As tough as it was to face, the debriefing process that followed seemed like it would never end. But Frank had known what he was in for and that it had to start somewhere.

The way was now open for the law to turn the tide in its favor in the war against Tony Spilotro and his associates. It didn't happen overnight, though. Progress had to be made one small step at a time.

. . .

In order to get the ball rolling, Frank needed to switch lawyers. That meant replacing John Momot, who would likely represent some of the people Frank might have to testify against. It was a task he had to perform himself. After the initial meeting with Charlie Parsons, he summoned Momot to the jail to break the news that changes were being made.

When Momot came to see him, Frank told him to sit down, because he had something important to tell him. Frank said, "John, this is the most difficult thing I've ever had to tell anybody in my life. Only one person knows what I'm about to say and he's with the FBI, so you probably know where I'm coming from. Tony has done me wrong and I've rolled over. I'm deeply hurt by the way he's treated me and what he's done to me. The worst that can happen to him is some years in prison. I'll either be in jail the rest of my life or take a bullet in my head. Tony has had this all planned. I'd prefer it if you didn't represent me."

Momot was in shock. With tears in his eyes, he asked, "What did they [the cops] do to you? Did they torture you?"

"No, they haven't done anything to me. But Tony has. He deceived me and lied to me to protect his own ass. Now he wants me dead. This is the decision I've made and nothing can possibly change it. There's no turning back."

Momot appeared stunned. But he accepted Frank's decision and left the meeting without trying to talk him out of it. The lawyer issue over with, Frank contacted his wife, mother, and brother. He told each of them what was going on and why.

Eileen asked, "Are you sure you're doing the right thing?"

"There's no other choice; this is the only way. I've already made arrangements for you and the kids to go into the Witness Protection Program; I'll join you later. If you don't want to go, if you want to stay behind, I'll understand."

She said, "I'm with you until the end. Tony wants to hurt you and I know you're doing what you have to do. I'm on your side."

Frank's mother was concerned for his safety and about her other son. She also wondered if someone had forced Frank into his decision. He told her it was entirely his own choice. He assured her that he knew how the mob operated and that Joey would not be in any physical danger.

Frank told his brother that he'd probably lose a lot of friends when the word got out. "I'm sorry about that, Joey, but this is something I have to do."

Joey said, "You raised me right. It's your decision and I'll always be proud of you. You'll always be my big brother."

· · ·

Frank Cullotta wasn't the first mobster to switch sides and he wouldn't be the last. Among those who preceded him were Joe

Valachi and Aladena "Jimmy the Weasel" Fratiano. They and others like them were often referred to as "turncoats" or "rats."

Joe Valachi was a soldier within New York City's Genovese crime family. His main duties for the family were as a driver, carting upper-echelon mobsters around to their various meetings and other functions. The assignment put him in a position to know a lot about the family's businesses and how they operated.

In 1962, both Valachi and his boss, Vito Genovese, were serving time in prison after being convicted of heroin trafficking. The story goes that Genovese believed Valachi had ratted on him in return for a lighter sentence. That August, Valachi killed another inmate whom he mistakenly thought was going to murder him on Genovese's behalf.

In October 1963, Valachi burst upon the national scene when he voluntarily testified before Senator John McClellan's congressional committee on organized crime. The precise motive for his decision to cooperate is unknown. He could have been seeking to avoid the death penalty for killing his fellow prisoner or simply doing what he felt was his civic duty.

Whatever the reason, Valachi's testimony, which was broadcast live on radio and television, raised the eyebrows of the politicians, law-enforcement authorities, and general public. For the first time, a mob insider told America that the Mafia existed right in the United States. Up until then, even noted lawmen such as FBI Director J. Edgar Hoover had refused to even admit there was such a thing as organized crime. He used the phrase *cosa nostra*, meaning "our thing," which caught on and soon became a household term. The witness described mob rituals, such as the ceremony of becoming a "made man," to his stunned listeners. He identified the major crime families and named many of their top members.

Although Valachi's disclosures did serious harm to the mob by bringing it out of the shadows and into the spotlight, no organized-crime figures were prosecuted as a result of his turning.

In 1968, journalist Peter Maas published Valachi's biography, *The Valachi Papers*. The former mobster died of a heart attack in 1971 while incarcerated in a federal prison.

Jimmy "Weasel" Fratiano was originally from Cleveland. He reportedly made his bones in the early 1940s when he carried out a contract hit for then-Los Angeles crime boss, Jack Dragna. He became a made man in the Dragna crime family in 1947. The Weasel's star continued to rise and he eventually served as acting boss of the Los Angeles crime family for a time. Along the way it's believed he put at least 11 notches on his gun.

However, in the 1970s, Fratiano began having disagreements with his superiors and the bosses of other families. After receiving word that a contract had been issued on his life, the Weasel became a government informant. Over the next several years, he testified in a number of mob trials in various venues. His testimony was instrumental in obtaining numerous convictions against organized-crime figures.

Fratiano entered the federal Witness Protection Program and, as far as is known, didn't go back to his criminal ways. His biography, *The Last Mafioso* by Ovid Demaris, was published in 1980. The Weasel passed away from natural causes in 1993.

Having once been an acting boss, Fratiano had the distinction of being the highest-ranking mob defector ever, until 1991. That year Salvatore "Sammy the Bull" Gravano, John Gotti's underboss, turned on his master.

The head of the powerful New York City Gambino family, Gotti had earned the nickname "Teflon Don" because he beat the feds every time they hauled him into court. Gotti was facing another racketeering trial and the law wanted him bad. They were willing to make a deal with the devil, if they had to, in order to get him. In this case, the devil was Sammy the Bull, a 19-time killer.

It worked out well for the prosecutors. With Sammy's testimony, they were able to convict Gotti and get him a sentence of life without parole. As one of the government lawyers said later, "The Teflon turned to Velcro. Every charge stuck."

In the case of Valachi, his decision to talk served to make the authorities and public aware of organized crime and how it operated. The roles of Fratiano and Gravano were geared more toward sending people to jail. And in Gravano's case, the law had a very specific target.

Before Cullotta was through, his words would both educate and convict.

. . .

While Frank's new lawyer, a government-paid public defender, was still negotiating the details of his deal with the law, the debriefing process got into full swing. Frank was taken out of general population, put in an isolation cell, and talked with the feds. When he was alone, he did a lot of thinking. He'd grown up with only one set of values. Now he'd rolled and become a Judas. It was a hard thing for him to deal with; he hated himself for a while and even contemplated suicide. That would have saved Tony a bullet and he could have gone out with his reputation intact. But then he realized that after three decades of stealing what people had worked for, and following a code that sometimes required the use of violence, he was finally doing the right thing. After surviving the first few days, he began to get a grip on things. It got gradually easier for him. Not easy, but easier.

Metro got in on the act right away, too. The detectives initially brought Don Campbell with them, but Frank didn't like the prosecutor and refused to talk with him. Campbell left and things were okay after that.

Frank understood up front that he had to tell the complete truth. Any deal he ended up making with local and federal prosecutors depended on his being honest. Neither the FBI nor Metro wanted to hear any lies or embellishments, only things that he knew for sure. And there was a lot of paperwork. Frank had to take evaluation and psychological tests and a polygraph was administered. He was impressed with how thorough his captors were. He had to prove to them he was a valuable witness before they'd let him into their program.

Within a few days, Eileen and her 12-year-old son Kent entered Witness Protection; Kimberly elected to stay in Las Vegas. The two were flown to Minnesota where they stayed a couple of weeks. From there they were taken to Virginia Beach.

Frank's brother-in-law, Jerry, learned about Frank's decision from Eileen even before Tony Spilotro heard the news. Fearing for his own safety, he went to My Place and talked with Tony. "I don't know if you've heard about this yet, but Frank's rolled and my sister will be going into Witness Protection."

Tony laughed so hard he almost fell out of the booth. "You're fucking crazy! Frankie would never do anything like that."

He wasn't laughing for long.

. . .

Frank was soon released from jail, but he remained in the custody of Clark County, staying in Las Vegas for two or three weeks. He was put up in hotels, and for security reasons was relocated every couple of days. To him, it felt like he stayed in about every hotel room in town. His debriefing was constant, running from about 9 a.m. until 6 p.m. Then he went out to dinner surrounded by his security detail of detectives and FBI agents. He was even taken to Lake Mead to do some fishing. Eating in restaurants and fishing didn't completely ease his anguish, but it helped to make his life a little more bearable.

As Frank adjusted to the changes, a rather ironic twist took place. Gene Smith, the same cop Frank had considered killing after the Frank Bluestein shooting, was put in charge of providing his security.

Smith took the task of keeping Frank alive seriously. He once told his men, only somewhat tongue in cheek, "If Cullotta gets killed, there better be a number of dead cops around his body to keep it company."

During the Metro phase of his debriefing, Frank provided information that allowed the police to clear about 50 of their previously unsolved burglaries.

In less than a month, Frank was officially turned over to the feds. The FBI's Dennis Arnoldy took over from Charlie Parsons as the chief debriefer. The tenacious investigator, who had been pursuing Frank only days earlier, now worked with him on an almost daily basis. According to Arnoldy, there was never any animosity in their relationship.

After taking control of Frank, the feds got him out of Las Vegas. From then on, he was brought back only for legal proceedings. For his protection, he was moved around regularly. Arnoldy met with Frank hundreds of times during the following months in various locations across the country.

During the countless hours the two men spent together, they developed a bond that far outlasted the five or so years they were officially connected. From the earliest days of debriefing, Arnoldy developed a respect for Frank's honesty in regard to the information he provided.

The agent and his colleagues knew that any information prosecutors used that came from Frank would be vigorously attacked by defense attorneys. Thus, anything he told them had to be double- or triple-checked for accuracy before it was acted on. If it didn't pass that test, it wouldn't be used.

One of the ways Frank's veracity was verified was by matching police reports with his descriptions of crimes committed. For example, when he supplied the date and location of a burglary and the items taken, his statement was compared with police incident reports on file. Additionally, he'd be driven past the site of the burglary and asked to identify the specific house. Arnoldy found that when Frank was asked about something he had no knowledge of, he'd say he didn't know. He didn't try to tell his interviewers what he thought they wanted to hear.

Strike Force attorney Stan Hunterton also felt Cullotta was a good catch for the government, so he made sure that Frank was treated accordingly. In his opinion, Frank was one of the best-protected witnesses he ever dealt with.

Frank's positive impression on those who were interrogating and evaluating him didn't land him in a bed of roses, though. Soon after being taken out of Las Vegas, he was locked up in San Diego in a place where the government put all the other turncoats. The protected witnesses were housed in a special unit on one floor of the prison. For their own safety, they were kept segregated from the inmates in general population. Frank doesn't know if it was true, but he heard that their food was prepared in a special area to guard against poisoning.

Frank had turned because he had no other choice. He never wore a wire or tried to entrap anyone and he found it deplorable to live in a unit with 60 stool pigeons. These inmates were just as dangerous as the hardcore cons in Stateville, but in a different way. They got you with their ears and mouth rather than a shiv. Everyone wanted to rat on everyone else. They were always eavesdropping on conversations, trying to pick up any information that could be dealt to the authorities in return for a reduced sentence. It was a cesspool in which he spent two years.

· · ·

The government tried to keep Frank's cooperation as quiet as possible for as long as possible. Certainly the Las Vegas underworld knew what was going on, but the media and the general public remained in the dark for some time.

The law knew that as long as Larry Neumann remained free, he posed a threat to the public in general and to potential witnesses in particular. Frank Cullotta was providing information that prosecutors felt would put Neumann away for a long long time. What they needed to do was to get him off the streets until Frank's information could be pursued in the courts.

The 1981 charge of an ex-felon in possession of a concealed weapon against Neumann was all they had on him at the moment. Stan Hunterton prosecuted the case vigorously and won a conviction against Neumann on that charge, resulting in a sentence of two years, the maximum term that could be imposed at the time. Neumann's lawyer filed a motion to get his client out on bond while the conviction was appealed. Obviously, that couldn't be allowed to happen.

At the subsequent bail hearing, prosecutors had to demonstrate that Neumann presented a danger if released, thus his request for bond should be denied. As part of their presentation, Charlie Parsons testified about Neumann's plan to kill Ernie Davino. During his testimony, he had to reveal that the source of his information was Frank Cullotta. A gasp went up from the spectators in the courtroom. The word was out.

• • •

The *Review-Journal* and *Las Vegas Sun* treated the news of Frank's defection as a major event. Both papers speculated about how much damage his cooperation with prosecutors would do to the mob in general and Tony Spilotro in particular. Using named and anonymous law-enforcement sources, the reports said Cullotta was providing information that would blow the lid off Spilotro's street-crime rackets. He was also allegedly saying things about casino employees who had functioned as tipsters to the gang, including some in executive positions.

After hearing from the lawmen, one of the first people on the journalists' interview lists was Oscar Goodman. The lawyer's reaction was low key, conveying the impression that the revelation didn't amount to much. He essentially dismissed the matter as a non-event, telling a reporter that he wasn't concerned about Frank saying anything detrimental about his client, Tony Spilotro, because there wasn't anything detrimental to say. He added that Tony wished his old pal the best.

Later, Goodman became more critical of his client's one-time confidant. He told author John L. Smith that in his opinion, Frank was never effective as a government witness. Goodman is quoted as saying: "Although you'll never get them to admit it, the government never got squat in the way of convictions for turning Frank Cullotta." However, as time went on, Frank's testimony began to lead to indictments and convictions against Tony and others.

• • •

Frank knew that from the law's point of view, he'd been a bad guy most of his life. He'd admittedly committed myriad crimes, including murder. He knew there was no way he was going to get a free pass. On the other hand, he didn't want to be locked in a cell and have the key thrown away, either. There had to be a mechanism by which he could testify about his most serious transgressions without being exposed to the full criminal penalties. By July 1982, Frank and his lawyer finalized an agreement with prosecutors. Sentencing was scheduled for July 7.

The agreement included both incentives and punishment.

Frank was given immunity for any previously uncharged crimes he testified to. To settle his pending cases, he had to enter guilty pleas, but all sentences would run concurrent with whatever term he received for his conviction on possession of stolen property for the furniture he'd used in his house. Since that was a local charge, the best the federal prosecutors could do was to make a sentencing recommendation to the court, asking that Frank's cooperation be taken into account. With that kind of backing, the defendant was expecting a somewhat lenient disposition.

On the sentencing date, Frank was flown to Las Vegas and transported by helicopter to the courthouse roof. The presiding judge had no sympathy for Cullotta and was about to hand down a sentence of 10 years in prison.

Frank stood up. "Ten years? I don't think so. I'm a valuable witness and I'm helping you guys a lot more than you're trying to help me. I'm not going to go for ten years. You can stick everything in your ass. Put me back on the street and let them kill me. I'd rather be dead anyway."

His rant, essentially a bargaining ploy, did some good. After a lot of back and forth between the federal and local prosecutors, the sentence was reduced to eight years, with all other sentences running concurrently. In addition, he'd serve his time in a federal facility with an opportunity for parole. Overall, he was satisfied.

Frank ended up serving two years at the federal lockup in San Diego. He was paroled to the Witness Protection Program in 1984 and placed on two years of probation. He was totally free in 1986. He was 48 years old.

• • •

On July 8, 1982, the *Review Journal* ran a story about Frank's sentencing hearing under the headline, "Cullotta gets eight-year prison term." The reporter's description of the scene at the courthouse captured the importance government prosecutors placed on Frank and the tense atmosphere surrounding his appearance.

"District Judge Paul Goldman sentenced the 43-year-old Cullotta while Metro officers and federal agents blanketed the courtroom with heavy security. Three agents sat in the jury box, two guarded the rear courtroom entrance, two more guarded the front entrance and four formed a line between the defendant and the spectator section. In addition to the guards in the courtroom, two more were positioned on the courthouse roof.

"All who entered the courtroom, even reporters and courthouse observers known to the officers, were searched.

"Although the formal sentence was to the state prison, Cullotta will serve his time in a federal institution."

. . .

The torment Frank endured during his two years in San Diego wasn't due solely to what it was like behind the walls. During that time, he had to testify in public against some of his former friends. His appearances as a witness forced him into the unpleasant position of having to come face to face with those he was helping to put in prison. He not only had to look into their eyes, but he also had to endure withering attacks from their lawyers.

Those were the toughest two years of his life: Back and forth to witness stands, facing all the people he'd grown up with and dealing with their lawyers. Knowing he had a violent temper, the attorneys tried to provoke him into losing his composure. They called him a serpent, a rat, and a devil. They said he was stupid and a jerk. They even accused him of raping other inmates. But through it all, he kept his cool. And he honored his promise to the prosecutors: He never lied to them during interviews and he never perjured himself under oath.

· · ·

Initially, the mobsters and crooks to whom Frank posed a threat tried to make him an offer he couldn't refuse: He always had a death threat hanging over his head. Then they sicced their lawyers on him, who used any and all means available to discredit or intimidate him.

Michael Spilotro reached out to Frank through his brother Joey. He said, "Tell your brother not to testify against Tony and we'll give you enough money to fill a good-size house." Frank told Joey to tell Michael that he wasn't interested.

When intimidation and bribery failed, the Spilotro forces tried a different approach. Tony's lawyers threatened to subpoena Frank's mother as a defense witness. Their plan to have Josephine testify against her own son was never carried out. Although the reason she wasn't called to the stand is unknown, Frank suspects the lawyers thought it over and decided it could backfire and turn into a public-relations disaster.

In spite of the pressures, Frank testified in a number of venues around the country, including Illinois and Florida. In all cases he took the stand under the protection of state and federal immunity. His testimony resulted in several indictments and convictions.

Dennis Griffin and Frank Cullotta

Two particular cases that Frank was instrumental in and warrant specific mention are Larry Neumann's murder trial and the M&M murders. One was a clear win. The other went into the books as a loss, but it may have been a case that couldn't have been won under any circumstances.

• • •

Based on Frank's grand-jury testimony, Larry Neumann was charged in the murder of Chicago jeweler Bob Brown. Neumann was tried twice and Frank testified at both. The first trial ended in a hung jury. The second resulted in a conviction and a sentence of life in prison without the possibility of parole. Lurch Neumann had breathed his last free air.

When Frank was escorted into court for one of his appearances against Neumann, he had to walk past the holding cell that held the defendant.

"Turn your back," one of Frank's escorts told Neumann.

"Fuck you, you cocksuckers! I know who you've got there!" Neumann yelled.

As Frank passed by the cell, Neumann didn't say anything to him directly, but their eyes met for a moment. Frank's impression was that his former friend couldn't believe what he was doing to him. It was a very uncomfortable few seconds.

• • •

On January 27, 1983, Richard Daley, state's attorney for Cook County, Illinois, and Chicago mayoral candidate, held a press conference. He announced publicly that Tony Spilotro had been indicted for the 1962 torture killings of James Miraglia and William McCarthy, the so-called M&M murders. The indictment was based in large part on the grand-jury testimony of Frank Cullotta. According to Daley, Cullotta had testified that he helped Tony set up the slayings, but hadn't actually been present when the murders were committed. Following the press conference, Spilotro was arrested in Las Vegas and jailed without bail to await extradition to Illinois.

Oscar Goodman learned of Tony's troubles when he returned to Vegas after winning a major but unrelated case in Florida. He rushed from the airport to his office, then over to the jail to see his client. A few hours later, the accused murderer was released on bail. Goodman's ability to spring a client facing extradition on such serious charges raised some eyebrows in law-enforcement and legal circles.

Preparing for the trial, Goodman conferred regularly with Herb Barsy, an attorney who had long represented Spilotro in Chicago. Barsy had the reputation of knowing how to work the system and being able to get things done.

When Judge Thomas J. Maloney was assigned to hear the case, Barsy and Spilotro were so impressed that they convinced Goodman to forego a jury trial in favor of letting Maloney decide Tony's guilt or innocence. It was an idea that didn't initially sit well with the Las Vegas attorney.

Goodman explained his feelings about trying a murder case without a jury to author John L. Smith: "Tony liked the idea, but in my career I'd tried it only once, and that was in Las Vegas at the insistence of a client who was up on income–tax charges and had drawn Harry Claiborne as a judge in federal court. I knew Harry. The client knew Harry. He insisted they were close friends and that the judge would never rule against him because of that friendship. I refused at first, but he insisted. And I'm convinced that Claiborne was harder on him than he would have been had my client taken a damn jury trial. Claiborne convicted him and threw the book at him."

In spite of his doubts, Goodman went along with the wishes of Spilotro and Barsy. However, his preparation was virtually the same as it would have been if Tony were being judged by a jury of his peers: His strategy was to discredit the testimony of the government's chief witness, Frank Cullotta.

In the end, Judge Maloney ruled that the prosecution hadn't proved its case beyond a reasonable doubt.

Goodman claimed that the decision surprised him, but Frank wasn't the least bit shocked by the acquittal. He knew from the start that getting a guilty verdict in a 21-year-old case would be difficult. And when he heard Tony had opted for a bench trial and who the judge was, he was pretty sure the case was lost. He expressed his concerns to the FBI and said there was virtually no chance of getting a conviction. They sensed problems, too, but it was too late to do anything about it.

After the verdict, it may have looked as though Oscar Goodman's strategy had worked due to good lawyering and a weak prosecution case. It appeared on the surface that the judge hadn't found Frank's testimony credible, which was why Tony Spilotro was a free man once again. But there were questions. Did Frank really fail to convince Judge Maloney of Tony's guilt? Or had the outcome of the trial been pre-determined?

• • •

In 1993, ten years after the M&M trial, Thomas Maloney, the presiding judge, had the dubious distinction of being the only Illinois judge ever convicted of fixing a murder case. Although Maloney wasn't charged in conjunction with the Spilotro trial, a closer look at his history and the Chicago court system of the time may help explain why Spilotro and Barsy insisted on foregoing a jury trial.

Thomas Maloney was a practicing defense attorney in Chicago in 1977 when he was appointed by the Illinois Supreme Court to fill a vacancy in the Circuit Court. One year later, he ran for that office and was elected by the voters. Maloney retained the position until his retirement in 1990.

In the early 1980s, the feds launched Operation Greylord, designed to investigate suspicions of corruption in the Chicago courts. One of the key players in a subsequent probe, Operation Gambat, which began in 1986, was Robert Cooley, a Chicago criminal-defense lawyer in the 1970s and '80s. Cooley represented, and fixed cases for, organized-crime figures. He was highly successful in purchasing influence in the courts and didn't lose a case for approximately four years.

"I had no problem paying people money to make sure I got a decision in a case. In fact, I wanted to win all my cases and I did," Cooley explained. But all that changed in the late 1980s when a client asked the attorney to arrange to have a witness murdered. That's when Robert Cooley became an FBI informant.

As a result of Operations Greylord and Gambat, 92 people, including defense attorneys, bailiffs, clerks, and 13 judges, were indicted. One of those 13 was Thomas Maloney. Maloney was convicted in 1993 on charges of racketeering conspiracy, racketeering, extortion under color of official right, and obstruction of justice. These violations of the law all arose from three cases in which Judge Maloney took bribes. In 1994 he was sentenced to 15 years in prison and fined $200,000.

The first of the three cases took place in 1981. Three hit men were accused of attempted murder. During the course of the trial, the victim died and the charges were elevated to murder. Defense attorney Robert Cooley was retained by political friends of the defendants. He assured his clients that Judge Maloney could be bought, but that the price would be high. The politicians contributed $100,000 to grease the various wheels involved in the fix, including Maloney. At trial, the judge admitted as evidence a declaration from the dying victim identifying the defendants as his killers. But he then ruled that the declaration was unreliable, resulting in acquittals for all three defendants. After turning informant, Cooley covertly taped a conversation with one of the politicians who acknowledged the case had been fixed.

The next charged bribe occurred in 1982 and was also a murder case. This time a single defendant and a different defense attorney were involved. Maloney wasn't able to let the defendant off completely, because the case was receiving a lot of media attention and was considered too hot for an out-and-out acquittal. But that didn't mean the judge couldn't be of service. As a compromise, he acquitted on felony murder, convicted on voluntary manslaughter, and imposed a nine-year sentence, greatly reduced from the 20 years at least that would have resulted from a murder conviction

The third case consisted of two defendants accused of murdering two men in 1985. This time the fix was arranged, but it didn't come to fruition. A middleman negotiated a fee of $10,000 for the defendants to receive acquittals after a bench trial. Things fell apart when the prosecution put on such a strong case—including three credible eyewitnesses to the murders—that Judge Maloney saw no way he could let the defendants off. Through the middleman, he sent word that he was going to return the bribe money. Maloney was talked into hanging onto the cash until the defense put on its case. If they could discredit the government's evidence, perhaps Maloney could still deliver. The defense flopped. Maloney found both men guilty and sentenced them to death.

Does Maloney's conviction mean conclusively that the Spilotro trial was fixed? No, it doesn't. It simply raises a possibility that can logically be considered. But at least two people believe that Tony was in no danger when he faced Judge Maloney.

On November 11, 2003, Las Vegas TV station KVBC aired a segment on its nightly news show called "Another Side of Oscar Goodman." The focus of the piece was the M&M murder trial, whether Tony Spilotro had beaten the rap due to a crooked judge, and if so, had Goodman been aware of it. One of the guests interviewed was former mob lawyer-turned-informant Robert Cooley.

The question of the validity of the verdict was posed to Cooley, who said, "Absolutely it was fixed. I saw Tony on many occasions before and after. Tony made it clear the case was fixed and he had no problems with the case."

As for whether or not Oscar Goodman could have been unaware the fix was in, Cooley said, "Well, it's possible I'll be seven feet tall when I wake up in the morning. But the odds are pretty good against it."

Joe Yablonsky, the former Las Vegas FBI chief, had earlier expressed his reservations about the legitimacy of the M&M trial. In a letter to the editor of the *Las Vegas Review-Journal* in April 1999, Yablonsky, talking about Oscar Goodman, said, "Why did he and his co-counsel in Chicago waive a jury in the M&M boys' homicide case (the victim's head was placed in a vise, popping his eyeballs) perpetrated by his beloved client, gentle Tony the Ant Spilotro? Waiving a jury trial in a homicide case is virtually unheard of. It places the fate of the defendant in the judgment of one person, the judge, as opposed to 12 jurors. The judge in that case was subsequently convicted of corruption in an FBI sting operation known as Greylord."

• • •

Though Oscar Goodman claims that Frank was a total flop as a government witness, Dennis Arnoldy has an entirely different opinion. He's convinced Frank delivered for prosecutors in a big way.

To support his argument, Arnoldy cites statistics of Frank's productivity between 1982 and 1988. During that time, his testimony in front of various federal and state grand juries and trials was instrumental in indicting 19 people on federal racketeering-related charges, in four Illinois murder indictments, and in five Nevada burglary and armed-robbery indictments. These charges resulted in 15 federal convictions, including the Florida home invasion, one Illinois murder conviction, and five Nevada burglary and armed-robbery convictions.

Eighteen of the 19 federal racketeering indictments and 14 of the 15 federal convictions were related to Tony Spilotro's street-crime activities. They included burglary, robbery, arson, interstate transportation of stolen property, and murder. Two of the named defendants were Tony Spilotro and Cullotta himself. The other 16 were either members of, or associated with, the Hole in the Wall Gang or people who'd conspired with them in the commission of criminal acts. Included in the latter were a Las Vegas merchant and a casino executive.

On September 15, 1983, the *Review-Journal* reported the indictments. According to the article, reputed mobster Anthony Spilotro was accused of ordering a murder and overseeing a multi-million-dollar burglary ring in two federal indictments unsealed the previous day in Las Vegas.

FBI officials believed the burglars struck at least 200 homes or businesses in 1980 and 1981, making it the largest organized burglary operation in Las Vegas.

Tony and Michael Spilotro, along with 16 other men, were charged with 17 counts of racketeering. The charges included conspiracy, illegal transportation of a slot machine, interstate transportation of stolen property, possession of stolen Air Force radio equipment, mail fraud, extortion, and the use of a firearm in the commission of a felony. Tony Spilotro and alleged hit man Wayne Matecki, of Northridge, Illinois, were also accused in a separate indictment of violating the civil rights of a suspected con man-turned-government-witness, Jerry Lisner, by plotting to kill him.

The burglary/racketeering indictments were based on the testimony of Frank Cullotta and federal informant, Salvatore Romano, a one-time member of the burglary ring.

Besides the Spilotro brothers, Matecki, and Cullotta, the other 14 men indicted included Larry Neumann, Leo Guardino, Ernie

Davino, Joe Blasko, Pete Basile, Herb Blitzstein, James Patrazzo, Elie Nader, Freddie Pandolfo, and five others.

Elie Nader, owner of Nader's Clothing Store, allegedly contacted Cullotta to torch his shop in May 1980. Cullotta, Leo Guardino, and Ernie Davino carried out the arson. Nader's filing of an insurance claim resulted in a charge of mail fraud.

Freddie Pandolfo, an assistant casino manager at the Stardust, was charged with conspiring with Spilotro and others to commit nine residential and two commercial burglaries during 1980 and 1981.

Between the issuing of the indictments and the first trial, which ended in a mistrial on April 7, 1986, some of the defendants were dropped from the case. Others extricated themselves by making plea deals. The remaining defendants, including the Bertha's burglars, all entered guilty pleas. Prosecutors believe the rapid succession of admissions of guilt was a clear indication of the strength of their case.

Wayne Matecki was sentenced to five years for his racketeering conviction and five years for violating Jerry Lisner's civil rights.

The same five Hole in the Wall Gang members were also convicted on state charges of burglary and armed robbery, thanks to Frank's testimony.

The other federal indictment credited to Frank was against the man who had driven the getaway car the night of the home-invasion robbery in Florida. He was charged with interstate transportation of stolen property for going along with Frank when the hot ring was delivered to Michael Spilotro in Chicago. Frank's testimony led to his conviction at trial.

Besides the cases brought as a result of Frank's grand-jury appearances, he was called to Chicago to take the stand against Peanuts, the man who had organized the Brinks armored truck robbery, and another defendant in an unrelated case.

In another appearance in Illinois, Frank testified against Carl Messino. He was the Elmwood Park cop who stopped Frank while he was transporting a stolen safe and let him go in return for 10% of the score. Messino eventually became the chief of police and was allegedly involved in criminal activity on the side. The case against him was later dropped due to a lack of evidence.

In addition to prosecutors, politicians and lawmakers also sought Frank's knowledge. He appeared before a session of the President's Commission on Organized Crime held in New York City. Seated behind a screen to conceal his appearance, he explained the structure of organized crime.

The Florida Governor's Commission on Organized Crime wanted to talk with him, too. Besides his knowledge of organized crime, they wanted to hear from a criminal's perspective what effect legalized gambling had on the community.

· · ·

However, Frank's first appearance as a government witness in open court wasn't to help win a guilty verdict at trial. His debut was to provide character evidence at a pre-sentencing hearing in Chicago in February 1983. The defendant was his old acquaintance, Joey "the Clown" Lombardo, the same man who had authorized Frank's beating at the hands of Louie the Mooch years earlier. Lombardo had been convicted of bribery and was facing up to 55 years in prison. Prosecutors called on Frank to tell what he knew

Dennis Griffin and Frank Cullotta

about Lombardo's ties to the Outfit and his position within the organization.

On February 9, the *Chicago Tribune* described the court appearance of the previous day: "Former mobster Frank Cullotta testified that he sought permission from Joseph 'Joey the Clown' Lombardo to kill a man for causing a disruption at his disco. But Lombardo approved only breaking the man's hands and legs.

"'What I want you to do is break his hands, break his legs,' Cullotta said Lombardo told him. 'Then if he don't get the message, later on you can kill him.'

"The disclosures were made in a tightly guarded federal courtroom during Cullotta's public debut as a government witness.

"The testimony was central to the government's effort to portray Lombardo as a top mob figure before he is sentenced for his role in the conspiracy to bribe former U.S. Sen. Howard Cannon [D., Nev.].

"The 44-year-old, bearded Chicago native then recounted a criminal career dating to his days as a teenager. He said he has committed 50 armed robberies, 200 burglaries and 25 arsons. And, he said, he participated in two murders and arranged two others.

"In 1976, Cullotta had been running a disco called Spanky's in Schiller Park, a Chicago suburb. One night, he recalled, a chronic troublemaker supposedly started a fight that damaged the club and left several people hurt.

"'I decided to get an okay to get him killed,' Cullotta said.

"He said he went to see Lombardo, meeting him on a street near the mobster's home at 2210 West Ohio Street. He said Lombardo told him to come back the next day with a photo of the troublemaker.

"When he returned with the photo, he said, Lombardo told him that he couldn't kill the man. He told him he would have to be satisfied with breaking the man's hands and legs, Cullotta testified."

Lombardo drew a 15-year sentence.

Other lawmen also disagree with Mr. Goodman's assessment of Frank's usefulness as a government witness. Sheriff John McCarthy compared Frank's decision to become a government witness with similar actions by Jimmy Fratiano and Joseph Valachi. He said Frank was having a rippling effect on both those in law-enforcement and in the Mafia all across the country. It was educating the lawmen and scaring the mobsters. "It's opened up a new facet to organized crime being involved and tied to a lot of crimes— something many law enforcement professionals, including myself, didn't understand."

. . .

Frank may have been granted immunity from criminal prosecution while wearing his witness hat, but he wasn't immune from life's other trials. To begin with, while he was still incarcerated in San Diego, his wife became disenchanted with Witness Protection.

Eileen was still in Virginia Beach with her son when she told Frank she wanted out of the program. She wanted to move to Pennsylvania and live with her sister. Frank knew she was lonely and unhappy. He told her if that was what she wanted to do, she should go ahead and do it.

Eileen made arrangements for her sister to pick up her and her son. Money was tight for her right then, so Frank asked the FBI if they could help out until she could get back on her feet again. They promised to help and they did.

Eileen and her son remained with her sister for two years while Frank was in prison. She experienced no incidents of mob threats or intimidation during that time.

. . .

Frank hadn't lived what most people would consider a normal life in decades. He'd either been out doing crimes or in jail. He had to wonder whether his phone was bugged, if there was a tracking device on his car, or if the guy he was talking with was wearing a wire. Whether he was at home or working in his restaurant, he never knew when the law would show up with a search or arrest warrant or when a stranger, or even a friend, might put a bullet in the back of his head. Life in Witness Protection may not have been totally normal, but it was as close to it as Frank had been in a long time.

When Frank was released from prison in 1984, he was moved to Texas. Eileen reentered Witness Protection and joined him, but her son went to live with his natural father for a while. Later the boy returned and his stepdaughter Kimberly arrived after that.

Kimberly was single and pregnant and suddenly Frank had a whole new life. He had a wife, kids, and a grandchild on the way. Neither the cops nor the G were after him. Nobody was out to get him, other than, possibly, some Outfit guys. He was part of a big happy family and it was great. Kimberly gave birth to a daughter, Ashley, in November 1985. She was a beautiful child, the light of Frank's life.

But old habits are hard to break and after the baby was born, Frank became a little uncomfortable again about everyone's safety. When he thought it over though, he realized it would take a big effort for the Outfit to find him and send someone to kill him. He thought he'd already testified against everyone he was going to, and they probably didn't want him bad enough anymore to exert that much energy.

Frank hadn't quite finished his courtroom obligations, however. On a trip back to Chicago to testify, a bizarre set of circumstances occurred that could have cost him his life.

• • •

While he was in Witness Protection, Frank's security, including when he was traveling to court appearances, was provided by the U.S. Marshals. Overall, they were quite efficient, but on one occasion there was a security breakdown. In the position Frank was in, one mistake could very well be one too many.

He had to return to Chicago to testify against a couple of his former associates: Peanuts, of the Brinks robbery, and a guy called Billy the Goat. Frank got out of court around 6 p.m. and a pair of marshals took him back to O'Hare to catch his flight. They drove out to the airplane in unmarked cars, then walked him up the stairs and into the plane. After they got him on board, they were supposed to hang around in their car until the plane taxied away.

All of a sudden an announcement was made: The plane was experiencing a mechanical problem and all the passengers had to disembark while the problem was being fixed. The delay was estimated at two hours. Frank looked out the window and the marshals were nowhere to be seen; he exited the plane with the rest of the passengers.

Inside the terminal Frank found a pay phone and called the marshal's office; there was no answer. He then tried the secret number he'd been given. That number had been changed! He couldn't believe it; the emergency number had been changed and nobody bothered to tell him. Getting a little nervous about loitering around the airport in Chicago, he went to a ticket agent and bought a ticket for the next departure to Dallas. It left in half an hour.

When Frank boarded that plane, he saw two familiar faces, both Outfit guys. One of them was Paul, the thief and hit man he'd worked with in Scottsdale, Arizona. Paul looked him right in the eye like he couldn't believe what he was seeing. Frank grabbed his things from the overhead compartment and got off the plane; inside the terminal he hid behind a pillar. Paul and his companion came out, looking all around. When they got back on the plane, Frank took a cab to Midway Airport. Between the ticket to Dallas and the cab ride, he'd gone through $200. He hoped he had enough money left to get another ticket out of town.

From Midway he called the local FBI office and left a message on their answering machine. Within five minutes an agent named Dave Kelly called him back. Frank explained what had happened and Kelly told him to get a hotel room, then call him. After securing a room near the airport, he again called Kelly. To Frank's relief, Kelly and his partner were at his door within 20 minutes.

Frank explained everything again. Kelly said, "My God! The Strike Force attorney is going to be pissed off when he hears this. I mean really pissed." The two agents took Frank back to the airport and got him on another flight. But his troubles weren't over yet.

He was in his seat when the flight attendant stopped and asked his name. He was traveling under an alias and gave her the name from his ticket. When she left him, she stopped and spoke to a man seated a few rows ahead. Upon landing in Dallas, Frank noticed that the guy the attendant had spoken with didn't leave his seat. As Frank walked past him the man said, "Hi, Frankie. How ya doin'?"

Pretending not to hear him, Frank kept moving. But the man spoke to him again. "Frankie Cullotta, didn't you hear me?"

This time Frank answered. "I'm afraid you're mistaken. I'm not this Cullotta person."

He said, "You're Frank Cullotta all right. I know you; I was a floorman at the Stardust."

"I'm sorry, but you're wrong," Frank said, and continued down the aisle.

A marshal met Frank inside the airport. Frank didn't say anything to him about his encounter with the man from the Stardust out of fear he and his family would be relocated. He did mention it to Eileen, though. She said, "Thank God you're safe. You had an awful streak of bad luck."

Frank replied, "It wasn't all that bad. After all, I came face to face with an Outfit hit man and I'm still alive."

• • •

The Witness Protection Program was good for Frank and his family in many respects, but it was far from a panacea. Charlie Parsons had told Frank that they probably wouldn't like it, and they didn't. They were given birth certificates and Social Security numbers to establish new identities, but other than that they were

Dennis Griffin and Frank Cullotta

pretty much on their own. Under their new identities, they had no history, so it was tough to establish credit. They had to put down extra deposits for rent and utilities and pay higher interest rates on anything they financed. They had to take their paperwork to the Department of Motor Vehicles to get driver's licenses and make up stories about where they had come from.

For Frank, who was used to having several new cars each year, it was particularly tough having to drive an old jalopy. He found a way around that embarrassment in short order, however. Using money he'd stashed during better times, he bought a Mercedes that he kept in a rented garage. His neighbors or passing marshals saw an unimpressive used car in the driveway, but he was able to travel in luxury when the situation warranted or the mood struck.

Frank felt the Chicago incident was a fluke and continued to believe that the Outfit probably wouldn't actively pursue him or his family. But with a new baby on the scene, his wife and step-daughter didn't share his confidence in their safety.

In spring 1986, Eileen told Frank they needed to talk. She said, "I'm afraid for our safety; we need to break up. I love you and I hope you understand. Maybe somewhere down the road we can get back together. But for now it's the best thing." Shortly thereaf-ter, Eileen, her two kids, and her granddaughter departed for parts unknown.

Before she left, Frank told her he understood, but it put him through another major change. After Eileen and Frank agreed to split, Frank, still in Witness Protection, made arrangements to be relocated. He was flown to a remote location and housed in a cabin for three or four weeks. Then he was moved to another temporary location where he stayed in a motel. He had only a little money with him, just his monthly funding from the feds. He'd given everything else to Eileen. It was there that he first became aware he wasn't the only Las Vegan in trouble with the Outfit.

Frank's life was in turmoil, but Tony Spilotro was experiencing much more serious problems. He was under tremendous pressure from the law and the Chicago bosses were disenchanted with him. The only question was which side would get to him first.

14

The End of
Tony Spilotro

As Frank Cullotta was doing his duty as a government witness, his testimony placed additional pressure on Tony Spilotro. But he wasn't the only thorn in his former friend's skin; Tony was under assault from other quarters as well. Tony and Oscar Goodman fought back, but it was an uphill battle.

By June 1986, Tony Spilotro had three open cases hanging over his head, all of them federal. Two of the cases were being tried in Las Vegas. In those, Tony was being prosecuted under the Racketeer Influenced and Corrupt Organizations Act (RICO). He stood accused of being the mastermind behind the Hole in the Wall Gang. Many of the crimes committed by the HITWG, including the burglary of Bertha's and the robbery of the Rose Bowl sports book, served as the predicate offenses upon which the RICO case was based. Lawmen and government lawyers referred to that prosecution as the "Bertha's trial." The other pending Las Vegas case alleged that Tony had ordered the murder of federal defendant and witness Jerry Lisner. He'd also been indicted in the casino-skimming investigations and those charges remained unresolved.

The first Bertha's trial ended in a mistrial. Frank overheard prosecutors say that prior to the start of that trial, Spilotro was offered a sentence of 10 years in return for a guilty plea. Tony and Oscar Goodman rejected the offer. A retrial was scheduled to begin on June 16, 1986. Most experts thought the evidence against Tony was overwhelming. They believed the second trial would result in a conviction. The prosecution seemed to have a strong case in the Lisner matter, too.

Those in the know also thought Tony was in dire trouble in the casino-skimming case. Thanks to agent Lynn Ferrin in Las Vegas and his colleagues in other offices, on September 30, 1983, a federal grand jury in Kansas City returned an eight-count indictment against 15 defendants, including Tony Spilotro. Tony got his case severed from the other defendants and didn't stand trial with them. But their court cases, which ended in early 1986, resulted in convictions against mob bosses in several Midwest cities. A couple of the big names found guilty were Joe "Doves" Aiuppa of Chicago and Frank "Frankie Bal" Balistrieri of Milwaukee. Kansas City's Nick Civella was spared the ordeal of a trial and likely conviction only when it was learned he was suffering from terminal cancer. Based on those results, Tony's chances at trial didn't look too good.

• • •

In early June 1986, Tony's 41-year-old brother Michael, who lived and owned a restaurant in Chicago, was contacted by an underling of Outfit boss Joe Ferriola and asked to get in touch with

Tony. Michael was to ask Tony to come to Chicago for a meeting. The get-together was scheduled for June 14, two days before the start of the second Bertha's trial in Las Vegas. Tony responded to the invitation. He and Michael left for their meeting on that day, then failed to return home when they were expected.

In his motel room, Frank received a message to call the FBI. Dennis Arnoldy wanted to talk with him. Arnoldy said, "Tony and Michael Spilotro have disappeared. Have you got any idea where they would have run to?"

"They ain't run nowhere," Frank said with certainty. "Tony would never run. He fucked up and he's dead. If his brother is with him, he's dead too."

"What makes you so sure?"

"Tony's caused the Outfit a lot of problems and he'd stopped generating money. Michael is cocky and has caused problems, too. They aren't needed anymore. If you whack one, you gotta whack them both. I guarantee you they're both dead."

. . .

On Tuesday June 24, the *Las Vegas Review-Journal* ran the story on its front page. According to the Associated Press article, the Spilotro brothers were reported missing June 16 by Michael's wife Anne, who said she last saw them June 14 at her suburban Oak Park home. Several days later a farmer discovered the two badly beaten bodies in a shallow grave on his Indiana cornfield. The bodies were identified as those of Anthony and Michael Spilotro.

An Indiana State Police spokesman said the bodies, clad only in underwear, were buried one on top of the other in a five-foot grave.

An examination of the bodies by a forensic pathologist indicated blunt-force injuries, probably caused by hands or feet, resulted in the deaths. They'd been beaten senseless and there was some evidence that they may have been put in the ground while they were still breathing.

The grave was about five miles from a farm owned by mobster Joseph Aiuppa, who'd been convicted earlier that year on racketeering charges of skimming from a Las Vegas casino. Law-enforcement sources said there was no way to know if there was any connection between Aiuppa and the murders.

•   •   •

The news from Indiana wasn't totally unexpected in Las Vegas law-enforcement circles. In fact, some lawmen were surprised it hadn't happened earlier. Gene Smith expressed his feelings this way: "The department had been receiving intelligence that Tony's days were numbered. He'd been falling out of favor with the bosses for quite a while, because he wouldn't give up his street rackets and keep a low profile. But he was real tight with Joe Lombardo and that probably extended his life. When Lombardo and the others went to prison on [racketeering] convictions, Tony lost his protection. He wasn't liked or trusted by the new regime and that sealed his fate. It was just a matter of when.

"As for Michael, the word was that he was running a protection racket without the approval of the Outfit and not cutting them in on the profits. There was also the possibility that if they only hit Tony, Michael might want revenge. The best solution for the boys in Chicago was to get rid of both of them at the same time."

Dennis Griffin and Frank Cullotta

Kent Clifford believed Tony himself, and law-enforcement's efforts against him, led to the murders. "Tony's ego and his ambitions caused most of his problems with the mob. By us [Metro] and the FBI keeping him in the news, he became too much of a liability. Either the law was going to put him away or the mob would take care of him. For Spilotro, those were the only two possible outcomes."

· · ·

When Frank learned officially that Tony and Michael had been killed, he was troubled by the method of execution. During another phone conversation with Dennis Arnoldy, he expressed his opinion. "The way Tony and Michael were killed was terrible. They were beaten to death! Not shot, no cut throats. They were beaten, beaten to death. That's a hell of a way to die. Nobody should go like that. That was the Outfit's way of showing Tony wasn't that tough a guy."

"Have you got any idea why they were buried the way they were?" Arnoldy asked.

"The Outfit didn't intend for the bodies to be discovered so soon; they weren't looking for any more heat. The bodies were buried okay; no mistakes were made there. It was just that the farmer knew his land too well and spotted the fresh dig."

· · ·

In the years that followed the killings, Nancy Spilotro and Oscar Goodman expressed the opinion that the FBI wasn't exerting much effort to find the murderers. However, records show that the FBI did do a lengthy investigation in an attempt to identify and prosecute the killers. In a redacted report dated May 19, 1993, the FBI summarized the results of their investigation:

"For information of the Bureau, in June of 1986, Anthony Spilotro, a known Chicago LCN (La Cosa Nostra) member and his brother, Michael Spilotro, a known LCN associate and suspected LCN member, were murdered and buried in an Indiana cornfield located at the outskirts of Enos, Indiana. Autopsies conducted showed that both Spilotros were beaten. The cause of death was listed for each as asphyxia, due to blunt forced trauma about the head, neck and chest. The bodies of the Spilotros were positively identified through dental records supplied by Patrick Spilotro, DDS, and brother of the two deceased.

"As in most gangland slayings, cooperation with law enforcement officials by associates and members of the Chicago LCN is virtually non-existent. Several cooperating witnesses and sources were developed in this matter and have provided the following information concerning the time and period just prior to the Spilotros disappearance and subsequent murders and events that followed the murders.

"Approximately 10 days before the murders, Anthony Spilotro arrived in Chicago, Illinois, with a female companion identified as (redacted), of (redacted), currently residing in (redacted). Information from (redacted) indicates that a meeting was scheduled between Anthony Spilotro and (redacted) on the date the Spilotros were last seen alive, June 14, 1986. On June 13, 1986, Michael Spilotro received two important phone calls from (redacted). After the second of these calls, Michael Spilotro was heard telling (redacted) that he had a meeting the next day. It is known from interviews conducted with (redacted) that (redacted) contacted Michael Spilotro at Hoagie's Restaurant during the evening of June 13, 1986. Hoagie's Restaurant was owned by Michael Spilotro. During the same evening, Michael Spilotro informed (redacted) that he had a meeting the next day with (redacted). Michael Spilotro said that if he didn't come back from that meeting, 'It's no good.'

"On June 14, 1986, Anthony and Michael Spilotro departed Michael's residence at approximately 4:00 p.m. and were never seen alive again. Prior to leaving the residence both Spilotros removed all valuables and identifying papers from their persons.

"It is speculated that the brothers met with associates they trusted implicitly and proceeded to the meeting place. Upon arrival at the meeting the Spilotros were beaten and strangled.

"Comments by (redacted) as well as (redacted) and confidential informants seem to indicate the following information regarding the murder of the Spilotro brothers:

"(redacted) and (redacted) participated in the murder of the Spilotro brothers.

"The Spilotro brothers may have been picked up at a motel in Schiller Park on the afternoon of June 14, 1986, by (redacted) and possibly (redacted). The last sighting of the brothers by witnesses was in the bar of the motel at approximately 3:00 p.m. Tony Spilotro's vehicle was later recovered at the motel parking lot. Because of the close relationship of (redacted) and Tony Spilotro, it is believed that the brothers may have voluntarily entered (redacted).

"It is believed that the six subjects beat the Spilotro brothers to death at a location believed to be near the burial site, located in Enos, Indiana. At least part of the reason for the killings was to get money from Tony Spilotro.

"Redacted paragraph.

"Redacted paragraph.

"Albert Tocco is currently serving a 200-year sentence on a conviction out of the Northern District of Illinois (NDI). An attempt was made to indict Tocco by a Newton County, Indiana, grand jury to enable the state prosecution of Tocco in a Newton County Superior Court, located in Kentland, Indiana. An Assistant United States Attorney (AUSA) from the NDI was to be cross-designated to handle the state prosecution of Tocco. The purpose behind the state prosecution of Tocco was to enable Tocco to receive a death penalty sentence, should he be convicted at the state level. It was hoped that this possibility for the death sentence would convince Tocco to cooperate in the Spilotro murder investigation. However, to date, there has been an inability to make arrangements for the payment of the anticipated high cost of this prosecution to be covered by federal funds.

"On November 2, 1992, Gary Shapiro, Criminal Chief, United States Attorney's Office, Chicago, Illinois, and David Capp, United States Attorney's Office, Northern District of Indiana, Dyer, Indiana, advised that they are both in agreement that at that time, there was no viable prosecution in either the Northern District of Indiana or Newton County, Indiana.

"Chicago Division is awaiting (redacted).

"Chicago will notify Headquarters upon the completion of the above and will then re-contact the United States Attorney's Office, NDI, for a final prosecutive opinion on this matter."

As additional years passed with no apparent progress in the investigation, it appeared that the murders of the Spilotro brothers would remain another unsolved gangland mystery.

• • •

Frank got off probation in 1986, soon after Tony's murder. He moved once again and sent the U. S. Marshals a letter telling them he was out of the program. Witness Protection had served its purpose, but as soon as he could he ditched it and became himself again.

Free of the constraints of Witness Protection, Frank's wife, stepdaughter, and granddaughter rejoined him. That was good news for Frank. The bad news was about the baby. Ashley suffered from a congenitally weak liver and spleen. She had one medical problem after another, putting her mother and grandparents through hell.

Frank and his family struggled for several years with the girl's health problems and the related costs for treatment. While that was going on, Frank experienced a devastating loss in 1990 when Josephine Cullotta, his mother and best friend, passed away.

And then the FBI called. This time, however, they didn't want Frank to testify or to interview him in conjunction with some investigation. Instead, the feds were conveying a job offer.

At a time when money was in short supply, the message the FBI gave Frank was that an author had contacted them concerning a book he wanted to write about Las Vegas and the casinos run by Lefty Rosenthal. The author was looking for technical help with the project and if Frank was interested, he should call the writer, Nick Pileggi.

Frank met with Pileggi several times, always flying to different places to talk. After about a year and a half, Pileggi produced a book, then hooked up with movie director Martin Scorsese for a screenplay resulting in the film *Casino*. Frank worked as a technical consultant on the movie. He tried to instill as much reality as he could in regard to personalities and incidents. He even appeared in six or seven scenes; it was a lot of fun for him.

Frank was in Las Vegas for around four months working on the movie. Eileen and the kids were worried about his safety and his in-laws, who were still living in Vegas, didn't have much to do with him. He understood that some people still resented him for rolling on Tony, so it didn't bother him. He wasn't very worried himself, though. He knew how much of an effort it would take to off him, especially with the number of people working on a movie set and the security that was in place. Unless it was a suicide mission, it wasn't going to happen.

Frank did get an opportunity to have a little extra protection, however. One of the private security people was a nice attractive girl named Rebecca. One day she told him she'd like to be his body-guard and, if he requested it, she'd be able to get authorization to carry a concealed weapon.

As a convicted felon, Frank wasn't allowed to carry a gun himself. He considered what Rebecca had said and thought: *If she can carry one gun, she can carry two. One for her and one for me.* He requested that she be assigned to guard him, then had her carry two snub-nosed .38s. She asked why she had to have two guns. Frank didn't want to hurt her feelings, so he didn't tell her that if anything did happen, he'd feel much better if he could take care of himself.

The fact that Frank was in Vegas was no big secret. The newspapers wrote about him and the son of one of his old partners came to see him. He hugged Frank and said that both he and his father respected him. Some of the wiseguys showed up on the set, too.

They told Frank he didn't have to explain what he'd done; it was over. He was even able to get a couple of them spots in the movie.

Only one wiseguy made any waves. He knew one of the stars and mouthed off about Frank. But that was the end of it.

One other guy tried to cause a problem. The driver for one of the stars, he was also the son of an Outfit guy. Frank was using the name Joe Russo, but the driver knew his real identity. He started telling people who Frank was, but it backfired. Instead of trouble, it resulted in Frank becoming a celebrity on the set. He got along well with all the stars and they treated him with respect. As far as Frank was concerned, Martin Scorsese was a real gentleman, a great man. Even with the former hit man on the set, Scorsese never once got nervous.

After the movie wrapped, Frank returned home. A liver donor became available for his granddaughter and he used the money he'd made from the movie to pay for the operation. The transplant was a success and Frank considered it the best money he ever spent.

Ashley, who'd lugged an oxygen tank around with her for over nine years and never had a childhood, enjoyed several good years after the liver transplant. But her health problems returned. Complications developed during the 19-year-old's treatment, and the light of Frank's life dimmed forever in October 2005.

Today, Frank Cullotta resides in an undisclosed location and runs a legitimate small business. He makes an occasional appearance in public as himself. But for the most part, he lives his life out of the spotlight and is at peace with himself.

15

Looking Back

Dennis Arnoldy retired from the FBI in 1997. He and his family remained in Las Vegas where he worked as a private investigator. Today he has his own polygraph business, Arnoldy & Associates.

Following are his thoughts regarding some of the people and events that impacted his career.

Tony Spilotro

"It's my belief that beyond putting criminals in jail, the FBI's Spilotro investigations were important in removing the public image of his invincibility. For years he and his men were the faces of organized crime in Vegas and appeared to be above the law. They were able to operate as they pleased, attesting to the strength of their operation and the apparent weakness of law enforcement. I think the public had come to believe the law was incapable of bringing them to justice.

"As the law-enforcement pressure increased, that facade began to crumble; we dismantled Spilotro's organization piece by piece. His Chicago bosses eventually found him to be expendable, leading to his murder in 1986."

Las Vegas Metropolitan Police Department

"The first time I ever worked on a task force with a local police agency was during the Spilotro investigations. I found the Metropolitan Police Department's Intelligence Bureau, under the direction of Commander Kent Clifford, to be an outstanding organization. I worked closely with detectives Gene Smith and David Groover. They were two of the best investigators I ever dealt with. It was a pleasure working with them and I learned a lot."

Sal Romano

"In my opinion, three major incidents during the Spilotro investigations contributed to the end of Spilotro's reign. They were the murder of Jerry Lisner, the Bertha's burglary, and the turning of Frank Cullotta. Sal Romano was an invaluable asset to us, because he was able to infiltrate Spilotro's organization and furnish up-to-date information on their activities. Without him, the arrests at Bertha's and the resultant prosecutions wouldn't have happened."

Frank Cullotta

"When Frank first became a government witness, I looked at him as just another tool to use in our effort to arrest and convict criminals. In fact, that's the only way to view that type of cooperating witness; to do otherwise is asking for trouble. During the debriefing process, I developed a respect for Frank's commitment to tell the truth. We knew his credibility would be an issue in any prosecution in which he was involved, and double- or triple-checked whatever he told us. Some people in Frank's position will tell you whatever they think you want to hear, believing they'll make themselves more valuable as witnesses. In Frank's case, if he didn't have information about a specific incident, he'd say he didn't know. When he did provide information, we were able to independently verify its accuracy. I never lied to him and he was honest with me.

"I worked closely with Frank while he was in custody and when he testified in various venues around the country. Even after his obligations as a witness had been fulfilled, we remained in contact. Over the years a friendship developed between us that continues to this day."

. . .

It has been many years since Frank made the decision that turned his life around. Today he runs a successful small business and continues to enjoy a very close relationship with Eileen and his stepchildren.

Below he offers his current feelings about some of the people and events from his past.

Gene Smith

"Gene Smith was a tough guy. I think in some ways we were similar. We were both dedicated to what we did and would do whatever we had to in order to get the job done. I think if he'd become a criminal instead of a cop, he'd have been good at that, too.

He had the guts and determination to be successful at whatever he decided to try."

Sal Romano

"There was a big difference between Sal and me. I rolled as a matter of self-preservation; he became an informant because he liked it. The guy should have been an undercover cop, wearing a wire and setting people up. I may have testified against people, but I never wore a wire; I never trapped anybody. I don't wish Sal any bad luck. However, I don't respect him and we could never be friends."

The Outfit

"I never wanted to become too involved with those guys and I'm glad I didn't. If I'd taken Tony's route, I'm sure I could have become a main man. If nobody whacked me, I might even have been one of the bosses. I have absolutely no regrets that I decided to be a renegade, though.

"The Outfit bosses were usually pretty sharp. But they weren't right all the time, like when John Kennedy ran against Richard Nixon. Sam Giancana made a real miscalculation on that one. It was common knowledge in the Chicago underworld that Joe Kennedy reached out to the Outfit through Frank Sinatra. Giancana put out the word that it was important to get Kennedy elected, because he'd be a friend to the Outfit if he got into office. We did a big get-out-the-vote thing concentrating on the Italians. We figure we got Kennedy about a hundred thousand votes in Chicago. That helped him carry Illinois and got him into the White House. Then he made his brother Bobby the top cop. Bobby went after the Outfit big-time, trying to lock up all the dagos. A lot of guys were pissed off at Giancana over that deal. They said he never should have gotten involved with those goddamn Irishmen."

Larry Neumann

"From a crook's perspective, I felt that Larry was an honorable man. He was loyal, but a little tough to control as far as his taste for violence. Tony Spilotro was a dangerous guy, but Larry was much more dangerous. He was smart, almost a genius. I think he could have been a professor if he'd wanted to. He had money and didn't need to be a criminal. He did it because he liked it."

Oscar Goodman

"I thought there were several lawyers in Vegas better than Oscar. Tony really liked him, though, and paid him a lot of money over the years. I remember one day I was riding with Tony when he stopped at Oscar's office. When we pulled up, Tony said, 'See that building, Frankie? I paid for it.'

"One thing Oscar was good at was getting delays. In Tony's case he prolonged things until everything piled up. And I know that the government offered Tony a deal before the first Bertha's trial. As I remember it, their first proposal was for him to do ten years, and then I think they lowered it to five. But Oscar wouldn't go for it; he kept telling Tony they could beat the case. If Tony had taken that deal, he'd have been out of the picture and there would have been a lot less pressure on him. He may have gone to prison, but he'd probably be alive today.

"I understand that a defense lawyer has to fight for his client. He has to say what he has to say and do what he has to do. Be that as it may, I don't have much use for Oscar Goodman."

Bertha's

"I'd say this was the most important event that led to my rolling. We'd always been a step ahead of the cops and FBI. But when they got Sal Romano working with them, we lost that edge. They used him well and put a nice operation together to get us that night. I'll say this, though, and I believe it with all my heart. If it hadn't been for Sal, we'd have gotten away with it. They'd have suspected us of doing the job, sure. And they'd have put the heat on. But I know in my soul that they would never have been able to prove it."

Tony Spilotro

"I always liked Tony from the time we were kids in the same neighborhood in Chicago. I know that he wanted to have me killed, but I understand the spot he was in and I can forgive him for that. I'm still bothered today about the way they killed him. It showed total disrespect for him and his brother. They could have done it another way. Tony and I each had choices to make back then and we did what we did. It happened, and now it's over."

Dennis Arnoldy

"To this day, I consider Dennis to be my best friend. When I was going through the toughest time of my life, he was there. He treated me fairly and with respect. He never lied to me and I came to trust him completely. Until you've been between the proverbial rock and a hard place like I was, you might not be able to appreciate how important it is to find someone you can trust and have confidence in. In my opinion, he's a great man."

Dennis Griffin and Frank Cullotta

Frank Cullotta

"Everything in this book is the truth; it happened just as I told it. At times, putting it all together was difficult. It brought back a lot of memories and not all of them were pleasant. In some cases it was like resurrecting the dead.

"I had a good mother. She tried very hard to make me walk the straight and narrow. I had two sets of friends, the good ones and the bad ones; I chose the wrong group. Once I went the way I did, I became a good crook. I think that if I'd put my efforts into something legitimate, I might have been a millionaire today. But I didn't, and I'm not. I don't think it does any good to go down the 'what-if' route anyway. What's done is done.

"All I know now is that it's a wonderful feeling to be legit, to be a working stiff. When I wake up every day, I go to work. I don't have to look over my shoulder anymore. I'm not worried that someone I consider a friend is going to take me for that final walk just to put a bullet in my head.

"As far as my becoming a government witness, I have no regrets about what I did under the circumstances I was in. I'm a survivor and I did what I had to do to keep me and my family alive. I can count forty-four of my former friends and associates who were killed either by their own kind or by the police. Many more are still in prison or have done long prison terms. Any reasonable person will understand why I chose not to be included on that list.

"People always want to know if the mob is in Las Vegas today. They're not. At least not the Outfit, and not in the same form as when I was there. And nobody's [organized-crime families] running the casinos. You'll still see some mob-connected guys in Vegas, but they're on vacation. And a few might live there. They aren't the criminals, though. What you've got in Vegas today are renegades, bookies and drug dealers mostly. But it's not organized like it used to be. Those days are gone.

"Now, the street gangs have taken over. Most of them are from Los Angeles, unemployed kids looking for status. We only killed when we thought it was necessary. These guys will kill a person, any person, just to get recognition, to build a reputation. They're much more dangerous to the general public than we ever thought of being.

"And today you've got the white-collar criminals. They don't use guns, but they'll empty your pockets and bank account and put you in the soup line without batting an eye. Maybe some day they'll all be gone—the mob, the gangs, and the scam artists. And then the world will truly be a better place."

16

Where Are They Now?

The current status of some of the other key players in this book was obtained from confidential sources, newspaper archives, and public records. It's believed to be as accurate as is reasonably possible.

The Chicago Bosses

Joseph Ferriola, the man who allegedly ordered Tony Spilotro's execution, had only a three-year stint as boss of the Outfit. He died of natural causes in 1989.

Tony Accardo died in 1992 at the age of 86. Unlike many of his colleagues, he avoided serving any lengthy prison terms and his death was the result of natural causes.

Joseph Aiuppa passed away in February 1997. At the time of his death, the 89-year-old was in prison as a result of his convictions in the casino-skimming cases.

Sam Giancana was murdered in his Oak Park home on June 19,

1975, in an apparent mob hit.

The Other Bertha's Burglars

Wayne Matecki was found not guilty of burglary by a jury verdict. He is now living in Illinois.

Leo Guardino pled guilty to burglary. After serving a prison sentence, he left Nevada. He is now deceased.

Ernest Davino pled guilty to burglary. He is out of prison and residing in New Jersey.

Larry Neumann died in prison on January 9, 2007, of advanced cardiac disease. His body was cremated.

Joe Blasko, the former cop, served five years in state and federal prisons for his crimes while working with the Spilotro gang. He died of natural causes in November 2002 at the age of 67.

Others Associated with Tony Spilotro

Oscar Goodman, the defense attorney who represented Tony Spilotro and several other alleged mobsters, was elected Mayor of Las Vegas in June 1999. He began serving his second term in April 2003 and has enjoyed high approval ratings while in office. Mr. Goodman often describes himself as "the happiest mayor in America."

Spilotro associate Herb Blitzstein was convicted of credit-card fraud in 1987 and received a five-year prison sentence. After his release in 1991, he resumed loansharking and fencing stolen property in Las Vegas. He was found dead in his Vegas townhouse in January 1997, shot execution-style. Two men were arrested for the murder and pled guilty prior to going to trial. Two other men with ties to the Los Angeles and Buffalo organized-crime families were subsequently charged with hiring the hit men to kill Blitzstein so

Dennis Griffin and Frank Cullotta

they could take over his illegal businesses. They were acquitted of those charges, but were convicted of running an extortion scheme to take over Herbie's loansharking and insurance-fraud operations. Blitzstein's death marked the passing of one of the last remnants of the Spilotro gang in Las Vegas.

Frank "Lefty" Rosenthal lives in Florida and is still involved with the world of sports betting. He has a sports-related Web site at www.frankrosenthal.com.

The Law

Charlie Parsons, the agent who visited Frank Cullotta in jail and informed him there was a contract on him, is the Executive Director and COO of the Drug Abuse Resistance Education (DARE) program, headquartered in Los Angeles.

Emmett Michaels, the FBI electronics and surveillance expert, retired in May 2006 from his position as the Vice President of Corporate Security & Surveillance for Station Casinos, Inc.

Gene Smith is enjoying retirement and lives north of Las Vegas.

Kent Clifford obtained a real-estate license while working for Metro. After leaving the department he considered attending law school and an attorney had agreed to hire him upon graduation. As he was contemplating his future, he closed his first escrow on a vacant parcel of land. His commission on that one transaction was nearly what his potential employer had quoted him as an annual salary. Today Clifford owns and operates Clifford Commercial Real Estate in Las Vegas.

Stan Hunterton, former Strike Force attorney, has his own law practice in Las Vegas.

Surprise Indictments

On April 25, 2005, federal indictments were announced charging 14 reputed members and associates of Chicago organized crime with running a decades-old criminal enterprise that was responsible for 18 murders. The slayings included those of Tony and Michael Spilotro.

Among those named as a result of the FBI-led investigation dubbed "Operation Family Secrets" was Joseph "the Clown" Lombardo. Mr. Lombardo was allegedly one of Tony's superiors during Spilotro's Las Vegas years. He was considered by many to have been a friend of the Spilotro family.

After nearly 19 years, how was this news received by some of those who knew Tony best? In order to find out, I reached three such people by telephone on April 25 and 26, 2005. Following are their comments.

Nancy Spilotro: "I'm thrilled, absolutely thrilled." Tony's widow had been critical of the government's efforts to solve the killings of her husband and brother-in-law over the years. She explained: "I never said the FBI was doing nothing to solve the murders. But Tony and Michael weren't the Kennedys."

Regarding Joseph Lombardo, she said: "I've known him like a cousin for forty years. But I'm going to withhold comment until I learn more details."

Vincent Spilotro: Although there had been rumors of indictments in his father's murder for some time, Vincent was pleasantly surprised when they actually happened. "I couldn't be happier," he said. In the weeks prior to the announcements, Chicago and Las Vegas reporters had contacted Vincent and his mother, hinting that major developments were pending and requesting interviews. No interviews were granted, however. The government gave them no prior warning of the indictments.

Another person quite familiar with the Spilotro case is Dennis Arnoldy, the former FBI Las Vegas case agent for the Spilotro investigations. On April 27, Mr. Arnoldy provided his comments.

"The orders to kill Tony and Michael likely came down from Joe Ferriola. Lombardo would have had little choice but to carry them out. Remember, when it comes to protecting the Outfit, its bosses, or business interests, there is no such thing as friendship or even blood ties. Even if Lombardo was a personal friend to Tony and Nancy, it would have made no difference."

Joseph Lombardo was not immediately arrested after the indictments were issued. Instead, he went into hiding and became a fugitive from justice. For nine months he avoided the law, but his luck finally ran out. On Friday January 13, 2006, FBI agents nabbed him in Elmwood Park, Illinois, a Chicago suburb.

As the charges against Lombardo and the other defendants

move forward (they're scheduled to go on trial in Chicago on May 15, 2007), perhaps the complete story of the demise of Tony and Michael Spilotro will at last be told.

31 BLANK
291
31
___
260 ACTUAL
PAGES

ABOUT 7135

Index

About the Author

In 1994, Dennis N. Griffin retired after a 20-year career in investigations and law enforcement in New York and moved to Las Vegas. In 1996 he wrote his first novel, *The Morgue*, based on an actual case he investigated. He currently has six mystery thrillers in print.

In 2002, Griffin turned his attention to non-fiction. *Policing Las Vegas* (Huntington Press, 2005) chronicles the evolution of law enforcement in Las Vegas. *The Battle for Las Vegas—The Law vs. the Mob* (Huntington Press, 2006) tells the story of Chicago Outfit enforcer Tony Spilotro's reign in Vegas from the law-enforcement perspective.

For more information, visit:

www.authorsden.com/dennisngriffin